COXEY'S CRUSADE FOR JOBS

Northern Illinois University Press, DeKalb 60115

© 2016 by Northern Illinois University Press

25 24 23 22 21 20 19 18 17 16   1 2 3 4 5

978-0-87580-498-9 (paper)

978-1-60909-197-2 (ebook)

Design by Shaun Allshouse

Cover by Yuni Dorr

Library of Congress Cataloging-in-Publication Data

Names: Prout, Jerry, author.

Title: Coxey's crusade for jobs : unemployment in the Gilded Age / Jerry Prout.

Description: Dekalb : Northern Illinois University Press, [2016]

Identifiers: LCCN 2016005090| ISBN 9780875804989 (paperback) | ISBN
   9781609091972 (electronic)

Subjects: LCSH: Coxey, Jacob Sechler, 1854-1951. | Coxey's Army. |
   Labor—United States—History—19th century. | Unemployment—United
   States—History—19th century. | Working class—United
   States—History—19th century. | Unemployed—United States—History—19th
   century. | BISAC: HISTORY / United States / 19th Century.

Classification: LCC HD8072 .P897 2016 | DDC 331.13/797309034--dc23

LC record available at http://lccn.loc.gov/2016005090

COXEY'S CRUSADE FOR JOBS

UNEMPLOYMENT IN THE GILDED AGE

JERRY PROUT

NIU PRESS / DEKALB

for our grandchildren

Contents

The Cause of the Unemployed

"The aim and object of this march to Washington has been to awaken the attention of the whole people to a sense of their duty in impressing upon Congress the necessity for giving immediate relief to the four million of unemployed people."[1]

Jacob Coxey, 1894

L IKE MANY AMERICANS FACING the ravages of an economic depression that began in 1893, John Schrum's face was hollowed out from hunger. Having lost one eye, his tall, gaunt visage seemed all the more emblematic of the conditions that plagued millions of Americans in the new industrial era. For Schrum, his wife, and their one-year-old child, every day turned into a struggle for survival. Living in tiny Brazil, Iowa, Schrum worked in the local coal mines. But when the railroad construction bubble burst, many of the steel mills that supplied the rails closed. Then those coal mines that provided the coke for the steel shuttered as well. Like millions of other Americans, Schrum found himself suddenly without work and alone, to fend for himself and family.[2]

As the depression grew worse in the winter of 1894, Schrum became more desperate. Though he had joined the Iowa Miners and Mine Laborers Association, one of the many newly formed fraternal brotherhoods of workers dedicated to improving working conditions and bettering wages, the union could not help those like Schrum once they lost their jobs. As the winter wore on, one author described, "The silence of distress is more tragic than its loudest clamor. This is, indeed, the winter of our discontent." Out of work and, as Schrum would later describe to a reporter, "because starvation was staring me in the face," this unemployed coal miner picked up and traveled to Massillon, Ohio, to join a march of the unemployed to Washington, DC, a march ironically being organized by a successful businessman and employer named Jacob Sechler Coxey.[3]

No one seemed to know exactly how many men like Schrum were searching for work following the collapse of the stock market on May 5, 1893.

However, three months after the market's disastrous failure, the reputable business journal *Bradstreets* suggested that about nine hundred thousand were without jobs. By December Samuel Gompers, head of the newly formed American Federation of Labor, estimated that three million workers were on the streets. In the new and still unfamiliar corporate economy, America was awash in statistics but none that accurately measured employment. The 459 pages of the 1894 *Statistical Abstract of the United States* dutifully reported measurements of the tons of exports and imports, the value of precious farm and mineral commodities, and the assets and liabilities of banks, among others. However, statistics on the number of jobless were lacking.[4]

Sporadic efforts to count the poor began as early as 1824, when the state of New York determined that some seven thousand of its citizens were living in poverty. But not until 1878 did the state of Massachusetts Bureau of Labor Statistics attempt to count how many in that state actually were out of work. The US Census Bureau posed questions about employment as early as 1880, but the disappointing and confusing data it collected discouraged any official estimate. In 1884 the newly established federal Bureau of Labor began an investigation into the causes of the economic malaise and what it called the "surplus of labor," rather than "unemployment." Similar studies were conducted in many of the nation's largest cities. But such inquiries failed to reach definitive conclusions, nor did they suggest any remedies.[5]

Moreover, there was simply no sense of urgency to getting the numbers right. Indeed, the very idea of being unemployed was at odds with the dominant laissez-faire business ideology of the nineteenth century that revered individual enterprise and self-reliance. Everyone who wanted to work was supposed to be able to find a job. Those without jobs were generally frowned upon and viewed as indolent, or even worse, naturally flawed. Even the most prominent charitable groups conducted anti-tramp campaigns in an effort to distinguish what they considered a more select group of "worthy poor," those generally thought to have respect for the work ethic but who had temporarily fallen on hard times. In a few cities the Charity Organization Society (COS) tried to engage this subset of the unemployed in make-work jobs at newly created homes called the Wayfarer's Lodges. They wanted to demonstrate that a hand-selected group of poor, under strict authority, might quickly redeem their lives and distinguish themselves from the increasing armies of pathetic hoboes that endlessly roamed the countryside.[6]

To change such deeply entrenched attitudes of disdain toward the roaming unemployed was an immense challenge, as Coxey would soon discover. The self-reliant, resourceful individual remained the embodiment of the Puritan work ethic and deeply ingrained in the American ethos. In his

Gospel of Wealth, the self-made steel tycoon Andrew Carnegie praised the uncluttered, free market, citing as proof for its capacity his own rise from a mere "bobbin boy" in the textile mills to steel magnate. Carnegie viewed himself as living proof that the "rags to riches" story was not just the fiction of the sensationally popular Horatio Alger novels but living testament to the real prospect of upward mobility for any hardworking American. The steel magnate became a devout follower of the British philosopher Herbert Spencer, whose Social Darwinism proclaimed an economic hierarchy of the fittest. Unbridled greed was a manifestation of natural selection, governed by what Carnegie extolled as the "Law of Competition." Carnegie observed that though unconstrained competition "may be sometimes hard for the individual, it is best for the race, because it insures the survival of the fittest in every department."[7]

An Alternative Path

If he had chosen to do so, Coxey could have told his own "rags to riches" story. As he organized this march of the unemployed at his home near Massillon, Ohio, the forty-year-old Coxey was the respected owner of two prosperous quarries and horse farms in Ohio, Kentucky, and Oklahoma. Typically adorned in a white Edwardian wing-collared shirt and stylish business suit, he was described as confident, affable, and straightforward. Yet, as successful as he was in 1894, Coxey recalled how his own luck had once been not much different from that of Schrum and the other "tramps" who arrived in Massillon as the embodiment of his cause.[8]

During a depression twenty years earlier, Jacob Coxey, then a nineteen-year-old mechanic in the iron mills of Pennsylvania, lost his job and thus came face-to-face with the reality of unemployment. Throughout his long life (Coxey would live to be ninety-seven), he continued to recall what it was like to be without work. Even after his Horatio Alger–like rise, Coxey simply could not shed the memory of this earlier experience. As Guy McNeill Wells of the *Wall Street Journal* noted, "Under his shirt beat a heart that bled for millions of miserable and pitiful American citizens, and a patriotism that raged at an economic system that, in a land of peace and plenty, could produce nothing but hunger and poverty." In harboring his own personal experience without work, Coxey would become fully committed to his own solution to the unemployment crisis.[9]

Coxey developed his own Good Roads Plan, which would provide every unemployed American with a job that would pay $1.50 a day, the very salary he paid his own workers. As he described in a seemingly endless stream of promotional bulletins and pamphlets, Coxey's $500 million Good Roads Plan called on the federal government to issue non-interest-bearing bonds that could be issued by any subdivision of government for the purpose of raising money to build roads or other public works. Coxey was convinced that his plan, one that totaled more than the size of the annual federal budget itself, would not only restore jobs but also create a much-needed national system of roads.[10]

Coxey's bold plan, offered more than a decade before the automobile took hold, seemed outlandish. Even bicyclists, who comprised the core constituency of the nascent Good Roads movement, were stunned by Coxey's temerity. As Coxey's Army marched toward the nation's capital, the Reverend William Alvin Bartlett of Washington's New York Avenue Presbyterian Church seemed to summarize the prevailing attitude toward Coxey's March. Bartlett told his congregation that "no honest laborer would ever think to march to Washington to ask for a job." With state and local governments reluctant to fund public works, asking the federal government for a roads program of this magnitude seemed nothing short of lunacy. No wonder press headlines amusingly referred to Coxey as "Ohio's Don Quixote," suggested he was a "candidate for the lunatic asylum," and referred to his plan as "idiocy."[11]

Coxey preferred to call himself a Populist, and his plan, like those of other notable Populist reformers, was noteworthy for its breadth and imagination. However, what set Coxey apart from many of his fellow reform-minded colleagues was his willingness to take his argument outside the meetinghouses and convention halls where Populist reformers often spoke to one another or argued among themselves over platform planks and the wording of resolutions. Coxey was not content to see his ideas encompassed in party declarations that went nowhere. Encouraged by his eccentric and flamboyant sidekick, Carl Browne, Coxey realized that the Populists needed new tactics to realize their bold visions for reform. Following the emphatic drubbing that the Peoples Party endured in the 1892 presidential election, the remnants of the Populist political apparatus, including the fourteen Populists in Congress, had already begun to turn to the established parties to find common ground. By contrast Coxey, who remained stubbornly steadfast in his commitment to put the unemployed back to work, was in no mood for compromise. Rather, he sought new means to focus political attention on the plight of the unemployed. With this first-ever march to Washington, Coxey would set a precedent for subsequent unpopular political and social causes, from paying wartime bonuses to civil rights.[12]

Unintended Consequences

Yet, for all their careful planning and preparation, neither Coxey nor Browne could have foreseen exactly how the unprecedented press coverage of the spectacle they staged helped them to achieve their goal. Over the five-week duration of the march, it became the most covered news story since the Civil War. While the actual numbers of unemployed in its ranks fell far short of expectations, thousands of newspaper stories about the march splashed across America's front pages and familiarized millions of readers with these unemployed men. The dozen reporters embedded in the Commonweal created a journalistic prism that projected a myriad of colorful individual stories about the characters and everyday episodes that comprised it. Though they had carefully planned this event, Coxey and Browne were unable to foresee how these reporters, with their interesting stories about the marchers' foibles and frailties, humanized the very ill-understood concept of the unemployed.[13]

The young *Chicago Daily Record* reporter Ray Stannard Baker, on his first major out-of-town assignment, was one of the intrepid reporters who stayed with the march for its duration. It left him with a sense of the power of the press, one he used to advantage later as a muckraker for *McClure's*, a devoted progressive reformer, and aide to President Woodrow Wilson. Baker acknowledged that the unemployed walking alongside him became friends. "I began to know some of them as Joe and Bill and George," he noted later. "I soon had them talking about their homes in Iowa and Colorado and Illinois and Chicago and Pittsburgh—and the real problems they had to meet." Baker's articles, like those of the other reporters who marched with Coxey—replete with humorous incidents and colorful descriptions consistent with a new journalistic style—thus helped portray the marchers as human beings, not as the tramps and vagabonds the public conceived. Readers came to see the marchers as genuine farmers or workingmen searching for the next job.[14]

The Gilded Age had already witnessed a remarkable number of academics, reformers, and journalists who sought to bridge the era's economic divide by entering the work zone of the "down and outers," attempting to live with them and understand their challenges. Even before Coxey marched, a number of literary notables had crossed class boundaries to experience *How the Other Half Lives*, as Jacob Riis would entitle his best-selling volume. During the march itself, author Jack London enlisted in Kelly's Army, out of San Francisco, one of the nine copycat industrial armies that joined Coxey's cause, marching west from as far away as Portland and Los Angeles.[15]

Yet, unlike these artists who chose to cross class lines, Coxey was satisfied to maintain his identity as a wealthy businessman. His goal was not to learn about the "unemployed," as if they were part of a laboratory experiment, but to actually help them find jobs. By financing and staging a spectacle, Coxey hoped to dramatize the plight of the unemployed and have Congress adopt his Good Roads program. In doing so, he not only brought the unemployed to the steps of the Capitol but, with the aid of unprecedented news coverage, he brought the unemployed into the homes of millions of Americans.

Telling the Coxey Story

The story of Coxey's March has already been well told by historians. However, each of the four previous treatments of Coxey's March have viewed it as emblematic of the larger Populist movement and as a window through which to better understand the energy and turmoil created by the era's producer uprising. The very word "populism" had only recently come into the vernacular when Henry Vincent, himself a member of a radical Kansas Populist group, the Viddettes, wrote his contemporaneous account, *The Story of the Commonweal* (1894). Vincent clearly found the march to be an expression of a "positive populism," since it sought the enactment of laws to help the unemployed. Yet, thirty-five years later Donald McMurry struggled to place Coxey's March into a populist context. The prevailing historical literature of his time viewed populism as an exclusively agrarian phenomenon. Thus, in his *Coxey's Army* (1929), McMurry escapes this dilemma by using the term "Coxeyism" to explain what he considered an industrial derivation of the broader populist movement.[16]

Though Richard Hofstadter's important interpretation of populism in his renowned *Age of Reform* (1955) seemed to cement the Populist movement's place as a nostalgic attempt to recapture a vanishing rural America, the subsequent important works of Norman Pollack (1962) and Lawrence Goodwyn (1976), among others, saw the critical role that a nascent labor movement played in fortifying the producer's rebellion. The existence of an underclass of unemployed tramps, Pollack argues, revealed a deeper crisis in capitalist development. He sees Coxey as representative of this growing farmer-industrial alliance. Thus by the time Carlos Schwantes wrote his own account of *Coxey's Army* (1985), the historiography of Populism had evolved to allow the author to state that the event was "a dramatic vehicle by which to conduct readers through the mainstream of American life in the 1890s, as well as into some of its bizarre and now forgotten byways."

Benjamin Alexander takes this same periodization approach in the most recent account. In his *Coxey's Army* (2015), much like Schwantes, he sees the march as "the physical manifestation of the long annals of debate over inequities in the American economic order and the proper role of government in response to economic privation."[17]

Thus, by now the Coxey story is well placed within its own historical context. However, this book will argue that the event's historical significance transcends its place in the Populist moment. In this interpretation Coxey's March is characterized as significant because it represents an important transitional event. With its racial diversity, visionary ideas, and conflation of religious and political themes, it blurs neat chronological divides. Despite the ridicule that the march invited with its eclectic array of characters and messages, the impressions rendered by its embedded newspaper reporters endeared these unemployed to a vast national readership. This same warmth poured out onto the roadsides as people cheered the marchers, whether passing in rural Salem, Ohio, or parading near the steelworks at Homestead, Pennsylvania. The spectacle of jobless men marching to their nation's capital in search of work reified the importance of addressing the little-understood phenomenon of unemployment. In the transient jobs environment of a new industrial economy, Coxey turned the spotlight on the human casualties of capitalism that most of his business contemporaries wished to rationalize as weak or incapable. As newspaperman Stanley Waterloo said of Coxey's men, "They are peaceful and earnest, and there is an eloquence in the patient dreariness of their plodding." It was an unfamiliar image that the march helped propel forward—and that future reformers who tread in Coxey's footsteps would not let history erase as they carried forward his crusade for the unemployed.[18]

CHAPTER ONE

They Sleep on Marble Floors

"It's the crazy people who move the world forward and make progress a possibility."[1]

Chicago Mayor Carter Harrison Sr.

THE WORLD'S COLUMBIAN EXPOSITION, occupying some six hundred acres of Chicago's Jackson Park, opened its doors on May 1, 1893. Meant to commemorate the four-hundredth anniversary of the founding of the New World, this spectacle trumpeted the triumph of an industrialized, modern America. With its ten thousand electric lights gleaming against splendid white edifices, the very symmetry of design and function of this magnificent "White City," as it came to be known, stood as the apotheosis of the Gilded Age. Chicago journalist George Ade proclaimed the exposition "the world's greatest achievement of the departing century." Architect Daniel Burnham's neoclassical design represented an attempt to unify a confusing array of diverse exhibits and a dizzying montage of images. This magnificent display of technology seemed to the Boston Brahmin Henry Adams a testament to the power of the new corporate capitalism that was transforming the American economy.[2]

The tides of visitors thronging to Chicago that summer from a still predominantly rural nation witnessed the splendors not only of the exposition but also of a teeming Midwestern city that embodied the raw contours of America's exploding industrial growth. A city of just over three hundred thousand at the time of a devastating fire in 1871, in two decades Chicago had quickly quadrupled in size. The city's new streets, with their chaotic combinations of vehicles and shops and varied smells and sounds, captured the restlessness of its surging immigrant population and fast-growing, ethnically distinct neighborhoods. Just like the fair itself, Chicago represented a "sprawling carnival of cultures."[3]

Yet immediately beyond the exposition's acres of perfectly aligned waterways and boulevards, pavilions and palaces, the streets of Chicago became home to an increasing corps of unemployed workers. Out of work and homeless, they slept on the marble-slab steps of city hall, stood in line to receive food at local shelters, and took to the streets in protest and riots. This burgeoning Midwestern city that reflected the triumph of technology and capitalism also presented the foreboding specter of those that the new American economy had failed. British minister and writer William Stead, living among the poor in Chicago, lamented, "The unemployed are our industrial deficit which yawns wider and wider and refuses to be choked." As with other relief efforts across the country, the patchwork of Chicago's volunteer programs could not keep up with the needs of the unemployed. Stead estimated that only about five thousand persons in the city received relief from a makeshift, volunteer welfare network. As he observed, the saloons provided more free lunches to the poor than did the Chicago Central Relief Association.[4]

Eating Their Own Grass

As the summer wore on, the numbers and plight of the jobless and homeless in Chicago grew worse. In what turned out to be a perverse irony of timing, on May 5, just four days after the exposition opened its gates, an already wobbly stock market collapsed. This massive collapse of the stock market came to be called the Panic of 1893 and marked the beginning of a four-year depression. One newspaper account of the ensuing Wall Street mayhem reported men and boys moving on the streets at frenetic speed, "diving in here and darting out there—rushing in or hurrying out of the place where their interests centered," desperately trying to save their businesses from financial ruin. Another observer described the mayhem this way:

> Crowds gathered around the trading posts of active stocks, swinging their arms and yelling themselves hoarse in an attempt to sell, and brokers and messengers running as if Satan were after them. Nobody thought of walking, and the gravity of the situation was accented by the pale anxious faces of the struggling brokers.

In the ensuing days, though there would be bullish talk and an occasional weak rally, the stock market's continued decline reflected a nation sliding into depression. National Cordage, a company that had assured itself of a virtual monopoly in hemp and rope only two years before, now went bankrupt, triggering a broad sell-off. It became the headline example for hundreds of other collapsing stocks. Beginning the year at seventy-five dollars a share, at the market's close on May 5, it sold for fifteen dollars.[5]

The market's cratering reflected the depth of an economic calamity that had been simmering for years. As with earlier and later depressions, once a few threads began to unravel, the whole tangled fabric of the economy began to fray, finally tearing open at the seams. The seeds for the Panic may well have been planted in an agricultural expansion during the 1880s. As a result of promised handsome profits offered by corporate middlemen, farmers responded by overproducing, which led to declining prices. However, rather than realizing the prosperity they were promised, growers in the South and the Midwest suddenly found themselves the victims of increasing debt. Under pressure to produce more, farmers found themselves overleveraged, with expenditures that outpaced the credits from future crops. The decline in prices meant that farmers could not pay the interest on their loans. Caught in this vice, they simply mortgaged more and more, sometimes everything they had. The last entry in one bankrupt farmer's ledger listed the expenses for his own burial supplies and coffin.[6]

The agricultural downturn was a major contributor to the Panic of 1893, and its impacts soon were felt in other sectors of the economy. With crop prices tumbling, farm foreclosures multiplied. As the volumes of commodities being shipped declined, so too did the amount of new railroad track being laid. Since railroads accounted for 90 percent of America's rolled steel output, the increasing failure of the rail lines also shook the foundations of America's industrial economy. The Reading Rail Line and Richmond Terminal had already failed by February 1893, well before the market's collapse. By the end of 1893, the US government had reported the failure of some 15,242 businesses. And yet, the worst was still to come.[7]

As the depression took hold, the industrial cities of the Northeast and Midwest increasingly felt the effects. In this unsettled economy the angry urban unemployed sometimes turned to violence, breaking store windows, raiding farms, and taking to the road in a desperate search for shelter, food, and work. The number of hungry steadily increased, particularly among the new immigrant population. Evictions from tenements rose in the cities, just as many farmers left their lands in the plains. With no discrimination in the hollowing out of farm and factory, the nation, as described in *Harper's Weekly*, seemed visited by increasing "poverty, gaunt hunger, physical and mental anguish, and brooding despair." On the July 4 weekend following the market panic, President Grover Cleveland made his own journey by train from Washington to New York for a secret operation to remove a tumor from his mouth. As he stared out the windows at shantytowns along the trackside, he saw firsthand many of the most impoverished, who were often called "the mudsill." It was even reported that these poorest of the poor could be seen eating the grass from their own yards.[8]

The human toll from the growing depression greeted wealthy Ohio businessman Jacob Sechler Coxey as he arrived in Chicago by train on the evening of July 30. Like hundreds of so-called silver men and soft-money enthusiasts, Coxey had journeyed north to attend a hastily called national convention of the American Bimetallic League, or simply the "Silver Convention," as the press preferred. The rowdy delegates had gathered in their fervent opposition to the repeal of the 1890 Sherman Silver Purchase Act. Though arguing among themselves as to the right monetary policy, the delegates united in full-throated opposition to constricting the nation's money supply by ceasing government purchase of silver. Chicago mayor Carter Harrison Sr. welcomed the delegates to the opening session on August 1. "Some of you may be rather wild—it is said you are silver lunatics," he said, to laughter and agreeable cheers. Meeting in the Methodist Street Church Auditorium, the delegates quickly formed into committees to begin their hasty deliberations. Though there was no scheduled adjournment date, there was a sense of urgency. President Cleveland had called a special session of Congress, and it was reportedly set to begin the very next week; congress would debate the repeal of the Sherman Act, legislation that seemed inevitable.[9]

The Sound-Money Debate

The deteriorating economy only helped fuel the argument among regions and sectors of the economy over how much currency should be in circulation and how it should be valued. For all intents and purposes, with the Coinage Act of 1873 Congress had returned the United States to a gold-only standard, replacing the historic bimetal standard established in 1792. After 1879 and the final retirement of greenbacks, America was essentially on a gold standard, though it might pretend otherwise. The politics dictated that even the staunchest silver advocates were sparing in their mention of an alternate money standard. The Bland Allison Act (1878) and then more than a decade later the Sherman Silver Purchase Act (1890) would allow for purchase of silver stocks and the authorization of some limited silver coinage. While these acts were no substitute for a bimetal standard, for groups such as the Farmer Alliances the opposition to a bimetal standard was so fierce in Congress that they realized the free coinage of silver or increased silver purchase (which was tantamount to the same thing) represented the only practical course for political action. And of course, gold-standard traditionalists, particularly Republicans, opposed both. These so-called goldbugs saw the purchase of silver as a precipitating cause of the depression. By the spring of 1893, American investors, heavily invested in

US dollars, had followed the British rush to convert their paper dollars into gold specie. Soon, overextended banks in the United States began to fail, and some 642 of them had shuttered their doors by the end of the year.[10]

Since the Civil War the debate about what constituted "sound money" had become a surrogate conversation about who controlled the economy. Was the future to belong to the very wealthiest barons who controlled the ascendant corporations or to an eclectic group of reformers whose bold ideas captured a new populist energy sweeping across the South and the plains? The gold-standard advocates consisted mostly of bankers and wealthy industrialists in the Northeast, as well as the prosperous merchants concentrated in the trading centers of the Eastern Seaboard. In addition to those in the silver-mining business, those in favor of silver included the farmers of the Midwest and the South, many of whom had joined the newly formed Peoples Party, the Populists as they were conveniently, often derisively, called. The farmers, long feeling the effects of an agricultural depression, supported a more expansive money supply that bimetal advocates from the silver-producing Western states offered.

Coxey represented an even more extreme version of those seeking to expand the money supply. In many ways he stood as a remnant from the days of an active Greenback Labor Party. Following the Civil War these soft-money enthusiasts waged a fight to prevent the elimination of some $450 million in outstanding greenback paper currency issued to finance the Northern victory. After the war, these "legal tender" greenbacks, supported only by the "full faith and credit" of the government and not by specie, became a subject of ridicule by gold advocates. The so-called goldbugs viewed greenbacks as "rag" money. These self-proclaimed "sound-money men" scoffed at the very notion that there could be any value in paper literally made from rags! They viewed greenbacks as a form of money that was even worse than silver and an embarrassment to a nation that was now the world's largest economy. Thus, no sooner did the war end than an Eastern-dominated Republican majority in Congress quickly sought to allow redemption of these "worthless" greenbacks and end this embarrassment.[11]

The gold ideology resonated particularly among an estimated two hundred thousand Americans who possessed over 70 percent of the nation's wealth. For this Upper Ten it made little sense to expand the money supply. As the numbers of unemployed steadily rose, the iconic tycoons of this Gilded Age, men such as Carnegie, Rockefeller, Morgan, Vanderbilt, and Mellon, grew increasingly insulated against the impacts of the depression and those few reformers who now tried to draw attention to the plight of the unemployed. These wealthy Wall Street and corporate elites clung to their established beliefs in the gold standard and high tariffs to protect their domestic banking, manufacturing, and railroad empires. They saw the depression as just growing pains of a rapidly industrializing economy. An editorial critical of the Bimetallic Convention in *Harper's Weekly* noted that states further west were woefully unsophisticated in their backwards notions of capital and monetary supply when compared with their more civilized Eastern counterparts. Alas, the *Harper's* editors concluded, "A young country, left to itself, rarely resists the temptation to issue money to excess." The article chided the bimetallists' demands for continuance of the Sherman Act as an example of this expansionist folly.[12]

The bimetallists were accustomed to this sort of condescension. However, it did not diminish their boisterous enthusiasm for speaker after speaker who came to the rostrum to denounce the moneyed elites. From the opening of the convention in the steamy Music Hall, General A. J. Warner, the president of the American Bimetallic League, sounded the call for the continued use of silver to keep more rather than less money in circulation. He acknowledged that, though the economy might be good for some, the plight of the jobless grew ever more menacing:

> Never before in the history of the country has there been such widespread fear and distress, never before such loss of confidence and destruction to credit. The industries are everywhere breaking down and laborers by tens of thousands are thrown workless on the streets with want staring them in the face.

As he concluded his opening speech, the delegates stood on their chairs and waved banners railing against the goldbugs' opposition to silver. However, the unruly assemblage saved their most raucous reception for ex-Tennessee Congressman Rice Pierce who boldly attacked President Cleveland's pro-repeal position and brought the delegates to their feet, chanting, "He [President Cleveland] represents Wall Street!"[13]

After four days of endless speeches, the delegates realized they needed a specific and forceful platform to convey their outrage. Thus, they turned to a famous author and agitator in their midst, Ignatius Donnelly. Donnelly's writing skill was unquestioned. The previous summer in Omaha, the author of the best-selling, dystopian novel *Caesar's Column*, penned the words of the energetic People's Party Platform. Now this avowed Populist would artfully capture the obligatory disdain for the Sherman Act's insistence that silver was a metal of lesser value. Like Coxey a former Greenback–Labor Party (GLP) devotee, the former Minnesota Congressman proclaimed in the Bimetallic League Resolution:

> We are convinced that as bad as is the state of affairs in this country, it would have been still worse but for the Sherman act, by which the nation has obtained to some extent the expanding circulation to meet the demands of a continent in process of colonization and the business exigencies of the most industrious race that ever dwelt on the earth.

Donnelly's punctuation to the five-day gathering, much like his Omaha Platform preamble the year before, captured the energy of a two-decade-old protest movement that in the end brought together a coalition of industrial workers, artisans, and miners as well as farmers under the Populist banner.[14]

Indeed, throughout the convention, the press frequently referred to the delegates as "Populists," as if the word invited scorn. Donnelly did not back away from the newly invented label. Instead, the Bimetal platform captured the Populists' distrust for the Gilded Age wealthy who would extend their control over the economy by contracting the currency at the very time when it should be expanding. In the platform Donnelly warned about the growing chasm between the haves and the have-nots. "To every person except a capitalist out of debt, or salaried officer, or annuitant, it is a period of loss, danger, lassitude of trade, fall of wages, suspension of enterprise, bankruptcy, and disaster." Donnelly gave voice to the bimetallists in their last hurrah to maintain the value of silver and inflate the money supply as a way to balance the scales of economic justice.[15]

Throughout the convention Coxey listened intently. It might seem as if Coxey's status as a wealthy businessman would put him at odds with his fellow Populists. Whether calling for the nationalization of the banks and railroads or eliminating all taxes in favor of a single tax, these bold-thinking reformers were most concerned with doing what they thought was right, rather than what was politically expedient. The loose-knit confederation of reformers who formed the heart of late nineteenth-century populism thought boldly and spoke loudly. As one historian subsequently concluded, "The populist genius lay in protest rather than in performance." However, despite his wealth and his status, Coxey embodied the spirit of this eclectic array of reformers. He had his own bold plan to help those like the growing numbers of homeless and jobless souls sleeping on the marble slabs of Chicago's City Hall. Coxey knew there were others like them, tramps as they were derisively called, wandering America's decrepit roads in search of work. From his own hard-bitten past he had a genuine affinity for the common man, even though he now was among the wealthiest Americans.[16]

The Heart of a Producer

As a young entrepreneur wealthy enough to dabble in buying horse farms and pace his prize trotters throughout the Midwest, Coxey seemed a much more likely candidate to adopt the standard Gilded Age orthodoxy that assumed that wealth accrued to the fittest. Indeed the young entrepreneur Coxey demonstrated just the sort of superior fitness that Carnegie described in his *Gospel of Wealth*, one whom the law of competition deemed "essential to the future progress of the race." Like other rags-to-riches tycoons, Coxey stood as a testament to the Social Darwinist theory Carnegie so admired. Measured by his success as a businessman, Coxey seemed to be living proof that, just as in nature, in the Gilded Age economy the fittest thrived. In ascending the economic ladder, he had undoubtedly heard and read words he could have readily adopted as moral justification for his own sudden wealth. He could easily have taken comfort that his fortune in the sand and silica business outside Massillon resulted from his "natural selection." Coxey represented the classic rags-to-riches story that so many of his peers used to turn their backs on those less fortunate. So why did Coxey follow another path?[17]

Coxey's father was born in 1800 on a boat coming from England, and his German mother's lineage could be traced to soldiers in the Revolutionary War. Coxey was born in 1854 in Selinsgrove, Pennsylvania, and he spent eight years in public schools and at least one in a private academy. But by the age of sixteen, Coxey took his first job as a water boy in the iron mills in nearby Danville. He steadily worked his way through a series of jobs and after eight years was promoted to stationary engineer. His father worked the night shift, and Coxey worked during the day. Coxey grew up reading voraciously and seemed always to be delighted to discuss his political views with his fellow workers. From the age of twenty, and while still working in the steel industry in Pennsylvania, Coxey joined in the concerted efforts to prevent Resumption (i.e., the earlier post–Civil War redemption of greenback paper currency with enactment of the 1875 Resumption Act) and to allow for greenback currency to remain in circulation. After the 1876 election, increasingly concerned about the Democrats' failure to prevent the retirement of greenbacks, he dropped his Democratic allegiance and joined the Greenback Party. As with everything he would do over a career of political agitation and activism, Coxey became thoroughly engaged. Though working full-time in the mill, he found the time to become a successful ward organizer in this region of Pennsylvania, which represented the core of Greenback support in the state.[18]

Coxey left the Danville mill in 1878 to join his uncle in a new scrap-iron company in Harrisburg. No longer a wage laborer, Coxey became a full-fledged partner in this new joint venture. This entrepreneurial role brought him to Massillon in 1881, where he spotted an opportunity that changed his life. He visited an idled sandstone quarry some four and a half miles outside this tranquil northeastern Ohio town. Knowing the iron-and-steel business as he did, Coxey saw the immediate potential for real value. Displaying a keen business savvy, he immediately determined that he could restore the moribund quarry to a more profitable venture. For one, he knew that the nearby steel companies valued a high-grade form of silica sand. He also reckoned that building a crushing mill to the right specifications next to the idled quarry would allow him to take full advantage of the Baltimore and Ohio railroads that ran alongside the quarry to conveniently ship his valuable product to steel producers throughout Ohio and Pennsylvania. Coxey's hunch proved correct. He would later acquire another quarry in nearby Dundee, Ohio, and as his wealth grew, he also found the wherewithal to satiate his appetite for racehorses, acquiring three ranches, one as far away as Guthrie, Oklahoma.[19]

Coxey quickly became a very rich man from his new ventures. To put his wealth in perspective, by 1885, at age of thirty-one, he had made some $40,000 a year from what was previously an idled gravel pit. As he arrived in Chicago for the Bimetallic Convention, his own fortune was estimated to be about a quarter of a million dollars. By comparison, in the late nineteenth century, 80 percent of America's households earned less than $500 a year, while the one hundred wealthiest Americans earned over a million. Coxey might not ultimately be considered in the same breath with other tycoons of the era, but he clearly was a wealthy man even by the demanding standards of Gilded Age America.[20]

Yet for all his sudden success, Coxey resisted the natural temptation to adopt the conventional views of other wealthy individuals of his era. He refused to believe that his own success derived from his being genetically superior. In fact, his worldview remained at heart the same as when he worked in the factories of Pennsylvania. He remained true to his earlier conversion to the Greenback-Labor ideology that championed the common producer over the monopolist. Coxey never wavered from his belief that money should be divorced from specie and its value based instead on the assurance of the full faith and credit of the United States. While it might seem unusual for a businessman to take what represented a radical position, there was ample precedent established by other well-heeled businessmen to advocate in favor of soft money. Earlier in the nineteenth century, three prosperous Northeastern businessmen, Edward Kellogg, Henry Carey, and Peter Cooper, each saw their own self-interest as well as economic growth and job creation as being naturally tied to a growing money supply.[21]

Edward Kellogg (1790–1858), a wealthy dry-goods merchant, argued for a system of currency loaned to individuals on the basis of local real estate values. The self-taught economist conceived of a monetary "Safety Fund" that would limit the interest rates of banks based on the value of mortgages and real estate. This fund would, in turn, expand the availability of currency, and thus economic opportunity. Philadelphia publisher Henry Carey (1793–1879) with his straight talk reduced his own economic philosophy to a simple premise. In his *Principles of Political Economy* he unequivocally championed the producer with his simple observation that "labour is the sole cause of value." Carey's views helped shape those of a generation of soft-money men, including his contemporary Peter Cooper (1791–1883). Despite his meteoric ascent as an ironmaster in the mid-nineteenth century, Cooper turned from being a hard-money advocate to being an inflationist. He became such a champion for soft-money policies that he ran for president as the Greenback–Labor Party candidate in 1876, which found that its real strength lay in the Pennsylvania iron industry where the young Coxey helped the party to organize.[22]

The echoes of these three soft-money proponents—Kellogg, Carey, and Cooper—reverberated in the region where Coxey grew up. The intellectual tradition of "producerism," so ingrained in Pennsylvania iron-and-steel country, shaped young Coxey's outlook not only on monetary policy but also on the importance of producing jobs. Thus, even though Coxey steadfastly claimed that his ideas were his own, his early experience in the Greenback politics of this region undoubtedly exposed him to the ideas of these thinkers. Indeed, the very leaders of the iron-and-steel industry where Coxey worked constituted a forceful lobby against Resumption. As Joseph Wharton, Bethlehem Steel magnate, opined on Resumption policy, "Nothing more deadly to the soldiers and champions of the nation who are in mine, mill and farm desperately fighting for her independence could be devised." The roots of Coxey's lifelong expansionist monetary philosophy were well established before he became a successful businessman.[23]

While Coxey's Greenback allegiance was shaped by his Pennsylvania labor experience, when he arrived in Ohio he found that it too possessed its own claim to Greenback enthusiasm. George Hunt Pendleton, who ran as vice president on the Democratic ticket in 1864, abandoned his own conventional hard-money notions in light of postbellum economic realities, to devise what became known as the "Ohio Idea." Concerned by the impact of removing such a large amount of currency from circulation, Pendleton recommended that the government continue to issue greenbacks as a way to retire the substantial war debt. The Ohio congressman suggested a companion bond plan that he felt could buffer any inflationary impacts. Pendleton's Democratic friends quickly dismissed the idea. However, Washington McLean, a wealthy manufacturing scion and the editor of the *Cincinnati Enquirer*, actively promoted Pendleton's plan, and it soon became popular among Ohio's still largely rural population. Adopting the slogan "the same currency for the plow holder and the bondholder," Pendleton's supporters contributed to the strong Ohio greenback legacy that greeted Coxey as he moved to Ohio.[24]

However, Coxey was not a greenback advocate just for the sake of monetary principle. For him it was an important means to stoke the economy and provide jobs. As he developed his own business, Coxey paid his employees wages that typically exceeded those of the average non-farm wage earner. Even when the depression set in during the summer of 1893, Coxey did not want to have his own workforce experience what had happened to him earlier in his career. During an earlier panic in 1873, Coxey had temporarily lost his job as a skilled mechanic at the Danville iron mill. This experience with unemployment apparently left an indelible mark. Twenty years after his brief experience, Coxey felt a special tie to those now left behind by the Panic of 1893. Though he tried to sell his horse farms to avoid laying off workers, the decline in orders from the steel industry eventually forced him to temporarily idle much of his workforce. This seemed to motivate him even more to take up the soft-money cause. A Cleveland correspondent to the *Wall Street Journal*, reflecting on Coxey's steadfast Populist advocacy, noted that Coxey "was no stuffed shirt," but rather a reformer who understood what it was like to be without a job."[25]

The Conestoga Cowboy

Thus as the Chicago silver convention wore on, Coxey would sometimes leave the rowdy and raucous floor debates to join the even more boisterous polemics at Lake Front Park, where talk of the growing depression filled the air. In this tumultuous summer, the park on the shores of Lake Michigan became Chicago's equivalent of Speakers' Corner in Hyde Park, London. Populist agitators with all manner of ideas took special aim at bankers and speculators. The wealthy and the privileged were portrayed as the "real anarchists" who threatened democracy by demeaning the hardworking producer. Those who witnessed the intensity of these diatribes recalled how eight years earlier the bombing at nearby Haymarket Square brought to a fiery culmination another workers' protest. The same ominous threats now stoked a growing anxiety. Rather than being frightened, Coxey found himself drawn to the incendiary words of one speaker. The flamboyant Carl Browne had already gained a reputation with the Chicago press corps for his considerable rhetorical gifts and feigned cowboy appearance. Typically dressed in a sombrero and buckskin coat, by trade he was an itinerant painter but by avocation an activist. One reporter referred to him as the "flower of American demagoguism." That summer, Chicago newspapers went so far as to publish the times when he was scheduled to give one of his rabble-rousing speeches.[26]

In the previous decade Chicago had become a gathering point for radicals, intellectuals, and immigrant anarchists. The Haymarket protest literally and figuratively exploded before a national audience in 1886. Then the city reacted in near panic, fearful that the waves of immigrants were unraveling civil order. The widespread fear and anxiety led to Mayor Harrison's ouster during the "Red Scare" reaction that ensued. However, by 1893 Harrison was back in City Hall again, known for his tolerance for the very sort of protests that now gained Coxey's attention and a new friend.[27]

Coxey seemed particularly impressed that the deep-throated Browne chose to engage none other than the infamous Donnelly himself. The little-known Browne hardly seemed the match for this Populist icon. The Californian's resplendent appearance, marked by the Western garb that he donned as a bit actor in the popular "Wild and Wooly West Show" at the Columbian Exposition, made him seem larger than life. Indeed the exposition's popular Wild West Show itself seemed to satirize a frontier that, according to one historian, had simply exhausted its promise. The young Wisconsin professor Frederick Jackson Turner, who spoke at the exposition just a few weeks before Coxey arrived, based his talk on his meticulous examination of the census of 1890. As a result of his analysis, he boldly proclaimed to a thinning crowd in the frightfully warm Hall of Columbus that the American frontier had vanished. Americans would now need to find a new space to exercise their restless energy. Browne, the restless Californian, who now came eastward, seemed to embody the very energy that Turner described. Coxey would now invite Browne to help him in a new venture, and the two would turn their sights toward the nation's capital and ask government to restore the promise of this now-vanished physical frontier.[28]

The Chicago press referred to Browne as the "Cowboy from California" or the "Conestoga Cowboy." Other less complimentary descriptions noted that, though he seemed to have some force as a thinker and speaker, he lacked substance. Said one account, "He affects the cowboy style of dress to the extent of a disgustingly filthy leather suit set off by high boots and sombrero." However exaggerated the style, Browne's substantial rhetorical gifts helped him win his debate against Donnelly, at least in the eyes of some. Browne boldly challenged Donnelly's Populist pedigree and then insisted that land needed to be considered as an alternative form of currency. The message appealed to this Lake Front audience, including Coxey. To best Donnelly, "the Minnesota Sage," was no small accomplishment. Donnelly was not only a veteran politician and much-published author, but according to one contemporary, in any debate "no one could more easily make the worse appear the better reason, and no one delighted more in doing so."[29]

After the debate ended, Coxey was so impressed with Browne's performance that he wasted little time introducing himself to the artist turned orator. From the moment of this first encounter, the two apparently began to forge a friendship based on shared ideas. Though no evidence of their discussions that summer survives, we know that Coxey asked Browne to return with him to Massillon to help him promote his Good Roads plan. The relationship between Browne, the imaginative artist, and Coxey, the thoughtful businessman, grew deeper in the months that followed this first encounter. Coxey needed a dramatic way to draw enough national attention to his plan so that it might resonate with Congress. The two began discussing how they could create an event that would allow them to escape the concert halls, meetinghouses, and lecture rooms that confined political speech. How could they best express the frustrations of those who felt suffocated under the weight of a new form of corporate capitalism and a growing depression?[30]

The two posed a sharp contrast in style while agreeing on substance. The straight-laced Coxey, sporting his trademark winged collar and frock coat, did not hide his conventional business airs or his substantial wealth. Yet, in his devotion to soft money he also displayed an uncommon and steadfast devotion to expanding the nation's currency, infrastructure, and employment. Browne consistently agitated for the underdog, always comfortable creating the sort of controversy that drew attention. He harbored resentment of those bankers and monopolists who he believed suppressed the hardworking producer. Born in 1849 and six years Coxey's senior, he had apprenticed in a printing shop in Illinois and then, after the death of his mother, migrated to Iowa and trained to become an artist. Thus began an itinerant career that included stints as an artist, rancher, journalist, carnival barker, and labor organizer. While little information is available about his past, according to one account his first painting was of the Lord's Supper, foreshadowing his later religious turn. In 1869, inspired by reading about the West, he migrated in that direction, painting scenes in Yosemite and wandering throughout the region before eventually settling in Berkeley, California, in 1872 with his young wife, Alice Currier. One of his later paintings of the Civil War battle at Gettysburg was exhibited at Market Square in San Francisco and reportedly earned him a considerable sum of money.[31]

By his own admission, it was the Great Rail Strike of 1877 that transformed Browne from a wandering painter to an active reformer. The nationwide strike, he later acknowledged, "aroused his sympathies for his fellow men." He enthusiastically joined in the mob violence in San Francisco that summer, befriending the "sandlot" agitator Dennis Kearney. Browne became Kearney's secretary, much as he would become Coxey's trusted lieutenant. Kearney was an Irish immigrant who fast became the central figure in the formation of California's Workingman's Party, which rallied in support of organized labor during the 1877 strike. In sympathy with labor and its cause, Browne began writing, illustrating, and publishing his own paper called the *Great Strike*. When San Francisco vigilance authorities threatened him with hanging if he continued to publish, he started an openly anti-Chinese newspaper called *Open Letter*. Just as Browne would help Coxey project his ideas, this publication served as Kearney's mouthpiece in his fierce opposition to the railroads and their Chinese workers.[32]

Browne continued to use his acquired journalistic skills when he arrived at the Silver Convention. He ostensibly came as a reporter for the activist *San Francisco Argus*. However, he quickly left his press credentials at the door to declare himself a bona fide delegate from California. As his debate with Donnelly revealed, he could be among the most vocal of populists; well trained in the art of agitation from his days with Kearney, he now possessed a distinctly activist pedigree. Perhaps then, not surprisingly, Browne initially declined Coxey's offer to return to Massillon with him following the adjournment of the Bimetallic gathering, opting instead to stay in Chicago and join the nightly protest rallies of the unemployed along Chicago's lakefront.[33]

Against the backdrop of a worsening economy, and with its collateral damage in the form of homeless men, women, and children now in plain view on the crowded streets of Chicago, Browne unleashed his nightly rhetorical attacks against the Gilded Age elites. At the windy Lake Front Park, he would stand on a barrel and display his colorfully painted canvas murals, with their caricatures of Wall Street tycoons carrying plump politicians in their inflated pockets. Often his long speeches and those of other reformers aroused the crowds to take action. On August 28, well after Coxey had returned to Massillon, an unruly mob took to the streets. When one of the leaders, thought by many to be Browne, yelled "Siegel and Cooper's," the angry marchers turned and headed toward one of the city's largest department stores. As customers and employees of the store headed toward the exits, the police swooped in to make arrests. While others might have been more responsible for this incident, Browne, easily identifiable in his cowboy garb, received the blame.[34]

Meanwhile Mayor Harrison, who recalled all too well the harrowing details of the violence in the Haymarket in 1886, decided the time had come to put an end to the protests that were turning more violent each night. Having experienced weeks of Browne's unruly behavior, the unusually tolerant mayor lost patience. He summoned Browne to his office and harshly lectured him for half an hour before finally telling him that for the "good of the city, you better get out!" Browne and his fellow activists, who had continued to meet at the lakefront, were thus forced to discontinue their nightly gatherings. With his Chicago act suddenly closed, Browne took Coxey up on his earlier offer from the summer to come to Massillon.[35]

Off to Massillon

As Browne departed, he left a city that, not unlike the rest of America, was reeling from the ravages of an ever-widening depression. Dr. Isaac A. Hourwich, from the department of statistics at the University of Chicago, began interviewing those who now filled the corridors of City Hall and slept on its marble slab floors. Touring a hollowed-out neighborhood on West Van Horne Street, which many poor families could no longer afford, Hourwich found a few still eking out a living, though they were growing more desperate by the day. He described how one immigrant family from Poland tried to survive the harsh winter in the basement of one abandoned home:

> There was a little fire in the stove, but the head of the family was an old man, who depended on the earnings of his wife, who usually washed for fifty cents per day. Washing, she said, was hard to get, as people were doing their own washing. Her husband used to clean street pits, but owing to the general rush for such work was unable to secure regular employment.

Indeed, many of those suffering were immigrants or those who had come from the countryside to the big city to help with the boom in construction that accompanied the World's Fair. Of the one hundred or so whom Hourwich interviewed, only eight said they received aid from any charity. And charity did not provide jobs.[36]

Meanwhile, in spite of the obvious human toll the depression was taking, the Upper Ten continued about their business as usual. On December 10, 1893, the *Chicago Tribune* published the results of its own informal survey of wealthy Chicagoans. The *Tribune* posed the question, "What would you do if you were to strike a city like this [i.e., Chicago] homeless and penniless?" Many of those asked seemed stumped for an answer. When, for example, Lyman Gage, the president of Chicago's First National Bank was asked this question, the *Tribune* reported, "The man [Gage] who heard the question stopped as if he had been shot. He never had thought of it before." After thinking a bit and musing on the various shelters available as well as the possible work relief options, Gage dismissed the need for much in the way of relief. As he pondered the question he noted that so many of those who now found themselves destitute were frankly "undeserving" of assistance. Another banker, Melville Stone, said he too had come to Chicago penniless but, being resourceful and enterprising, "began to hustle." He thus found the question a useful way to separate himself from those obviously suffering the consequences of the depression because they were less fit to survive. A diamond merchant on State Street exhibited a similar callousness. When asked by the reporter, "But what if you couldn't get work," the diamond broker answered glibly, "There should be no such word in any man's dictionary, especially a poor man's, as the word 'couldn't.'" Consistently the wealthy displayed the prevailing attitude that those without jobs had themselves, not the economy, to blame.[37]

However, one wealthy soul, now back in Massillon, Ohio, looked at the plight of the poor much differently than did his wealthy peers. Perhaps recalling his own misfortune in an earlier panic, Coxey thought the infusion of new currency, unconstrained by any artificial metal standard, would allow communities to raise the money to build roads and create vast numbers of new jobs. He and his newfound partner saw the unemployed as victims of the economy, not their own weakness. They decided to organize the unemployed in a march to Washington. Working from his home in Paul's Station just outside Massillon, Coxey together with Browne began sending out pamphlets, bulletins, and circulars to a network of Greenbackers and Populists across the country. Even the *Los Angeles Times* advertised a forthcoming march to Washington. As the year turned, Coxey would spend nearly all his time during the first three months of 1894 raising money, resources, and men for this spectacle set to depart Massillon on May 1, International Labor Day, a year to the day after the Chicago World's Fair opened and the depression set in.[38]

CHAPTER TWO

The Good Roads Plan

"With the Good Roads Plan of $500,000,000 to provide the machinery whereby all the unemployed, skilled and unskilled, may be put to work."[1]

J. S. Coxey, Good Roads Association

AS THEY BEGAN TO make their plans for the march to Washington, Coxey and Browne faced seemingly insurmountable practical and political obstacles. Coxey's Good Roads plan not only defied conventional notions of what governments should do to help the jobless, but in order to draw attention to his solution, he would now be publicly parading "the idle tramp," the very object of that public scorn. No wonder, then, that the two companions, working side by side, constantly sought to distinguish how their army would consist of proud men seeking honest work, clearly distinguishable from the stereotypical tramp. "We want patriots, not bummers," Browne affirmed. Coxey also declared that they were not recruiting idle tramps. One *Boston Globe* reporter obligingly acknowledged that the men who joined the march were not "Huns and Slavs, and densely ignorant." Rather, they were typical skilled workers simply in need of work. Yet, in the lead-up to the departure and beyond, most newspapers would refer to "Coxey's tramp army."[2]

Coxey not only sought to defend his marchers with his words, but he sought to dignify the march by the very way in which it presented itself. He discouraged the sick and those of ill repute from joining. He emphasized that the journey would be a test and that all who joined would face rough conditions. Adopting the individualistic ethos that defined an America on the make, those joining would be expected "with true American grit, to grin and bear it." Coxey succeeded in recruiting an assemblage that was far from the popular stereotype of tramps as unskilled laborers, immigrants, and anarchists. Rather, most were either American- or English-born skilled workers representing some seventy different trades. Few indicated any allegiance to a union. Most of the men were married and had some formal schooling. One analysis suggested that most were skilled tradesmen who would depart the march for a job if one were offered.[3]

Shirley Plumer Austin's account in the popular *Chautauquan* magazine provided detailed character sketches of several of the marchers. Almost three-quarters of those he surveyed were skilled workmen who were simply put out of work by the Panic. Austin described an eclectic band of diverse marchers representing mostly out-of-work industrialists with minds of their own. For example, A. H. Blinn was described as a thirty-year-old married man, well dressed and intelligent looking, an iron molder and a member of the National Federation of Labor. He actually belonged to the Republican Party, seemed "disgusted" with Browne's Theosophy, and reportedly kept his distance from Coxey. Dan Thompson, a former racetrack employee, professed to not know very much at all about Coxey's proposals or Browne's "religious stuff." But he seemed to be enjoying the camaraderie, noting "I am having a whale of a time with the outfit." Charles Smith, a Pittsburgh wire drawer locked out of work since Christmas 1893, needed to support his wife and six children. He believed in Coxey's ideas and thought they would lead to full employment. Frank Ball seemed to Austin to be a man of some means. He had worked on Mississippi steamers and, like Coxey, had become attracted to Browne's ideas when he heard him speak on the Chicago waterfront the summer before. "I had been idle ten weeks before the Army started," he said. Though he voted Democratic, he believed a great political change was about to happen. "I am a Socialist and I want to see complete government ownership—that's the only way of saying the people's ownership."[4]

The Tramp Stereotype

Nonetheless, Coxey and Browne faced an enormous challenge in presenting these jobless marchers as no different in their essential humanity from those with a job. In the late nineteenth century the presence of the wandering unemployed often provoked severe reactions. In Anderson, Indiana, on March 29, 1889, the city's marshal ordered eight "tramps" to leave the town's only train station. Outside, thirty men armed with poles and barrel staves formed a gauntlet along the railroad track. As the *New York Times* reported, "The tramps were forced to run, their speed being accelerated by heavy blows well laid on by the men." Beaten until bloody, the men stumbled out of Anderson and toward the next town, many diving into empty train cars in their desperate search for food and shelter. If fortune shone upon them, perhaps they would soon land a job.[5]

As part of an army of wandering wage seekers these "down-and-outers," according to the prevailing Social Darwinist orthodoxy as popularized in America by Yale professor William Graham Sumner, were flawed in character and not deserving of handouts. At a National Conference of Charities and Correction in 1886, tramps were formally described as being afflicted with everything from drunkenness to love of roving to loss of self-respect. Even before the Panic of 1893, the new wage-based economy of the industrialized North could no longer provide enough work for those leaving their farms for the cities or those returning to the city from jobs in the mines and forests in the West. New waves of immigrants exacerbated the competition for jobs, and the legions of tramps seemed to grow steadily. When faced with no job and little opportunity for assistance, many took to the rails. This practice, known as "hopping," dated back to the Civil War, when rail cars hauled fresh troops to the front lines and brought wounded soldiers home. Now, in an increasingly industrialized country, where many factory jobs were often distant and seasonal, the railroads provided a convenient way for those without work to search for the next opportunity in the next town.[6]

Regardless, leaders from every walk of life seemed bent on holding the indigent responsible for their own misery. Not only were the jobless viewed as essentially flawed in character, but because of their perceived lack of self-discipline and inherent character flaws government intervention on their behalf seemed wholly inappropriate. In fact, governments acted to police tramp behavior. Some forty states adopted Tramp Acts. In New York alone, almost five thousand people were arrested as tramps in 1894. The very idea that Coxey planned to recruit such wayward souls to march with him to the steps of the Capitol insulted the bedrock Protestant work ethic. Even before Spencer's Darwinian sociology captured attention, the notion of "self-reliance" stood as a pillar of the American ethos, early on sanctified by the likes of Ralph Waldo Emerson. Emerson excused those hardworking citizens too preoccupied with their own livelihoods to tend to those less resourceful. If the "self-helping man" could not find the time or resources to help those in need, then, said America's philosopher, "attend your own work, and already the evil begins to be repaired."[7]

The word "tramp" had actually entered the lexicon as a term of disparagement following an earlier panic in 1873. "Tramping" evoked an image of the shiftless vagabond, a person not to be trusted. An 1878 novel by Lee Harris posed the tramp as one who deliberately sought to provoke conflicts between business owners and laborers. Elaborate taxonomies of tramp types were developed to better understand the menace. Tramps even became the subject of an undercover exposé. In 1891, then Princeton seminarian Walter Wyckoff disguised himself as a tramp and over a period of eighteen months roamed the countryside, all the while submitting articles and writing a book. The popularity of his first articles for *Scribner's* magazine was in fact symptomatic of a new genre of "tramp literature." Notable writers such as Stephen Crane and Jack London (who also covered Kelly's Army, one of the industrial armies moving eastward from Oakland) also left their comfortable lives to wander with the jobless. Yet, while sympathetic to his subjects, even Wyckoff marveled at his own ability to find work and in subsequent lectures would note skepticism about the government intervening to create jobs. "It is more a question of the individual than of society as a whole," he said, conforming to the dominant view.[8]

The reality was that tramping was born of necessity. Most nineteenth-century wage earners had to be able to walk to work. Without a public-transportation system of good roads, a man either found a job within walking distance of his home or set out wandering in search of one, usually without money and often hopping a rail car. Seasonality and fluctuating manufacturing cycles only served to increase the challenge of finding steady work. Often associated with gambling, alcohol, or infidelity, the wandering workforce had become a fixture since the Civil War. As William Moody, former printer turned labor reformer, observed:

> Today throughout our whole country,—on the plains and in the mountains; in the densest populations and on the most advanced frontiers; in town, country, and mining camp, are found armies of homeless wanderers, that can be numbered only by hundreds of thousands, if not by millions, vainly seeking work, begging or stealing their subsistence wherever they can find it, and rapidly sinking to the most callous vagabondage and crime.

As the Panic of 1893 turned to a full-fledged depression, local charities found it convenient to establish tests that might separate wandering itinerants like Coxey's from the native and more-deserving poor.[9]

The tramps thus became the example of those simply unable to pull themselves up by the bootstraps, the mirror opposites of the heroes in Horatio Alger's popular novels. Yale professor Francis Wayland, a colleague of Sumner, summarized what constituted the canonical interpretation of "tramping" when he spoke to a gathering of social scientists at Saratoga, New York, in 1877:

> As we utter the word tramp, there arises straightway before us the spectacle
> of a lazy, shiftless, sauntering or swaggering, ill-conditioned, irreclaimable,
> incorrigible, cowardly, utterly depraved savage. He fears not God, neither
> regards man. Indeed he seems to have wholly lost all the better instincts
> and attributes of manhood. He will outrage an unprotected female, or rob
> a defenseless child, or burn an isolated barn, or girdle fruit trees, or wreck
> a railway train, or set fire to a railroad bridge, or murder a cripple, or pilfer
> an umbrella, with equal indifference, if reasonably sure of equal impunity.

Wayland's words reflect a view that seemed congruent with the nation's meteoric economic trajectory and provided a ready explanation as to why millionaires should be extolled and tramps despised. Wayland's words soothed the consciences of the newly successful and the already rich.[10]

Even theologians joined in praising the virtues of the hardworking wealthy and questioning the character-flawed poor. Roswell Hitchcock, president of the prestigious Union Theological Seminary in New York, spoke to the predominant view that nature found ways to select the gifted: "Mankind are not equal in endowment," he asserted. "In stamina and constitution, one is strong and one is weak. Brains are larger or smaller, coarser or finer." This was, he suggested, simply the natural order of things and to be accepted. Meanwhile, Hitchcock also reflected the prevailing fear among the era's wealthy and privileged that the burgeoning new immigrant population brought with them from Europe a pitiable allegiance to socialism that only encouraged man's worst instincts. By rewarding the less fit, these European forms of political economy defied the natural order of things by attempting to create a wholly unnatural equality of result. Hitchcock begrudgingly admitted that governments might make some accommodation for the sick and those victims of accidents, though even here he noted with seeming despair that "society might have to be taxed for the deficit." The best the fit could do for the unfit was to offer what Hitchcock called a "Christian Socialism." More a consciousness than a system, this beneficent voluntarism asked the well-off to make appropriate, faith-based judgments of both rich and poor. Those few of superior intelligence and ability should demonstrate a Christian spirit toward the poor. Exactly how this translated into specific measures was left to the gifted to determine. Hitchcock urged the mutual recognition by laborer and management of their respective obligations to one another. Both rich and poor needed to act with "forethought and frugality," since the masses could not expect much more than a fair wage and the "favored few" needed to reach an understanding that they served one another by serving God.[11]

Changing Views

However, not all were in lockstep in their disdain for tramps. As far back as the Panic of 1873, the sheer numbers of those unemployed became a troublesome reality that seemed to beg for some different view. By the 1880s a few clergymen, like Washington Gladden, began actively preaching a social gospel and questioning the very morality of the commoditization of labor. In academia new concepts were also being offered to explain the conditions of the poor. University of Wisconsin sociologist Richard Ely rallied others to his American Institute of Christian Sociology with his writings on the deleterious effects of industrialization on employment. It was in this context of new concerns that the very word "unemployment" first entered the lexicon in the 1880s and began taking on new meaning.[12]

Under conventional economic theories of the time, employment equilibrium was assumed as the norm. Prominent nineteenth-century economists recognized that though machines might supplant certain jobs, they would create others and thus contribute to a balance in the supply of labor. Though they acknowledged that the industrial economy might result in temporary worker dislocations, or "underemployment," they were confident that the market's inherent dynamism would create a situation where the supply and demand for labor were generally always in harmony. The notion of unemployment, so familiar to us today, remained an emerging and unwelcome concept in a rapidly industrializing American economy.[13]

However, the nascent labor movement was increasingly aggressive in challenging these conventional notions. American Federation of Labor President Gompers testified before Congress as early as 1883, urging the creation of a national labor bureau that "would give our legislators an opportunity to know, not from mere conjecture, but actually, the condition of our industries, our production, and our consumption, and what could be done to improve both [sic]." A year after Gompers's testimony, the Bureau of Labor Statistics (BLS) was created to gather statistics on the "subject of labor." However, it was not empowered to count the actual number of men out of work, a phenomenon still more stigmatized than acknowledged. And, even a decade after formation of the BLS, as the Panic of 1893 turned into a four-year depression and the number of jobless grew, still no one knew for sure exactly how many were unemployed or what percentage of the working population they represented.[14]

The "gravity of the problem" so impressed economist Carlos C. Closson that in 1893 he conducted an extensive survey of the unemployed in America's major cities in an attempt to draw the larger picture. While unable to precisely determine the number of unemployed in total, his survey corroborated the sheer magnitude of those unemployed. He cataloged how New York state reached out to its manufacturing "establishments" in an effort to estimate the extent of the jobless problem, and he reported how in Massachusetts, as early as 1878, the chief of the Bureau of Statistics and Labor, Carroll D. Wright, decided to actually count those in his state without work. Despite his own pioneering effort to give the unemployed a statistical identity and legitimacy in the context of a new economy, Wright himself succumbed to the presumptive bias of his time. In suggesting what the remedy might be, he counseled, "Courage, patience, and faith in hard work will reward the worker in the near future with continued occupation." As for his efforts, Closson simply noted that restoring the vitality of the economy was the only way to put the idle back to work. Given the paucity of relief and public-works initiatives, it was hard to argue that an economic recovery was the best panacea.[15]

While the idea of "unemployment" seemed to gain a toehold, those doing the most to legitimize the concept still harbored traditional ideas on what to do about it. In 1894, the very year Coxey marched, the state of Massachusetts, again in the vanguard, seemed to take a major step forward, authorizing a commission to investigate the causes of "unemployment" and to explore measures to alleviate it. However, MIT professor David Dewey, who led the study, believed unemployment to be a temporary phenomenon. While his analysis was indeed a government-sanctioned initiative that drew attention to the jobless, he blithely concluded that "there have always been able-bodied poor, sturdy beggars, shiftless ne'er do wells, weaklings, intemperates [sic], feeble discarded units of society, whom society has carried on its shoulders." Not surprisingly, then, his final report modestly urged more in the way of local relief efforts and the need to gather better statistical information. It seemed that even those who advanced the use of the term "unemployment" could not bring themselves to do much about it. The idea that there might always be a group of idled laborers seemed an inconvenient reality in this new industrial age.[16]

Thus, in spite of a growing consciousness of the phenomenon of the unemployed, for the most part the callous attitudes toward the unemployed individual remained unchanged. The jobless were still held responsible for their decrepit state. Only gradually would the possibility that environmental factors played a defining role in their fate slowly creep into the public consciousness. As the depression of the nineties worsened, the disparaged tramp still faced bleak prospects when it came to relying on government for answers. Assistance, however it might be administered, remained subject to the vagaries of local officials or the random beneficence of local philanthropists. This was a growing challenge, since even in good times as much as a fourth of the workforce found themselves without a job for three months of the year. Coxey and Browne seemed to be presented with insurmountable odds to change public perception, let alone to get the public to adopt Coxey's bold solution.[17]

Flawed Souls and Poor Relief

In 1894 there was still no social safety net to catch those who fell out of work. In most communities, relief continued to come mainly through the generosity of local philanthropists. In cities like Chicago, New York, and Philadelphia, governments stepped in, but only reluctantly. They typically provided only meager funds to those existing voluntary and religiously inspired aid societies and community chests. Public hostility to welfare remained high, and any government intervention predictably brought rebuke.[18]

Communities that confronted pauperism did so with a combination of so-called outdoor relief and poorhouses. Outdoor relief efforts administered aid (food, clothes, medicine, cash) to the poor as they found them, in their homes or on the streets. However, poorhouses—those central buildings where the indigent were sent, lived, and sometimes worked—were thought to be a cheaper alternative. Regardless, each constituted a form of so-called poor relief and found their support from a mix of charities, wealthy donors, and modest taxes. These initiatives, however inadequate, nonetheless also received blame for the very ills they tried to eradicate. Outdoor relief was attacked as too expensive and too expansive, as a giveaway to those too lazy to work. Poorhouses similarly came to be discredited over the century, their costs subject to stinging criticism and their ability to resurrect the indigent ridiculed. By the 1880s they had mostly devolved into homes for the aged. The able-bodied poor increasingly sought refuge in police stations or city halls.[19]

This stinginess toward the poor not only reflected the predominant Social Darwinism that pulsed through late nineteenth-century intellectual circles, but it had deeper roots in a Protestant work ethic that became part of the American credo. None other than Benjamin Franklin in his *Autobiography* voiced his healthy skepticism toward aid for the poor. He observed that "the more public provisions were made for the poor, the less they provided for themselves, and of course became poorer." Even late nineteenth-century clergy joined in the exaltation of the business doctrine of laissez-faire. The enterprising and individualistic entrepreneur was seen as God's rightful shepherd on earth, improving the lot of his fellow man through his industrious enterprise, creating jobs, paying wages, and creating the products that provided for the welfare of his fellow man. In this world view, governments needed to operate in the shadows, never to interfere with the important tasks of the industrious, god-fearing captains of industry who bore the responsibilities entrusted to them because of their obvious genetic superiority. As the Baptist *Standard* suggested, the day would come when the successful Horatio Algers of this Gilded Age "can meet the master of all, as one at whose feet it will be an infinite joy to lay down the fruits of all his giving and all his doing." A devout Baptist, oil magnate John D. Rockefeller thought his strong faith inseparable from his business success and his riches tied to his disciplined use of money. As the acclaimed preacher Henry Ward Beecher said, "Generally the proposition is true that where you find the most religion, you find the most worldly prosperity."[20]

With poor relief viewed this cautiously and relief efforts haphazard and stingy, some reformers became committed to finding a better way to administer relief. They called the new approach "scientific charity." Settlement houses such as Jane Addams's Chicago Hull House provided refuge and solace for limited numbers. Other social workers took the view that, with a more systematic and efficient approach to charity, they could encourage those in need to find ways to help themselves. In her criticism of existing outdoor relief efforts such as the "dole," one of the foremost practitioners of scientific charity, Josephine Shaw Lowell, stated her belief that charity should first and foremost "help people to help themselves." Clearly any systemic approach to the problem was still years away.[21]

Despite the optimism of the scientific charity movement and substantial donations from the Gilded Age wealthy toward making it work, communities were ill prepared for what hit them with the Panic of 1893. As the depression grew worse in the winter of 1894, many of the benevolent emergency-relief associations found themselves stretched to their limits. States and localities that bore the burden were strapped for funds and thus often turned to new ways of providing jobs and work relief. As early as the Panic of 1857, public works were tried as a means for putting the unemployed back to work. But through the remainder of the century, public-works projects seemed a last resort, tried only on a local and very modest scale. Indeed, municipal governments, in addition to doling out medicines, food, and even money, in some instances put the unemployed to work paving streets or laying sewage pipes. In Detroit the situation grew so dire that unemployed Polish immigrants roamed the streets with picks and shovels looking for work on the spot. Four-term Republican progressive mayor Hazen Pingree decided the unemployed needed small plots of land, or what came to be known as "potato patches." He asked local churches to provide these newly created "urban farmers" with the seeds and plows they needed in an innovative effort to calm the stress of urban unemployment.[22]

But modest and inexpensive work relief initiatives like Pingree's experiment with city farming were limited in their reach and their results. In Milwaukee and Waterbury, Connecticut, men went to work for a few months improving the city streets. In Holyoke, Massachusetts's sewerage construction kept some three hundred men working until the summer. In Rochester, New York, the unemployed were allowed to make improvements to local parks. This pattern of small projects, typically underfunded, at least kept the notion of publicly funded works alive but gained scant attention from federal or even state officials. Even at this paltry local scale the use of public monies for such relief continued to be unpopular. In New York City, where over $1 million was appropriated for use on local parks, far fewer dollars made their way into the hands of the unemployed. As one contemporary observer noted, "Workers referred by social agencies were dropped more quickly than those sent by politicians; some men never appeared except on paydays, and carelessness, extravagance, and misappropriation in administration were rife."[23]

While communities continually experimented with public-works programs as a way to employ the jobless, these initiatives were typically poorly funded and short in duration. Neither state nor federal governments viewed public works as a way to put the unemployed back to work. Nor, more importantly, did they see it as their role to provide jobs in the first place. In Coxey's home state, when local unions asked the Ohio legislature to approve public-works initiatives using unclaimed land to construct public buildings, officials responded by declaring that there was no such unclaimed land, nor any need to construct new public buildings.[24]

Coxey's Plan

Such a lack of enthusiasm for public works did not discourage Coxey. His public-works plan was not only nationwide in its scope but it required the equivalent of the entire federal budget. Coxey's bold initiative charged past the modest ideas emanating from a two-decade-old Good Roads movement. As early as 1891 Coxey wrote a letter to both President Harrison and the Congress, noting that the "public roads of the United States generally are a national disgrace." In 1892 Coxey formed his own "Coxey Good Roads Association of the United States." He actively communicated with fellow Good Roads advocates and Populist clubs about his own bold plan for the construction of a national network of publicly funded roads. He formally presented his ideas before the Populist convention in St. Louis in February 1892 and sent a written petition to Congress containing his plan. On March 29 of that year, Ohio Congressman John George Warwick, who grew up working in a dry-goods store in Massillon, introduced a petition to Congress from "J. S. Coxey and others, for the issue of $500,000,000 of Treasury notes to improve public roads." The petition was referred to the Committee on Agriculture where, like most written petitions, it died (as did Congressman Warwick himself later that summer, still in his first term).[25]

Yet, the very next year California Democratic Congressman Thomas J. Geary and Kansas Populist Senator William Peffer introduced two separate and briefly worded pieces of legislation in their respective chambers that sought to translate Coxey's plan into the law of the land. The bills called for the Treasury to issue $500 million in what Coxey described as "full legal tender Treasury notes, making them full legal tender for all debts, public and private, and appropriate to each State and Territory pro rata with the number of miles of road in each state." The vague and confusing mechanics of Coxey's plan allowed each government entity the authority to assess up to one-half the property values in its jurisdiction and then to issue interest-free bonds on the basis of this assessment.[26]

This latter feature theoretically allowed for redundant assessments on behalf of overlapping jurisdictions. Since the plan was lacking in some details of execution, it was thus possible for a property to be assessed once by a county and then a second time by a township—or any other combination of entities that could lay claim. In other words, separate bonds could be issued by overlapping jurisdictions based on the same property assessment. Coxey minded less about this seemingly troublesome detail than he did the virtue of allowing the Treasury Department to issue legal tender currency to political subdivisions, regardless of their size or location, up to a combined total of $500 million. His only caveat was that, when issuing bonds, each government entity was required to hold back a small percentage of the revenue raised for its own administrative costs. By Coxey's estimate four million men, composing an industrial army under the command of the Secretary of War, could be returned to work, constructing a nationwide network of good roads. Moreover they would earn $1.50 a day in greenbacks backed by the deposit of low-interest-bearing, twenty-five-year bonds.[27]

In this pre-automobile era still dominated by the railroads, Coxey's idea seemed vaguely reminiscent of the "American system" advocated almost a century before by Senators Henry Clay and John Calhoun. The two envisioned development of a national economy united by roads and canals built with the assistance of the federal government. Treasury Secretary Albert Gallatin's 1808 report to Congress clearly stated the need for a system of national infrastructure with roads at its core. Yet, ever since Peter Cooper's small locomotive, the *Tom Thumb*, defeated a horse-drawn carriage in 1830, the national investment in rails had dwarfed that in roads. Throughout the nineteenth century the railroad came to symbolize America's emergence as an industrial power on the world stage. Governments at every level sought creative, if not corrupt incentives to aid railroad construction, and towns and villages throughout America seemed willing to pay any price to have railroads boost their local economies. Political corruption enabled railroad magnates such as James Hill and Jay Gould to eviscerate any remaining vision of a national system of roads. By the 1880s the nation had achieved an integrated network of railroad lines that employed thousands, yet ironically also transported the unemployed in search of work.[28]

The decrepit road conditions that Coxey's men would endure during their march on Washington reflected this century-long legacy of rail dominance. Though there was plenty of complaining about the state of the nation's roads, road construction needed a powerful political lobby. As evidence, Coxey's Army often found itself marching on the National Pike, a half-built and declining artifact of Clay and Calhoun's vision. In the spring of 1894, what was now referred to as the Cumberland Road symbolized the decline in America's roads throughout the nineteenth century. This was hardly the magnificent National Road that its proponents had envisioned stretching from the Maryland tidewaters well into the Ohio frontier. The road had not only become unworthy of its original name but had so deteriorated that it was not unusual to see bull dogs with their necks bulging against their collars, tied to stuck wagon wheels and straining to move their heavy loads forward on the road's most treacherous stretches.[29]

For those like Coxey, the path toward revitalizing our national road system remained rocky. Since Senator Martin Van Buren blocked additional National Pike funding in 1828, the federal government could not get out of the road-building business fast enough. By 1832 Congress handed its authority for the National Pike over to the states of Maryland, Virginia, Pennsylvania, and Ohio. Each state became responsible for developing its own system of tolls in order to finance road repair. Indeed, throughout

America, state and local governments were left to finance roads as a result of the federal government's relinquishment of any role in construction or upkeep. For example, the law in Coxey's Ohio, not untypical of many states, actually required farmers to perform two days of labor on highways, contiguous to their property just to keep them in some semblance of repair. Known as the "working out tax," this led to inconsistencies in road repair and reduced the amount that localities raised in revenues. It proved as ineffective a mechanism for Northern road maintenance as convict labor did for the upkeep of Southern roads.[30]

Before Coxey proposed his Good Roads plan, the impetus to revitalize the national infrastructure emerged from a most unlikely source. In 1877 Colonel Albert A. Pope, a decorated Civil War hero, began importing bicycles into the United States. When he began manufacturing them in America in 1879, the bicycle craze truly took hold. With the advent of the pneumatic (air-filled) tire, bicycle riding left the rinks for the roads. The seeds of what two decades later became "highway federalism" began to slowly take root with these early bicycle riders. By 1880 riders had formed their own association, the League of American Wheelmen (LAW). With chapters in virtually every state, these riders figuratively began paving the way for an improved road system throughout America. In the span of a decade, beginning with its formation when "a little band of gentlemen" met at the epicenter of Gilded Age elite culture in Newport, Rhode Island, to its later hard-earned engagement of farmers to help finance road repair, the LAW evolved from being an elitist recreational amusement into a broad national movement.[31]

Despite the momentum that the LAW generated, rural Americans generally did not see good roads as being in their economic best interest. Good Roads advocates as early as the 1860s perceived a widespread public acceptance of bad road conditions. But whether from stinginess or myopia, American farmers generally opposed road improvements they might have to pay for. Having grown accustomed to bad roads, they seemed not to realize that new technologies could dramatically improve their local roads. Occasionally, a wet winter in the Midwest would draw some passing attention to the economic impact of bad roads that were preventing essential goods from moving to market. Even city fathers frequently complained that the condition of rural roads prevented outlying residents from visiting their stores.[32]

Indeed, throughout the 1880s agitation for good roads increased in farm press commentaries, as did calls for state legislation to address the situation. "Let anyone drive over most American roads in the spring, with open eyes and wits, and see what unchecked destruction is at work," commented the syndicated "Country Gentleman" in April 1884. In October of that same year, the *American Farmer* expressed hope that soon Good Roads would be the rule rather than the exception. An Ohio farmer, losing money with every day that his goods could not reach market, calculated that maintaining one brief stretch of Ohio road that becomes impassable to any farm load during wet weather cost each of four road districts $1.50 a day to maintain. The farmer calculated that in twenty years, at this cost, he could buy more than enough gravel to repave the entire road.[33]

Coxey's own state of Ohio was typical of most states. It had taken little action to improve its road system. Ohio legislators contemplated the prospect of putting a charge on the weight of heavy wagons as a way to raise revenue for road improvements. But this proposal failed to move. In January 1893 the state's own chapter of the National Good Roads Association met to debate controversial alternatives to funding road repair and construction. But they adjourned with little resolution on how to solve the problem. For this very reason some of Coxey's fellow Ohioans were drawn to his plan to nationalize the costs of highway construction. A conference of farmers meeting in Athens warmed to the idea, and one reporter noted that a majority of the state's citizens seemed to like the notion of states and municipalities being able to borrow money from the federal government at low interest rates—or in the case of Coxey's plan at zero interest.[34]

Yet, it would be an understatement to say that Coxey's version of a Good Roads plan and that of the more conventional-thinking Good Roads movement were far apart. Coxey's expensive and expansive plan soared in the stratosphere, while the elitist-tinged LAW sought to take careful earthbound steps in their advocacy of a new road system. Longtime Good Roads champion General Roy Stone thought the movement should welcome virtually any financial plan for improvement, regardless of whether housed at the federal, state, county, or municipal level. Stone did not rule out the need for a federal role, and he clearly tried to encourage what he perceived to be some gathering momentum for federal support of local road improvements. "Public opinion is fast crystallizing in favor of national aid in building country roads and it can hardly be a debatable question that the government will again turn its attention to assisting the states in this work," he proclaimed at the November 1892 Chicago meeting of the newly formed National League for Good Roads (NLGR). Yet Stone's ideas and those of both the NLGR and the LAW for some federal engagement remained Lilliputian in scale when compared with Coxey's Brobdingnagian idea.

Stone modestly proposed that Good Roads could be financed by the issuance of county bonds to be guaranteed first by the state and ultimately, only if necessary and as a last resort, by the federal government. However, unlike

Coxey's bold plan, Stone, likely constrained by the lack of any reliable data, did not specify what amount would need to be raised to create a national road system. Moreover, he left it for local governments to choose to participate or not. Only if local governments defaulted on their obligations would these roads be mortgaged to the United States. Stone seemed to reflect the will of the Good Roads movement that the national government be in the rear rather than the lead, though he at least acknowledged that the federal government had a role to play.[35]

Thus, Stone was more enthusiastic, and perhaps far more realistic, in his support for legislation that would create a National Highway Commission to investigate the scope and costs of road repair. Stone wrote to Republican Senator Charles Manderson of Nebraska, who also served as the president of the NLGR, to insist that the federal government must lend its own faith and credit to states and localities for the purpose of constructing this national network of good roads. Senator Manderson would obligingly introduce his own legislation for a national commission to study the need for good roads, since he seemed less impressed by Stone's financing schemes.[36]

While Stone vigorously lobbied for passage of Manderson's bill, its ultimate defeat revealed the continued concerns over any national presence whatsoever in road building and the Herculean challenge confronting Coxey and Browne. The Speaker and his allies labeled Manderson's "study" bill "dangerous" and an abuse of "state's rights." They saw it as the proverbial nose under the tent. With Congress erecting this stonewall to any federal involvement, Stone and the NLGR quickly changed their tactics. The Good Roads lobby called upon the president to establish a separate Office of Road Inquiry in the Department of Agriculture, an idea laid out by none other than Pope himself. Pope had busily compiled a catalog of publications on good roads, which he made freely available to libraries across the country. In March 1893, a year after Congressman Warwick first introduced Coxey's behemoth Good Roads legislation, Pope, joined by Governor William McKinley of Ohio and twelve other governors, quietly petitioned Congress to establish a modest National Roads Department.[37]

Noting the growing momentum for Good Roads in an article in the March 1892 issue of *Forum*, Pope advocated that state governments take the lead role in owning, controlling, or maintaining roads in order to connect the main towns. He reported to the League that he had over one million signatures in support of his plan to empower the states to take the lead in road construction. Pope admitted that local governments might lose some control, but he extolled the public benefits that Good Roads potentially offered in the more economical movement of goods for an increasingly dispersed population.[38]

Pope's tactic of working directly with the executive branch resulted in more tangible success. On October 3, 1893, the new office, under the leadership of none other than Stone himself, received its authorization from the secretary of agriculture. It was chartered "to make investigations with regard to the best methods of road making." At its first meeting Office Director Stone received a letter of welcome from J. Sterling Morton, the secretary of agriculture. But the letter was more than a simple courtesy. Rather, the secretary admonished his new colleague that highway costs remained the responsibility of the states and that his department would not endorse any initiatives that would "furnish labor to the unemployed or to convicts." Stone was clearly constrained in his new role. His earlier vision of a modest federal financial role in road construction now seemed moot. For the time being it thus seemed clear that it would be left to state and local officials to take a lead in financing, building, and maintaining good roads.[39]

The struggle over forming even this modest position in the Department of Agriculture suggested the challenge now before Coxey. His bold Good Roads plan vaulted well past the insular debates over how new roads should be funded and who was responsible for their upkeep. His notion to enormously expand the money supply outsized the most ambitious contemporary notions of poor relief or public works. To be sure, given the fate of Manderson's bill and the Office of Road Inquiry, the legislation to implement Coxey's plan stood no chance. Coxey and Browne knew that they needed to combine their organizational and creative temperaments to create a spectacle that would draw attention to Coxey's plan to put the jobless back to work. The spectacle they created surpassed even their most ambitious expectations.[40]

CHAPTER THREE

A Millenarian Spectacle

"People are dissatisfied and if something is not done soon to satisfy the unemployed something will drop."[1]

Washington Bee

BEFORE THEY LEFT MASSILLON Browne declared that the very act of marching to Washington "would awaken the attention of the whole people to a sense of their duty in impressing upon Congress the importance of Coxey's Good Roads Plan." Though the idea to stage this first march on Washington was unique, political theatricality found strong traditions in Europe and America. Indeed, the visiting British journalist William Stead, who focused on the plight of the homeless in Chicago, likened the march to the mid-nineteenth-century English protest movement known as Chartism. Stead saw parallels between Coxey's petition of boots and the English Chartist petition movement to establish the franchise that had occurred some fifty years before. He noted, "We have Coxeyism as a kind of spurious Chartism of the New World to proclaim to the world the need for action other than that of laissez-faire, and of a religion more helpful than that of the worship of the almighty dollar."[2]

Coxey's first march on Washington also followed a rich tradition of political protest in colonial America. Crowd actions such as the Stamp Act riots arose out of a long-established tradition of mob violence begrudgingly accepted as a necessary consequence of British constitutionalism. Here there existed a blurred line between the theatrically spectacular and the brazenly violent. Acts such as the hanging of British authorities in effigy, the tarring and feathering of tax collectors, or the staging of mock stamping acts meted out their own "rough justice." Perhaps the singular most recognized and spectacular act of defiance in colonial America, the Boston Tea Party, challenged an accepted ritual of authority. In defiance of a genteel tradition, theatrically costumed Indians (a uniform deliberately chosen to symbolize a frontier disregard for custom and civility) mocked this long-cherished British custom.[3]

Later in the eighteenth century the earliest American versions of labor protest would often spill out of taverns and shops into the streets, gathering sympathetic bystanders who paraded to the seat of local authority. Like the later Coxey phenomenon, these moving protests drew strength from sympathizers who joined them as they passed by, if even for a few brief moments as a way to show support. The spontaneous strike parade would merrily march through the streets in an affirmation of worker identity. These protests became the antecedents for the sort of strike processions that would become more prevalent as a form of dissent throughout the nineteenth century. As craft and trade unions emerged in mid-nineteenth-century America, "the public meeting, the festive celebration, the mass demonstration and the protest procession all became tools for popularizing various causes."[4]

Growing up in the coal regions of Pennsylvania, Coxey undoubtedly heard the tales of the recurrent strikes that marked the region in the late nineteenth century. He would have been fourteen in 1868, when about two hundred coal strikers armed with clubs appeared one afternoon in the streets of nearby Wilkes Barre, about fifty-six miles from Danville where the Coxeys then resided. The miners were part of a larger labor protest moving from the Mahoney to the Schuylkill and then on to the Wyoming River Valley. The men marched between mines and shops, rallying others to stop work. As they approached the large Pittston mine, the protesters now numbered over five hundred. Armed, they successfully forced a Pennsylvania Coal Company train to stop dead on the tracks. Led by Irish immigrant James Lamlert, the angry workers continued toward Scranton, gaining in numbers along the way in their determination to change the horrific working conditions in the coal mines throughout northeast Pennsylvania. Much like Coxey's march later, Lamlert's encountered sympathetic and welcoming crowds along the way.[5]

Surrounded by labor protests like these as he came of age, Coxey may well have conceived the idea to march to the nation's capital on his own. According to the account of David Heizer, a former Kansas state legislator, Coxey broached the idea nearly two years before the departure from Massillon. We actually first see reference to the march in the first bulletin of the J. S. Coxey Good Roads Association of the United States. Issued on December 15, 1893, the bulletin makes specific mention of "a mass meeting in Washington City at 10 a.m. on May 1st of that year [1894] on the steps of the nation's capital at which all the petitions will be received." Indeed, by January of 1894, we know Coxey was fully committed. Coxey revealed the entire plan in the January 27 issue of the *Massillon Independent*. Speaking to reporter Robert Skinner, Coxey said:

There will be one hundred thousand of us. We shall leave Ohio about March 25th and our war cry will be "On to Washington." We shall reach Washington on May 1st, when we will hold a grand meeting on the steps of the Capitol, to demand in the name of the sovereign people the passage of the good roads bill and extension of the rights of municipalities to issue non-interest bearing bonds and secure notes thereon.

Thus, it appears that both Browne and Coxey, in their ongoing discussions in the fall of 1893, hatched the idea of carrying their message directly to Congress.[6]

Browne, however, in his own account of the march written in 1912, claimed to be the soul author of the idea to march. He had returned to Chicago in December 1893 to successfully gain the endorsement of the American Federation of Labor for the Coxey plan. Browne claimed that it was during that visit, after he witnessed the homeless sleeping inside Chicago's City Hall, that "the idea came to me to organize these idle men into a 'petition with boots on,' and march to Washington as an object lesson to Congress and the country as well." Notwithstanding Browne's penchant for self-promotion, he could well have been the one who first broached the idea.[7]

Just as with Coxey, many experiences in Browne's activist background would logically lead him to have the idea. After all, as Kearney's deputy in the sandlot demonstrations, Browne joined a march up Knob Hill in October 1877 to protest in front of rail magnate Charles Crocker's home. The next year Browne would accompany Kearney on a pilgrimage east to Washington. As head of the Workingman's Party in California, Kearney sought to petition Congress to put an end to the use of Asian labor in railroad construction. Kearney's journey to the nation's capital took him through St. Louis, Chicago, and Boston en route to Washington. Like Coxey's later march, Kearney toured for his cause during an industrial depression and the year after the Great Strike. Kearney, like Coxey, was concerned about unemployment but only to the extent it affected white men. During these ugly anti-Asian protests, Kearney kept Browne at his side, including when he entered the White House for an unproductive meeting with President Rutherford B. Hayes. Furious at Hayes's dismissiveness of the Asian labor issue, Kearney decided that the next day he would take his campaign to the steps of the Capitol. Arriving with Browne at the Capitol steps, Kearney dared authorities to arrest him for making a speech to what was described as "a very large crowd."[8]

By the time Browne wrote his own version, nineteen years after he first met Coxey, he and Coxey had had a falling out. Moreover, Browne may have chosen to place emphasis on his recollection of Coxey's entirely legitimate concern with how to finance the march, construing this as a reluctance to march rather than simply the prudent caution of a shrewd businessman. Coxey twice left by train to attend horse auctions and was reportedly willing to sell his nationally famous trotter, Acolyte. As the reformer Henry Demarest Lloyd noted, Coxey "left large property interests to suffer while he has devoted himself to educating the people about his 'Good Roads' Plan." In attempting to arbitrate who first had the idea to march, the Commonweal's chronicler, Kansas Populist Henry Vincent observed that Coxey and Browne became so intellectually and spiritually entwined that it was foolish to try to delineate whether it was Browne or Coxey who first hatched the idea. Vincent split the difference by saying, "Together they conceived the March to Washington."[9]

The Second Coming

Indeed in the weeks leading up to the departure of the march, Coxey and Browne were joined in their commitment to producing, directing, and staging an unfolding daily drama that might attract a large national audience. Since Coxey had returned to Massillon from Chicago the prior summer, his neighbors and friends in Massillon had found him speaking openly about his sudden conversion. Browne was already a devotee when the two met in Chicago. Indeed, many in Massillon, observing the two in almost constant close company, thought Coxey succumbed to Browne's charismatic spell. Rumors swirled when Coxey, a devout Episcopalian, suddenly and inexplicably announced his conversion to Theosophy. The *Chicago Record*'s Ray Baker discovered on his arrival in Massillon the week before the march that "the neighbors cannot believe that Coxey, known and reputed as the wealthiest and shrewdest farmer in the country, is the leader of an enterprise so peculiar as the *Commonweal Army*." Coxey's own father accused him of being "pig headed" and "stubborn" and was openly opposed to the whole affair. The familial criticism became so intense that "Jake," as his father called him, found it necessary to tell reporters that insanity did not run in his family.[10]

Coxey's sudden conversion to Theosophy was indicative of how much an impression Browne made. Browne began his own religious odyssey toward Theosophy two years after the death of his wife left him in deep mourning. Seeking to reunite with her, he took to believing in the possibility of reincarnation. Theosophy provided him with the religious pathway. This religion, which affirmed the universal brotherhood of all men regardless of race, allowed for man to progress through seven stages and finally to be joined to the "eternal spark." It was this millennial aspect of the religion that Browne and Coxey began to incorporate as they made their plans for the march, which they would thus fittingly entitle the Commonweal of Christ. Theosophy's mystic beliefs provided them wide latitude to connect the otherworldly with the earthly and to imbue the spectacle with a millenarian aspect. While more conventional Theosophists did not believe in literal reincarnation, they did believe that the "soul" returned intact from heaven to earth and then tried to perfect itself through successive lives. However, Browne developed his own idiosyncratic version, which stretched the theosophist reincarnation doctrine even further.[11]

Browne envisioned a person's body after death conveying itself into one reservoir while its soul then migrated to another. He stated without equivocation that a newborn infant thus represented the union of not one but many other souls that floated freely within the waters of these eternal reservoirs. In Browne's words, "Every person has a bit of the reincarnated soul of Christ." Browne was explicit about his own millennial persona—and Coxey's as well. "I believe that a part of the soul of Christ happened to come into my being by reincarnation. I believe also that another part of Christ's soul is in Brother Coxey by the same process, and that is what has brought us together, closer than two brothers," he told reporters without equivocation. Even more boldly, Browne stated that Coxey became the cerebrum and Browne the cerebellum of the reincarnated Christ. This fortuitous combination would thus make possible the Second Coming as the two approached the Capitol steps on their scheduled May Day arrival. Suspending not only Christian doctrine but orthodox Theosophy as well, in Browne's imaginative interpretation, the "remainder of the soul of Christ has been fully reincarnated" in the thousands of people who would support Coxey's march. Indeed, the triumphant final parade up Pennsylvania Avenue, Browne suggested, would mark the true celebration of the second coming of Christ.[12]

Before and during the march, Browne's nightly lectures were suffused with religious references both familiar and strange, including his favorite biblical passage, Revelations, chapter 13, verse 1. He would liken the behemoth corporate trusts to the beast with seven heads, ten horns, and ten crowns. Thus the "seven heads" of the biblical beast became the figurative seven great monopolies including "the Standard Oil Company, the railroads, the iron producers, the newspapers, the national banks, and the speculators in grain and the gold mining concerns." Surrounded by his own hand-painted banners bearing inscriptions such as, "the Kingdom of Heaven (on Earth) is at Hand," Browne warned that "like Cyrus of old, we are fast tunneling under the boodler's Euphrates, and will be soon able to march under the walls of the second Babylon and its mysteries too. The infernal blood sucking bank system will be overthrown, for the handwriting is on the wall." Browne allowed his Theosophy to permeate his politics, and he was unabashed in advertising the Commonweal as a religious spectacle.[13]

As outlandish as these ideas may seem, in late nineteenth-century America, Theosophy was hardly a marginal religious cult. By the time Browne and Coxey met in Chicago, it was already a center of attraction at the Chicago Exposition's World Religious Parliament. On successive nights Annie Besant, who made her reputation fighting for the "laboring classes" in England and now served as the religion's star attraction, drew over three thousand people to hear her presentation. Browne was among those, noting, "I had the pleasure of meeting Mrs. Besant and other lights of Theosophy … from which all branches of all the religions of the world have sprouted." Part of Besant's attraction, and that of Theosophy generally, stemmed from its intriguing origins. Its founder, Russian émigré Helena Blavatsky, spent considerable time in Tibet and had an affinity for Buddhist teachings. Like Besant, she, too, mesmerized her audiences with her affinity for the mystical and otherworldly. "When the spiritual entity breaks loose from every particle of matter, then only it enters upon the eternal and unchangeable Nirvana," she observed. Blavatsky, who would become an American citizen, founded the religion in her Irving Place parlor in New York City in 1875, and she quickly attracted a burgeoning and sophisticated group of young professional followers.[14]

Theosophy was only one form of millenarianism that in the late nineteenth century attracted some of the nation's most influential thinkers. Indeed another mystical and millenarian sect, so-called Swedenborgianism, like Theosophy, borrowed freely from Asian antecedents. It attracted a highly respectable following, proving influential to such notable thinkers as William James and his cohorts in the Metaphysical Club. Swedenborgianism relied heavily on communication with the supernatural and the approximation of mental states that appealed to the extrasensory. Indeed, the notion that man's terrestrial body might incorporate a part of the kingdom of heaven was not at all unfamiliar to intellectual circles of the late nineteenth century, even though it might be foreign to the hardworking citizens of Massillon. Like most American cities of its size, Massillon contained many Christian churches, with the contents of each week's sermons dutifully summarized in the city's principal newspaper, the *Evening Independent*. However, while seventy-five Theosophical chapters existed throughout the United States, there were none in God-fearing Massillon.[15]

Theater of the Industrials

While the Theosophist influence on the Commonweal might be alien to Coxey's friends and neighbors, the march's millennial trappings also possessed a connection to the much more popular late nineteenth century's fascination with utopianism. Though the press would largely abstain from using the title the "Commonweal of Christ," they did oblige by frequently employing the term "industrial army" to describe the assemblage. This term was inextricably linked to the highly popular utopian literature of the late nineteenth century and would help to reinforce the march's hopeful themes and thus broaden its appeal. The "industrial army" nomenclature dated from its first use by French philosopher Charles Fourier, who early in the nineteenth century envisioned a utopian society that would need "industrial armies," or phalanxes of peaceful workers dedicated to community purposes, including public works. However, far more relevant to Coxey and Browne was the use of the industrial-army terminology in the highly acclaimed and popular utopian novel *Looking Backward*, written by Edward Bellamy in 1888 and thought to have sold some two hundred thousand copies in its first year.[16]

In this enormously popular utopian novel, the futuristic Dr. Leete introduces time traveler Julian West to the perfect industrial state, where poverty no longer exists and workers amass in "industrial armies" in service to their country. Dr. Leete informs protagonist West that "the army of industry is an army not alone by virtue of its perfect organization but by reason also of the ardor of self-devotion which animates its members." During the late nineteenth-century heyday of utopian literature, Bellamy's vision of cooperation captured the nation's attention as no other. The famous Gilded Age author challenged the pervasive selfishness of the new corporate economy and offered an alternative where selflessness and cooperation became the norm. Bellamy's highly popular utopian vision spawned some 165 so-called Nationalist Clubs across the country, aimed at promoting the author's utopian vision of a unified nation that addressed every man's needs.[17]

Though not formally a "Nationalist," Browne in particular seemed drawn to Bellamy's communitarian ethos. In Bellamy's utopia public trusts replaced private monopolies, state-owned warehouses replaced merchant houses, and college education became free for all citizens. In Bulletin Number Three issued just prior to departure, Browne praised the utopian author. Two of the murals Browne would paint for the march meant to capture the spirit of Bellamy's harmonious industrial future. Browne entitled these *The Prayer* and *The Prayer Answered*, conflating his own Theosophical millennialism with Bellamy's utopian vision. The intricate drawings were replete with the common populist theme of prevailing economic injustice. Browne even produced copies of each, which he tried to sell for twenty-five cents each as a way to raise money.[18]

The artist Browne naturally seemed to understand the importance of this visual aspect of the march far better than the businessman Coxey. Browne became fully vested in presenting the march as a millenarian spectacle, leaving it to Coxey to fret over logistical details. Now the itinerant artist sought to apply this prowess to create an array of decorative murals and banners. He adorned the colorful "Panorama Wagon," a rickety old farm contraption that sported a set of outsized red wheels, with banners that covered its platform and draped from its sides. With inscriptions such as "the Kingdom of Heaven Is at Hand," "the Farmer Leads for He Feeds," "Workingmen Want Work Not Charity," and "Equal Rights to All, Special Privileges to None," Browne envisioned that these artistic creations would serve as the backdrop for his theatrical, stem-winder speeches. During the march the reporter Baker captured the essence of the theatrical Browne and "the spectacle of him speaking at night from his wagon with the kerosene flare uncertainly lighting his grotesque cartoons [referring to Browne's graphic murals, which he would display where he spoke], his coattails flying in the wind, while he demolished the Rothschilds and the Rockefellers." The wagon would also be stocked with loads of special Good Roads petition paper, which sympathizers along the way could sign to support Coxey's cause.[19]

Browne sought not only to use his art to draw attention but also to convey his message about the plight of the unemployed and the vision of better days ahead. The mural called *The Commune* almost looked like the detailed triptych of fifteenth-century Dutch painter Hieronymus Bosch. In this stunning montage Browne's cartoon-like images of religious and political figures were spiced with cryptic phrases scribbled beneath each scene. At one end a skull-and-crossbones image is labeled with the phrase "Gold Basis Money." Beneath another with the phrase "Causes the Many to Suffer," he drew the image of nude figures reaching helplessly to the heavens. Juxtaposed against these images stood a smiling caricature of Uncle Sam gleefully doling out "Legal Tender" (i.e., greenbacks) to a group of grateful farmers and workers and holding a sign saying "As you create value by great public improvements." This jumbled assortment of images also featured the reassuring image of a smiling Coxey riding in his phaeton.[20]

However, as important as Browne thought his artistry was to the presentation of millennial themes, the sheer unadorned presentation of the unemployed in flesh and bone would prove over the five weeks to be more than enough to draw national attention. In the new "culture of imitation," where art and performance sought to replicate life, the imagery of Coxey's humble body of men in drab frock coats and bowler hats quietly walking toward their nation's capital carrying crudely drawn banners challenged the sleek and ostentatious advertisements parading themselves across America's newspapers and magazines. This imagery comported perfectly with the new culture of realism. In the late nineteenth century the earlier romantic language and imagery embellishing the rugged American advancing across the frontier, embodied in such iconic works as John Gast's painting *American Progress* (1873), would give way to realistic representations of poverty such as those pictured in Riis's *How the Other Half Lives* (1890). As Coxey and Browne began to conceive of just how to present their own spectacle of the unemployed, this growing taste for the lifelike seemed to infuse virtually all forms of aesthetic experience and came to be known as the "New Naturalism." Challenging the sensibilities of the self-anointed Gilded Age custodians of art and literature who saw culture as "lifting us above the mire of degrading things," writers such as Hamlin Garland and William Dean Howells allowed their stories to expose the tawdry realities of life in the most ordinary of circumstances. Exposés of the routine challenged the reader with often shockingly disturbing and unsparingly banal depictions of reality.[21]

In the new "incorporated America" commercial interests sought to enlarge their share of the market by presenting new forms of appealing art and copy in the form of enticing advertisements. In doing so, they often borrowed a gaudy imagery that stressed fecundity rather than scarcity and created its own spectacle of abundance. In this separate commercial space individual identity came increasingly to be defined by what one consumed rather than what one produced. In stark contrast Coxey's March mirrored back the reality of scarcity rather than the fantasy of abundance. Unlike the new advertising, which often drew upon voluptuous female imagery, the male-dominated march seemed almost the anti-spectacle.[22]

This living representation of the unemployed would appear just as lifelike as the Chicago exposition's popular displays of great floods, burning buildings, and erupting volcanoes. In this era when P. T. Barnum's lifelike dioramas and panoramas of places as far-flung as Jerusalem and Paris created a reality inaccessible to most, this marching spectacle would mobilize the starker reality now being experienced by millions struggling for survival. Onlookers could witness the collateral damage of the depression as it paraded by their homes, stores, farms, and factories.[23]

Indeed, Browne and Coxey also sought to present a spectacle that would affirm the dignity of the humble industrial worker. In its quasi-martial, army-like appearance, the march also drew from the less formal military characteristics of the French commune. The legacy of the Parisian workers' revolt in 1871 also cast a long shadow over protest in late nineteenth-century America. Beginning with the Great Strike of 1877, newspapers consistently referred to labor uprisings by invoking the "commune" as a metaphor of populist protest. Parallels were often drawn between laborers organizing in America and the potential for eventual violence such as had occurred in Paris. Coxey and Browne appropriated the commune's nomenclature and its quasi-military connotations. For example, one available roster of individuals carefully arranges each in either the "Chicago" or "Philadelphia" communities, within which were separately organized communes comprised of five individuals each. As explained in *Carl's Camp Circular* and in a February 8, 1894, letter in Browne's tortured handwriting, the communes were originally designed to range in size from 30 to 105 men. These communes would then be "federated" into larger communities and then into even larger "cantons." Browne carefully delineated each unit to be led by a specified commune marshal, who would report to separate group marshals. Thus the march was not meant to be some ragtag assemblage of men ambling toward Washington, but rather a well-organized procession that would change people's attitudes about those who simply wanted a job.[24]

To add yet another veneer of organization, each participant was clearly designated with one of eight separate badges, each with a different design. Some were illustrated with greenbacks or with sheaves of wheat. Others were designed with clasped hands or with battle-axes and chains. In the initial planning the officers, or "marshals" as they were to be called, were to wear a badge on their hats bearing the number of their commune, the sign of their canton, and the name of their community. However, Browne went to great lengths to inform press reporters assembling in Massillon prior to the departure that officers would refrain from titles usually associated with army rank. Order number one issued on March 22 stated that, because the march would be a civic demonstration and because all marchers were equal in their citizenship, "the necessary authority should not cause any of us to feel big over our titles."[25]

Realizing the importance of maintaining order, a call went out for "100 old officers, Union and Confederate, to volunteer as marshals of divisions." In this initial advertising Coxey was careful to explicitly refrain from inviting anarchists and criminals. Coxey reinforced that, though the Commonweal would exhibit a martial order, it was in fact on a peaceful mission. "Every man will carry a milk white flag bearing the words 'Peace on Earth, good will to men, but death to interest bearing bonds,'" he noted. Browne also reinforced this by suggesting that men leave their firearms behind and bring only their manhood.[26]

Sustaining a Spectacle

As their plans unfolded in the winter of 1894, Coxey and Browne seemed comfortable in their respective roles in staging a drama they hoped would play to a large national audience. Coxey raised the money for its production while Browne designed the set, and both helped to recruit its actors. The two enthusiastically began mailing bulletins to potential sympathizers across the country. Beginning with Bulletin Number One on January 1, 1894, they called for the cooperation of Good Roads advocates throughout the land and enlisted their fellow citizens in petition drives endorsing Coxey's plan. "Send for your petition and get everybody to sign," the bulletin urged.[27]

As the days to the scheduled departure dwindled, Coxey became increasingly anxious about how the men would survive without stores of food and clothing. Adding to his anxiety, he could not predict with any certainty how many men would arrive in Massillon. This eastern Ohio town of ten thousand people had almost doubled in size in the previous decade. However, with predictions of up to a hundred thousand marchers arriving to join the Commonweal, Coxey's anxieties did not seem misplaced. He thus focused his considerable business acumen on making sure that the march could be sustained with supplies over four hundred miles. He solicited financial support from across the country. Like many other Populist reformers, Coxey created his own educational machine with attendant publications, spending over $2,000 in distributing them to networks of individuals who in turn, he hoped, would spread the message among their cohorts. The cover of his *Cause and Cure* "magazine," published by the J. S. Coxey's Good Roads Association, promoted the idea of Good Roads to a network of bicycle enthusiasts, soft-money advocates, and populist sympathizers. His postal campaign indeed reached from coast to coast. The Good Roads petition appeared in publications like the *Twentieth Century Farmer*, popular in the rural heartland. Yet it also turned up in the *Los Angeles Times* and other newspapers throughout the country. Large headlines implored those so inclined to "circulate this petition at once." As the association disseminated its information, Coxey urged communities along the route to support the march with food and shelter. From the outset, since no one could be sure how many men would eventually show up, he realized that he would have to draw on the goodwill of sympathizers. As wealthy as he was, the prosperous quarry owner could not finance this alone, particularly in the middle of a depression.[28]

For his part, Browne beseeched followers to recognize the sacrifices that "Brother Coxey" made to sustain this enterprise. He joined in asking potential followers to contribute whatever they could. "Let every farmer and townsmen along our line of march, when they come to our meeting, bring with them something they can spare—bread, butter, bacon, ham, fruit, grain and hay for horses; etc. to put in our commissary wagons and they will not regret it," Browne implored. Similarly, the assigned head of the commissary, Solon C. Thayer, who had lost on the Populist ticket in a race for Ohio secretary of state the year before, suggested that "people living west and elsewhere off our line of march can send to any railroad station freight, prepaid, near our line of march, or before we start from Massillon, about everything they choose." Thayer sensed the populist network would come out in support of Coxey, awkwardly proclaiming, "What a sublime spectacle it will be of a band of brothers who cannot go, sending to another band of brothers who can go, to enter upon a siege that will bring benefit to all."[29]

Coxey also oversaw the meticulous mapping of the route. As the scheduled departure approached, he demanded that a precise destination be selected for each night's campsite. He even hired a Pittsburgh engineer, J. H. Dippold, who was to carefully plot each day's mileage and destination based upon the assumption that the men could traverse twelve to fifteen miles a day depending on terrain. Coxey also decided it was necessary to have an advance party traveling a day ahead of the march in order to prepare for the next campsite and make the necessary preparations, including promoting the nightly Coxey-Browne lectures. Coxey decided that he and Browne should take advantage of these theatrical appearances as yet another way to raise money for the enterprise. With each night's take they just might secure enough supplies for one additional precious day.[30]

As meticulous as the preparation was in the weeks leading up to the departure, Coxey simply found it impossible to accurately estimate how many recruits would make their way to Massillon or how many might join the march along the way. Already other industrial armies, encouraged by the growing press accounts of Coxey's initiative, were forming in places as distant as Los Angeles and Spokane. Would they go directly to Washington or join Coxey's troops in Massillon? There was no way to tell. Rumors abound, and the press, now excited by the growing momentum of this story, fed the frenzy of random predictions. Estimates swirled in the press that as many as three million men might converge on Washington. At one point during an interview, Coxey suggested that five hundred thousand men would march on the capital. Others tempered such hyperbole. One observer close to the planning realistically suggested that only six hundred would actually depart from Ohio, though he quickly added that, by the time they reached Washington, fifty thousand more would have joined their ranks. On and on, the letters arrived each day at Paul's Station, fueling the growing energy now surrounding the imminent departure.[31]

In defense of Coxey, he had no reliable way of determining how large an army might assemble in Massillon. The sheer amount of mail from sympathizers caused him to have to hire a secretary simply to wade through all the correspondence. Hundreds of letters arrived each week, and it was difficult to gauge their authenticity. For example, on March 7, a letter from J. B. Aki of Washington, Pennsylvania, noted simply, "I will meet you at Pittsburgh and will have what provisions I can secure at Finleyville when you arrive." Another from Job Sealing from Belmont, New York, on March 10 said, "I am confident I can raise 100 farmers headed by a brass band to join you at Williamsport, PA, or nearest point." On March 12, C. H. Carroll wrote from Ludlow, Kentucky, that "I am organizing a company to meet you on the day appointed to depart for Washington. Send me badges and literature. I have at this writing forty-seven members enrolled." Many letters like these represented good intentions, never to be met; others were deliberate hoaxes containing hollow promises or often bogus contributions.[32]

In the days leading up to the departure, Coxey typically walked into Massillon with a canvas sack filled with such encouraging letters. Many of these promised recruits and sometimes contained money. Though Coxey carefully kept such contributions a secret, some were reported to be as much as a thousand dollars. On the day before the departure, Coxey exuberantly announced, "We have this morning received in cash, checks and promises over $1,400, and assurances that any financial aid we may require will be forthcoming." He showed the *Chicago Record*'s Baker a letter containing a check for $5,000. Yet he was also forced to acknowledge that some of the checks from apparently prominent people in New York and Chicago were nothing more than hoaxes. While some of the bona fide contributions were for large amounts, other envelopes contained only a dollar or two. Coxey actually urged that cash be sent, as opposed to checks or drafts. Some letters simply promised that volunteers would stage benefits, including baseball games or concerts in order to raise funds. One writer offered up all the hay grown on the Kankakee Meadow. Many letters were from fellow businessmen whom Coxey knew, promising both new enlistees and money.[33]

Not only were there hundreds of letters, carrying news of recruits or monetary contributions, but increasingly railroad men across the country began reporting that their trains were filled with men who said they were going to Massillon. However, as the day of departure grew nearer and the recruits failed to arrive, Coxey began to lower his expectations. On Sunday, March 11, two weeks before the scheduled departure, Coxey said that the Commonweal would leave with about five thousand recruits. But by Wednesday of that same week, he changed his mind, saying that his desire was to leave with only a small body of men and increase the group in size along the way. It appeared that Coxey simply could not predict from the various representations, some couched as good-faith promises and others as wildly speculative rumors, exactly what size army might finally leave.[34]

One reporter, performing his own meticulous review of the letters, estimated that precisely 9,469 recruits were en route to Massillon. Despite this good-faith analysis, by Good Friday, just two days before departure, the press reported that Coxey's Army consisted of only two recent arrivals, who were apparently holed up in an abandoned freight car outside Massillon. Increasingly, the forty-some reporters who had excitedly descended on the eastern Ohio town to report on this suddenly national news story began openly speculating among themselves that they might just have to round up some of their own recruits from a nearby circus in order to keep their stories alive.

Yet, up until the very eve of the departure, both Coxey and Browne optimistically continued to create a sense of expectation. The lack of physical bodies did not deter the optimism of the two leaders. Until the very day of departure, promising letters and contributions continued to pour into Coxey's Good Roads headquarters. Surrounded by a flock of young boys as he came down West Main Street on Saturday morning, the very eve of the beginning of the march, Coxey responded to questions about the size of the army. "Oh, they'll be coming in to-morrow," he said confidently over his gold-rimmed spectacles, bedecked in his trademark mud-splashed mackintosh.[35]

The Easter Spectacle Departs

On Easter Sunday morning, March 25, 1894, as local residents made their way toward church services, some 120 or so other recruits, who had finally arrived the night before, awakened at a campsite along the Tuscarawas River. As the men shuffled from their tents, Windy Oliver, a bugler of sorts, tried to rally them with his version of "Boots and Saddles." But, he had drunk merrily with the newspaper correspondents the night before, and his pathetic attempt was reported to be more wind than sound. Gradually the men would begin moving toward the city's public square to begin forming for their departure from Massillon and the first day's carefully plotted tramp down the road to Canton. The pathetic number of men who finally formed dwindled even further from the night before when about fifty of the newly arrived recruits decided to leave and hopped a freight train bound for Chicago.

Browne assigned each of the recruits to their respective communes. He then proceeded to present them with his first written order detailing the sequence of events for this Easter Sunday. An hour before their scheduled departure, A. J. Thayer, atop the red, yellow, and black bandwagon that Browne had also decorated, began directing the seven-piece Commonweal of Christ Brass Band in its jangly tunes. The glee club, now nicknamed the "Hobo Brigade," with its lead soloist, music hall singer Frank Fenton, provided some songs as the marchers assembled. Browne came to the square astride a magnificent white stallion named Currier (after his departed wife), while a figure the press mysteriously dubbed "the Great Unknown," riding excitedly on a large brown horse, self-importantly barked all sorts of orders to the men huddled to shield themselves from the raw and nasty March weather.

Coxey and Browne looked weary after their weeks of intensive preparation. However, their spirits were buoyed by the arrival of yet another $2,000 and more letters from Coxey's network of business supporters in Chicago and Michigan City, Indiana, who responded favorably to Coxey's pleas for money. One Captain A. Bunch of Cincinnati even wrote to guarantee a delegation of shoemakers who could attend to the soles of the marchers as they made their way toward Washington. Based on other letters from local organizers, or perhaps embarrassed by his earlier more grandiose predictions, Coxey said he was convinced that about ten thousand more recruits would be joining the march over the next few days. Coxey himself now made his way to the town square in his phaeton and waved and bowed to the rapidly assembling crowd. Wearing his usual Edwardian business suit, he rode in one carriage while in another were his second wife, sister, and infant son, Legal Tender. Coxey's oldest son, Jesse, mounted on a blooded stallion, wore a blue-and-gray ensemble to signify the union of opposing forces in the Civil War. Symbolically, two years after the historic strike at Homestead, one of the strike's central leaders, Hugh O'Donnell, also took a prominent position at the head of the procession.

Adding to the theatrical send-off, some thirty colorful banners, prepared by the energetic Browne over the course of several weeks, now flapped in the breeze. This montage of illustrations and cartoons, images and sayings, included the Commonweal's catch phrase, "Peace on Earth, Good Will toward men, but death to interest bearing bonds." Quartermaster "Weary"

Bill Iler drove the colorful Panorama Wagon but remained despondent that he could not ride separately at the head of the parade. In all, the procession consisted of four covered wagons containing "camping outfits, baled straw, and several quarters of beef." As the hour for departure grew nearer, the self-proclaimed astrologer referred to as Kirkland confidently predicted this first march to Washington would "be a hummer in a cyclonic way."

As church services adjourned, many finely dressed townspeople wandered toward Main Street to watch the much-heralded departure. After months of planning, Coxey and Browne's spectacle of the unemployed was finally ready to depart. About eleven o'clock (though the precise time is as much at issue as the exact number of marchers), either the Great Unknown or Browne gave the command to march. Even its sympathetic chronicler, Vincent, described the sight as a "grotesque, if not to say pitiable assemblage." Leaving Massillon, the procession itself, with some marching two abreast, others single file, were followed by a crowd of some two thousand on foot, riding in carriages, and on horseback. The estimates of the precise number of marchers vary. At the outset, for example, Vincent reported 122 people on foot, horseback, and in wagons as comprising the core of the procession. However, some accounts estimate as few as seventy-five, and others more loosely at fewer than one hundred.

Whatever the exact number, snow flurries appeared as they made their first lunch stop in nearby Reedurban, just down the road from Massillon. Without overcoats the harsh Midwestern weather tested the marchers' resolve from the outset. Yet there appeared to be no more desertions, and by the time they reached Canton later that evening, an estimated twenty thousand people had already greeted the march from the roadsides. Coxey's efforts at spreading the word, coupled with what was now a steady stream of not just local but national daily news coverage, seemed to be raising the sort of attention that Coxey and Browne sought.

Ironically, the two creators who worked so hard to attract marchers, supplies, and money for this spectacle would now attract more national attention than they could have ever anticipated. Long before what they hoped would be a triumphant march down Pennsylvania Avenue to the steps of the Capitol, spontaneous audiences along the four-hundred-mile route enthusiastically found their own way of joining and supporting the men as they paraded past. People often ran in excited anticipation to the roadsides, waved bouquets from balconies, and enthusiastically welcomed their guests with food or clothing. Many found themselves so swept up in the moment that they would join in, if even just for a few miles. Like one of the new photographic images that might now hang on their walls, they became connected to the very spectacle they observed. They could belong to the march just by observing it. For all of its banners and murals, this spectacle portrayed at its core a reality that many of them knew too well. In the days ahead the public reach of Coxey's March would greatly exceed its physical size. In fact, as it proceeded, the physical size of the march came to matter less than the reality this spectacle represented and its hope for putting good men back to work building good roads.

Vincent noted that, despite their appearance, the "old and young, ragged and well clothed, hungry and well fed, the clean and the dirty were all there, but all seemed cheerful and determined of purpose." That sense of millennial hope and resolve would now carry them almost four hundred miles to the steps of the Capitol, where Coxey hoped to deliver his plan for jobs. No one seemed more resolute than Coxey about the Commonweal's intention. "They are travelling for a principle," he would say before their departure, "and nothing will daunt them." Vincent observed, "The world has never until that time witnessed such a *spectacle*," and indeed it appears that, up until this moment, no group had marched to Washington to petition for their cause.[36]

Reporters Ray Stannard Baker (*Chicago Record*), Clifton Sparks (*Chicago Tribune*), and Charlie Seymour (*Chicago Herald*) near Hancock MD, after their three day barge trip down the C&O canal. (Courtesy Massillon Museum, Ohio)

Carl Browne in his trademark western regalia that he wore throughout the march. (Courtesy Library of Congress)

Coxey's Army arrives on the outskirts of Pittsburgh near Homestead, PA, to a tumultuous welcome. (Courtesy Massillon Museum, Ohio)

Coxey's Army at a campsite near Hagerstown, MD. (Courtesy Ohio Historical Connection)

Coxey's Army entering Brightwood Park on April 29, 1894, their last encampment before the final march to the Capitol on May 1. (Courtesy Library of Congress)

Coxey entering Frederick Maryland on April 25, 1894. (Courtesy Montgomery County Historical Society)

Portrait of Jacob Sechler Coxey taken about the time of the march as he turned forty. (Courtesy Massillon Museum, Ohio)

Christopher Columbus Jones, Carl Browne, and Jacob Coxey stand outside the District of Columbia jail after serving a twenty-day sentence for trespassing on the Capitol Grounds. (Courtesy Massillon Museum, Ohio)

Portrait of Ray Stannard Baker who accompanied the march at age 24 for the *Chicago Record*. It was Baker's first major assignment outside Chicago. (Courtesy Library of Congress)

Portrait of Robert Peet Skinner who owned and edited the *Massillon Evening Independent,* and whose stories about preparations for Coxey's March, beginning in January 1894, attracted the attention of other newspapers. (Courtesy Massillon Museum, Ohio)

Portrait of "Dr. E. P. Pizzaro," who the press conveniently dubbed "The Great Unknown," to build reader interest in their daily dispatches, and who competed with Carl Browne in giving commands. (Courtesy Massillon Museum, Ohio)

CHAPTER FOUR

Through the Prism of the Argus-Eyed

"Journalists laugh at Coxeyism. The laboring people sympathize, and in the end it is the latter who will prevail."[1]

William Stead

AS HE LEFT MASSILLON with some forty other reporters on that Easter Sunday, the *Chicago Record*'s young Ray Baker would later recall how Coxey "did not impress me as a great leader of a revolutionary movement." And as for Browne, Baker described him as reminiscent of one of those "soap box orators and vendors of Kickapoo Indian remedies I had seen on the lakefront in Chicago." At the same time, as Coxey and Browne first gazed upon Baker across a kitchen table stacked high with sympathetic letters, the thought must have occurred to them that this young émigré from Chicago hardly looked the part of the stereotypical, hard-bitten city news reporter. Fresh from the University of Michigan Law School (which he did not finish), with his full mustache, steel-rimmed spectacles, and cleft chin, he radiated more an air of academic seriousness than serious city reporter.[2]

In February 1892, bored with his study of the law in Ann Arbor, Baker decided to sign up for a literature course taught by a legendary professor, Fred Newton Scott. Enthralled by Scott's dynamic approach, which combined adventure, imagination, and science, Baker decided to enroll in what the university subsequently claimed to be the first course offered by an American university in the techniques of newspaper writing. As an undergraduate Baker also immersed himself in the scientific curriculum. The then–widely taught methods of Harvard's Louis Agassiz attracted Baker. Agassiz, the empiricist, emphasized intense observation as the sine qua non of science. "The facts will eventually test all our theories," the legendary naturalist observed. Baker would soon find the challenge of digging out the facts and presenting them bald-faced was just as essential to good newspaper reporting. "My business as a reporter was to telegraph the facts as I found them," Baker would later say. As he left Ann Arbor to begin an apprenticeship with the *Chicago Record* in June 1892, Baker was emblematic of an emerging breed of young, college-educated men trying to become newspaper reporters. They helped define an age of new journalism with its emphasis on recounting the facts, even as, in the case of the Coxey story, those facts often appeared to resemble fiction.[3]

It did not take long for the *Record*'s editor, Charles Dennis, to be impressed by the way the young Baker tackled his first assignment, the plight of the homeless in Chicago. The *Record* was only four years old, but under Dennis's editorship its circulation grew rapidly. The upstart paper quickly gained a reputation for being more sympathetic to labor causes and the poor than its highbrow rivals the *Chicago Tribune* or the *Chicago Inter-Ocean*, and it was less sensationalistic than the flamboyant *Chicago Times*. When handed his first assignment, Baker acknowledged that his attitude conformed to the prevailing anti-tramp attitudes that permeated America. Baker's formative years had been spent in rural America, and like so many—as historian Turner noted—the vast expanses of land shaped his self-reliant attitude. He saw "the tramp" as needing to pull himself up by the bootstraps and go find a job, which was just over the next horizon:

> My attitude was that of the frontier where I had grown up. Bums, tramps! Why didn't they get out and hustle? Why didn't they quit Chicago? There was still plenty of work out on the frontier. Why didn't they go to work anywhere, at anything?

However, when he arrived in Chicago, Baker quickly became appalled at the lack of an effective social safety net. The alarmed young reporter recounted how "every day during that bitter winter the crowds of ragged, shivering, hopeless human beings in Chicago seemed to increase." His factual, yet provocatively descriptive narratives about the victims of the Panic, typified a "new journalism."[4]

Coined by famous British author Matthew Arnold in 1887, the term first appeared, as coincidence would have it, in a critique of the journalistic style of the British reporter William Stead, who was roaming and writing about the same Chicago as Baker. In his critique Arnold had rebuked the new journalistic genre as "featherweight," though he admitted he also found it "full of ability, novelty, sensation, sympathy, and generous instincts." The new journalism found itself precariously balanced between the antebellum, politicized penny press and an emerging sensationalistic yellow journalism already being practiced by Joseph Pulitzer at the *New York World*. In contrast, the new journalists found no need to overtly politicize or sensationalize.

Their novel journalistic style meshed well with the "New Naturalism" of William Dean Howells and Hamlin Garland, which placed a premium on vivid depictions of reality. The new journalistic genre found life more often than not replicating art and thus the perfect subject for reportage.

Keenly observant and often possessing the writing skills of good novelists, this new breed of reporters defined the new journalism by allowing their factual accounts to be stylistically spiced with an abundance of fictional finesse. The sheer facts were essential to the new journalism but so too was the way they were knit together in a compelling narrative. If a bit of clever storytelling crept in and slightly altered the accuracy of a story, then it was all in the name of competing for readership in order to grow circulation and advertising revenues. In covering the life of the destitute, Baker found that unpacking the stark conditions of slum life or vividly depicting the cold realities of standing in line for a meal or struggling to find a place to sleep was story enough.[5]

"What's Going On in Massillon?"

The new journalism was not just a big-city phenomenon. In Massillon another young newspaperman, twenty-eight-year-old Robert Peet Skinner, became intrigued by all the preparations at Coxey's home. Skinner, born into a wealthy local family, returned to his hometown from Cincinnati in 1887, and at the tender age of twenty he purchased the local newspaper, the *Evening Independent*. By the winter of 1894, the square-faced, balding young Skinner was well ensconced as its publisher and editor and had changed the paper from a struggling weekly to a thriving daily paper. Skinner was particularly enamored with the future of the state's Republican governor, William McKinley, who as president would later launch Skinner's diplomatic career. But in January 1894 the young editor became increasingly intrigued with the story unfolding before him in Massillon involving the city's prominent quarry owner.[6]

His first story about Coxey appeared on January 6. Headlined "Good Roads," it acknowledged how the "cartoon petitions" that Coxey and Browne distributed across the nation were actually coming back signed "by the multitude regardless of color, creed, religion, occupation, or politics." Noting that the movement appeared to be the "right thing at the right time," Skinner printed verbatim Bulletin Number One of the "J. S. Coxey Good Roads Association of the U.S." Yet by the time Skinner wrote his January 23 installment, his reporting took a different turn. In this detailed account he depicted the failed effort of Browne to lead a march on Massillon's City Hall in an effort to have the assembled city council vote a resolution in favor of the Coxey plan. Seemingly with tongue in cheek, Skinner reported how Browne and his quickly assembled fellow marchers arrived at City Hall, only to find that the forewarned councilmen had conveniently adjourned for the evening. This amusing story set the tone for how Skinner would report the Commonweal's preparations. Writing about it with increasing frequency over the coming weeks, his stories veered away from any substantive coverage of Coxey's Good Roads plan or the plight of the unemployed, leaning instead toward detailing the intense preparations going on at Coxey's home in Paul's Station.[7]

In an era in which human-interest stories first began to dominate the news, Skinner's coverage quickly turned to more reader-friendly topics, such as plotting the march's route, quoting from the letters received from well-wishers, and predicting how many recruits would show up in tiny Massillon. For example, on February 24, in what became his weekly front-page "Clippings from Coxiana," he quoted from several of the letters Coxey routinely made available to him. With his usual flourish he described how the "theosophists, financiers, road builders, horse breeders, and sellers of silica sand, continue to arrange for the March of the *Commonweal*." His articles inferred that the march might actually succeed, based upon the growing support it seemed to be receiving from across the nation. By reporting on the preparations in detail, Skinner began to lend the effort an air of credibility. Naturally, as Coxey tried to promote his adventurous endeavor, he was eager to give Skinner the daily scoop. And the young newspaperman obliged. Skinner concluded his February 24 dispatch with the prediction that if the Commonweal in fact did find some way to make it all the way to Washington, Coxey would reach "an eminence in public leadership at once undisputed."[8]

Almost as if Coxey had planned it, Skinner's stories began to attract widespread attention. Dispersed nationally across the new press wire services, these now-daily reports from Massillon began to catch the eye of other editors around the country. As he detailed the logistics, preparations, and general air of excitement growing each day, Skinner's stories created suspense around the coming departure. How many men would find their way to Massillon? Would the rumors of other "industrial armies" forming around the country materialize? Would the march encounter armed resistance, and how would it respond?

In Chicago, Skinner's "Coxiana" dispatches piqued the interest of the *Record*'s Dennis. Dennis decided it was just the sort of story that needed a good young reporter. Like other editors attracted by the possibility of a fascinating serial news story, he instinctively turned to his promising young city reporter as the natural choice to travel to the little town in faraway eastern Ohio. Dennis, who saw "poetry" in Baker's early stories, knew the young college graduate had grown interested in the "problems of unemployment and social unrest" as he roamed Chicago's streets. However, to this point in his career, he had little direct exposure to his managing editor. Thus, when summoned to the boss's office, Baker was not sure what was in store for him. "There is a queer chap down there in Massillon named Coxey," Dennis began. "Go down there and see what it all amounts to," he instructed his young reporter. The assignment thrilled Baker. Though he had never traveled east of Detroit, he wasted no time jumping on the evening train to Cleveland, later noting that his head was "swimming with excitement" as he headed toward a story he would now help create.[9]

Dennis was not the only editor who sensed that this event might make a good news story. When he arrived in Massillon, Baker found himself part of a growing cohort of some forty or so reporters who had similarly descended on the town. As Skinner wrote on the eve of the march's departure:

> Today it [the Coxey story] arrests the attention of the whole United States. From Massillon on Sunday night, seventeen operators sent 39,000 words of press matter contributed by dozens of special writers from all of the best papers in the country. Rarely except at national political conventions have so many newspapermen from the really leading papers assembled to cover a single event.

The local Massillon hotels were filled to capacity. The lobby of the Park Hotel had become a telegraphic nerve center dispatching stories across the country.[10]

The number of reporters who would stay on dwindled rapidly after the marchers departed Massillon. However, the dozen intrepid souls who would hang in with Coxey's men for the entirety of this unprecedented journey to the steps of the Capitol, including both Skinner and Baker, became in effect the Commonweal's de facto interlocutor with an ever-increasing national readership. This core group faced the same day-to-day physical hardships as the marchers. Yet every evening, while the marchers rested, the reporters busily responded to their editors' demand for the next day's dispatch. Thus at almost every stop along the way, they would make their way to a makeshift office set up by Western Union operators in order to send their accounts to news desks around the nation. E. P. Bishop of Western Union oversaw the telegraph operations. He made arrangements at each stop for a lineman to be on hand—someone who would make sure each dispatch could be sent. As Baker later reminisced about the challenges of getting his story back to Chicago:

> Imagine an old shed lighted by several feeble lamps or lanterns, with four telegraph instruments on goods boxes and the operators sitting on other goods boxes, ticking off with experienced fingers thousands of words and page after page to the four quarters of the country, while a dozen newspaper men's pencils are dashing over the paper in the gloom, the demons sitting on barrels or on the floor, and writing on anything and everything attainable.

The editors demanded that neither inclement weather nor remote geographies would be barriers to getting the story out. Once the stories arrived, utilizing an array of new printing technologies, the daily installment of the Coxey story could be printed instantaneously, catapulted onto the street as part of the latest edition, "hawked" by the omnipresent newspaper boys, and quickly grabbed up by readers anxious for the next episode.[11]

Over the course of the Commonweal's five-week journey, Baker himself would write some 75,000 words. The daily accounts of life from inside Coxey's March provided a ready-made, human-interest saga that entertained and thus served to expand readership, advertising, and revenues. The traveling journalistic troupe that accompanied the march would cast it more as a comical circus parade than a serious reform protest. The editors did not expect their reporters to write stories about the plight of the unemployed or how Coxey's good-roads plan would provide jobs. Rather, they wanted entertaining stories that would excite their readership and have them eagerly waiting for the ever-present newsboys hawking the next edition at street corners across America.[12]

The prism through which the reporters projected the Commonweal became at once its friend and a foe. On the one hand, the press popularized the march to an extent unimaginable by either Coxey or Browne. Though the two clearly planned a spectacle that they hoped would draw attention, they could not have foreseen or controlled the way in which the twelve embedded reporters would serve collectively as its voice. From Easter Sunday, when it left Massillon, until May Day, when the procession arrived on the Capitol steps, thousands of articles on Coxey's March or the other companion industrial armies moving eastward, appeared to a readership of untold millions. According to the analysis of one journalistic historian, no other single event since the Civil War, with the possible exception of the election of 1876, garnered as much news coverage. As Stead himself observed of the phenomenon, "The art of convincing the Press into a sounding board is one of the most indispensable for all those who would air their grievances and Coxey by instinct seems to have divined how to do it."[13]

New Reporters for a New Journalism

The reporters quickly discovered that they could not have made up any better stories if they were sitting at their city desks. The mere recitation of the facts created stories so colorful that they needed no embellishment. We know from an account that Baker later wrote for the *Baltimore American* that, in addition to Baker and Skinner, the reporters who endured the five-week march included Wilbur Miller of the *Cincinnati Enquirer*, Clifton Sparks of the *Chicago Tribune*, Charles Seymour of the *Chicago Herald*, W. H. McClean of the *Pittsburg Leader*, Austin Beech of the *Pittsburgh Times*, John Caldwell of the *New York Herald*, W. P. Babcock of the *New York World*, Hugh O'Donnell of the *Pittsburgh Dispatch*, Harold Calvert of the *United Press*, and Hamilton (no first name identified) of the *Pittsburgh Press*.[14]

This intrepid band of scribes freely navigated what often appeared to be a narrow divide between fiction and nonfiction. Whether writing about characters given nicknames such as "Tootin' Charley" or "Windy Oliver," their styles traversed the thin line between the new journalism and the new naturalism. Thus, the vivid account of the departure in Garet Garrett's 1922 novel *The Driver* is remarkably similar to Baker's contemporaneous account. Garrett described the array of characters assembled at Massillon as:

> A weird lot—a grim, one eyed miner from Ottumwa; a jockey from Lexington, a fanatical preacher of the raw gospel from Detroit, a heavy steel mill worker from Youngstown, a sinewy young farmer from near Sandusky, a Swede laborer from everywhere, one doctor, one lawyer, clerks, actors, paper hangers, blind ends, whatnots and tramps.

Yet, reading Baker's similarly colorful account of the Easter departure, a reader could just as easily be reading from Garrett's later novel:

> Windy Oliver and Carl Browne followed the colors and after them came a little gray tired looking man on a horse much too big for him. He wore a gray overcoat of the style in vogue fifty years ago, and the tails flapped far out on the horse's flanks. It was Dr. "Cyclone" Kirkland astrologer of Pittsburgh, so-called because he has a penchant for producing whirlwinds. He

also sells patent medicines. Oklahoma Sam of Three D ranch rode back and forth on his little nag and furnished sport for all the small boys. There were ten or fifteen other horsemen, variously attired to attract attention. One of them wore a blue velvet jacket and an enormous bouquet.

Just as Baker vividly depicted the plight of Chicago's slum dwellers at the height of the Panic, his journalistic accounts of the sundry characters that comprised the march often seem the stuff of fiction. The degree of separation between what a new journalism reporter might report and what a new naturalist author might write often seemed imperceptible.[15]

Straddling this thin divide, author-journalist Jack London, among the luminaries of the naturalist literary genre, actually wrote an account of his own experience marching with Kelly's Army, one of the twelve other industrial armies that Coxey's idea had spawned. "The March of Kelly's Army," which became a portion of London's anthology *My Life in the Underworld*, depicts mobs forming in Council Bluff, Iowa, raids on the Union Pacific rail yards, and the industrials' capture of a train engine as rail officials hurriedly tried to tear up the tracks to stop the protest's advance. London's richly descriptive account of how these California "Coxeyites" try to outwit the officials seems the stuff of later London fiction. But London did not have to make up the facts—nor did the journalists with Coxey. The march supplied all they needed to keep their editors happy and their readers enthralled.[16]

In this new journalistic milieu publishers such as Charles Dana of the *New York Sun* recognized that their newspapers could serve as incubators for the aspiring young journalist-author. Reporter Lincoln Steffens would later reflect in his own *Autobiography* how at the *New York Commercial* "reporters were sought out of the graduating classes of the best universities … Harvard, Yale, Princeton and Columbia … where we let it be known that writers were wanted—not newspaper men, but writers." Newspapers rewarded these good young reporters by allowing their bylines to appear and by publishing virtually every word they wrote. The emphasis on writing style attracted many tenacious young graduates fresh from schools such as the University of Missouri and Cornell that began offering "certificates of journalism." The field of newspaper writing began to take on the lineaments of a profession.[17]

While contemporaneously editors like Pulitzer developed their more sensationalistic "yellow journalism," the new journalists wrote stories that sought a more comfortable space between the extremes of the coldly objective informant and the tawdry salacious entertainer. More factual than sensational, the new journalism could also seem more literary than journalistic.

Just as Howells himself repeatedly expressed misgivings about oversensationalizing reality in works of fiction, so the new journalists were careful to let the facts speak for themselves. Howells's own works, the epitome of the new naturalism, were not about disasters, accidents, or wars. Rather Howells's reputation resulted from his precise descriptions of the subtle chance meetings of everyday acquaintances or the coincidental events that simply connected people. Similarly, then, for these new journalists, Coxey's March, seemingly at each turn in the road, provided just the right sort of everyday material. There was no need for contrivance. The sheer reality of it provided rich narrative.[18]

For this reason, the attempt of William Randolph Hearst's *New York World* to impose its yellow journalism made for an interesting footnote to the newspaper coverage. The legendary Nellie Bly, who five years before had made journalistic history with her accounts of a voyage around the world, clearly did not participate in the march. Nonetheless, she wrote her own self-serving account of its final leg down Pennsylvania Avenue, curiously datelined several days after the event. Pretentiously headlined "Nellie Bly and Coxey's Army," the piece she bylined makes the stunning claim that she actually *led* "Coxey's March up Pennsylvania Avenue." She even claimed to have tipped policeman, leading to Coxey's arrest. However, her account, even her presence, is corroborated by no other newspaper or account and, though entertaining, leads to doubts about its veracity and whether she was taking advantage of her own celebrity. It appears that she wrote the story sitting at her desk in New York, based on what she took from the many detailed accounts of the final day's drama.[19]

The march did not need Bly's embellishment, much less her celebrity imprimatur, to arouse readers' interest. Because Coxey's Army was making progress toward the steps of the Capitol each day, the story generated its own momentum. The much-anticipated daily installments describing such mundane events as what the men ate, how they shaved, or the lyrics to the songs they sang were set against the backdrop of new locations each day. Who knew much about Alliance, Ohio, or Jockey Hollow, Pennsylvania, or Hancock, Maryland? But at these and other stops along the way, the reporters only needed to report the facts to make for an interesting story. With each day's account the unemployed seemed not only closer to Washington but not all that much different from someone who had a job.

For example, in accounts dispatched two days out of Massillon, the marchers are described awakening to a breakfast of boiled potatoes and cold ham and then taking to the road about nine o'clock. They gave three rousing cheers to the Louisville, Ohio, mayor, who just the night before had greeted them with a shotgun but was soon won over by the peaceful spirit of the Commonweal. The accounts note that after the group shrank in size, immediately after the departure from Massillon, some fifty new recruits had brought the total to 143. An hour outside Louisville it began to snow, and the marchers began to quickstep toward Alliance. Already footsore after only two days on the road, they were greeted by some three thousand onlookers. The Alliance citizenry not only gave the men new shoes and some warmer clothes but provided a commissary stocked with plenty of food. Baker detailed how Dr. "Cyclone" Kirkland, not only the Commonweal's astrologer but also the designated weatherman, greeted a new recruit who listed his former occupation as simply "miner." Baker reported Kirkland as saying: "I see you labor in the bowels of the earth. Be faithful, and you shall receive your reward. You now belong to the greatest army on earth!" These were the sorts of verbal snapshots that characterized the reportage. Each day's story appeared as if a chapter in an unfolding novel.[20]

On the morning of April 12, roughly halfway to Washington, the reporters detailed how the march made its way over the Keyser Ridge of the Blue Ridge Mountains and then through tiny Jockey Hollow, which Baker described as looking like a postcard from the past. A posse of six deputies tensely greeted the arrival with Winchester rifles lining the beds of their wagons. That evening in Addison, with whiskey apparently flowing like "mountain dew," the situation grew more tense. For the first time on the route there was the threat of violence. To build the unfolding drama, Baker ominously noted, "It is not unlikely that there may be a bloody collision between the mountaineers and the Coxeyites before morning." And yet the Commonweal's peaceful nature again seemed to prevail. A prominent businessman, Jasper Augustine, diffused the situation by graciously allowing the men to sleep on the hay in his barn and then fed them well before they departed to cheers from the townspeople the next morning.[21]

By the time they approached Cumberland, Maryland, Coxey recognized that the rugged terrain over the remaining Blue Ridge might end the march. On April 15 the reporters noted Coxey quietly making final arrangements for boats to ferry the men down the Potomac River. Barging Coxey's Army, or "Coxey's Navy" as the reporters humorously designated it, added yet another interesting twist to the now-three-week-old story. Coxey decided to float down the Chesapeake and Ohio Canal to Hancock to make up lost time, rather than march over more difficult stretches of road in the Blue Ridge. Baker reported one grateful marcher saying, "We would have had a hard time of it if we had been compelled to walk over rough mountains where there are no towns." The news that they were about to take a boat ride picked up the spirits of the foot-weary soldiers. As Coxey spent the day arranging for the boats, the army spent a leisurely day lounging in the grass at their campsite, at a ball field two miles outside of Cumberland. Here streams of well-wishers numbering some four thousand visited them. They also ate well, as Cumberland's welcoming Mayor Hobb raised seventy-five pounds of cheese, sixty pounds of coffee, three hundred pounds of fresh beef, and six barrels of corn, among other supplies to replenish the empty commissary.[22]

And so it went. Each day the stories within this larger story seemed to multiply. Throughout its thirty-five days the march supplied plenty of colorful episodes. On a campground near Frederick, Maryland, as they neared Washington, the weary troupe relaxed on a sun-drenched baseball field. One of the more colorful characters, known only to the reporters as Oklahoma Sam, began bragging about his days herding cattle and then decided to prove his skills by riding one of the newfangled bicycles that typically welcomed the marchers at each stop. However, he found the "pneumatic steed" far more challenging than any bucking bronco. He repeatedly fell off the contraption supplied by the local wheelmen and crashed the bike in every way imaginable. The performance left his fellow marchers rollicking in laughter and undoubtedly many newspaper readers laughing as well.[23]

In only one exceptional instance did the core Coxey reporters obviously play with the truth. In this case they did so not by making up the facts or exaggerating them but by simply withholding from their readers the identity of the character they typically referred to as the "Great Unknown." They decided they could add to the interest their stories would generate by colluding to build a mystery around this larger-than-life character, who joined in Massillon and soon came to compete with Browne for the loyalty of the men.

At the outset the marchers heeded the Unknown's commands. Perched high on a large stallion, seated in a stunning red saddle, and wearing a blue overcoat, white trousers, and a yachting cap that all fit well on his tall frame, this dapper gentlemen exuded a decidedly military bearing. According to one reporter's accounts, the Unknown could "start and halt the column, direct them to right face, left and wheel, but cannot direct the execution of more intricate movements." The reporters first decided to reveal his true identity as Louis Smith, then as "Dr. Pizzaro." They enjoyed insinuating that he might be a German military officer, an anarchist, an undercover Pinkerton, or a leader of the 1886 Chicago Haymarket bombing. However, once the Coxey story took hold, the reporters decided to solve the mystery. They agreed to report that, despite their current hostilities, Browne had actually befriended Pizzaro in Chicago the summer before. It turned out that Pizzaro had recruited Browne to be a salesman for his quack cures.[24]

While the reporters knew these important facts all along, they initially saw it in their collective self-interest to build suspense and exploit the stormy confrontations between the Unknown and Browne. This created a separate subplot in their stories over who would win the respect and loyalty of the men, Browne or the Unknown. Yet, about halfway through the march this trumped-up mystery apparently no longer seemed necessary. The daily stories provided more than enough rich text and did not need any contrivance. Coxey's March was tailor-made for this era's new breed of journalists, who were accustomed to reporting on the thick of city life, replete with its scoundrels, scandals, and salacious affairs. As young men on the make, they thrived on the so-called space writing system, which put a premium on lengthy description and narrative. They had ample incentive to bring the ordinary to life because they were paid by the word. And to describe the daily machinations of the march, with all its characters and challenges, required lots of words—which is exactly what their editors wanted.[25]

It is not surprising, then, that the actual reportage was remarkably consistent across papers of diverse political stripe, both in its content and style. Collectively the embedded scribes portrayed Coxey's Army as almost innocently disconnected from any larger purpose. Thus, in comparing Baker's accounts in the *Chicago Record* with those of crosstown rival Clifton Sparks at the *Chicago Daily Tribune*, what stands out is the similarity not only as to the stories each chose to report but how they reported them. Both Sparks and Baker could comfortably ignore Coxey's plan for putting the unemployed back to work, choosing instead to vividly portray the unemployed as human characters facing daily challenges. Their reportage revealed a penchant for detailing the Commonweal's daily movement, the challenges of weather and terrain, and the reception from local officials and townspeople. More often than not, Sparks and Baker chose the same incident to lead their daily dispatches.[26]

For example, on April 9 they both started their reports by highlighting a tense though humorous confrontation with a stubborn toll keeper outside Brownsville, Pennsylvania. Unlike other toll keepers, the stalwart "Mrs. Clabaugh" seemed unpersuaded by Coxey and Browne's entreaties not to pay a toll for this "official procession." Even when Coxey threatened to get a lawyer to settle the matter, he was rebuffed, and when he finally relented and paid the toll, he did so in pennies and nickels. As the march passed the toll station, and in a voice loud enough for all to hear, Coxey threatened to sue the toll authority. For both Sparks and Baker, in covering this confrontation, just like the other dramatic and often semi-humorous incidents that occurred each day, the lines between fact and fiction seemed almost irrelevant. Suddenly the unemployed were cast into the living rooms and parlors of literally millions of Americans. Perhaps this made these victims of the Panic of 1893 more sympathetic—or perhaps more comic. No readership surveys exist that provide insight. Yet we know that all along the route the crowds turned out to express their sympathy and urge the marchers on to Washington.[27]

The Argus-Eyed Demons

Coxey and Browne reveled in this newfound attention, even if it was not exactly the attention they expected. In the very first week of the march, Coxey went from being an obscure Midwestern businessman to a national figure. As he took leave by train to auction some of his horses in Chicago in order to raise more money, Coxey ran squarely into his sudden celebrity. Almost instantaneously he had become a recognized figure. As crowds followed him down the same Chicago streets where he and Browne had begun forming their ideas in virtual anonymity the previous year, loud cheers now greeted him. Soon people gathered and began to chant for him to speak. Throughout the day, as Coxey moved about town, he greeted the admiring and the curious pressing him to comment on his plans. Even when he went to the auditorium for a luncheon, onlookers anxiously questioned him about the march. Coxey quickly embraced his newfound acclaim. Visiting the Chicago Press Club that afternoon, he decided to toast a few with a gaggle of local reporters, which caused him to miss the evening train back to Ohio.[28]

Coxey must have realized that it was the spectacle of the unemployed he had organized rather than the plan he had devised that was the cause of his sudden notoriety. Virtually every night of the march when he was not away raising money, Coxey would speak to those assembled on the importance of adopting his Good Roads plan. Yet the reporters typically gave only passing, if any, reference to speeches. For example, the *Chicago Tribune* perfunctorily noted on April 2 that at McKeesport, Pennsylvania, as on almost every night, "Coxey then spoke on the subject of Good Roads." The same day, the *Washington Post* similarly gave only a sentence mention to Coxey's speech on Good Roads. Understandably as each day presented the reporters with new human-interest stories, Coxey's Good Roads plan was "yesterday's news."[29]

Regardless of the national attention the reportage was creating, its two leaders became increasingly annoyed by the way the press characterized the march. The Commonweal's publicist Vincent himself explained that he thought the reporters were missing the larger story:

The first announcement of the movement was received with derision and sneers all over the land. The proclamation of J. Sechler Coxey demanding the expansion of the volume of currency, and the improvement of the highways over all the country, as well his expressed purpose to gather together, from east and west, and north and south, great masses of unemployed proletariat only served to evoke sarcasm and unrestrained laughter.

In Vincent's eyes, the reporters presented the march as a form of "low comedy." The Coxey drama indeed unfolded in the press as almost an "opéra bouffe" more than a serious political protest. The steady barrage of anecdotes featuring the array of characters that comprised Coxey's troupe drowned out the more serious message about the depth of unemployment and Coxey's plan to end it.[30]

The stories so annoyed Browne that in his nightly speech at Leetonia on April 6, he began a rant against the nearby reporters. What could one expect from the goldbugs and their editorial cronies, he asked rhetorically? "They have sent us representatives of a capitalistic press to dog our footsteps and wreck us if they can," he said, excoriating the press. "I can go nowhere now but that I am followed by forty argus-eyed demons of hell, eager to catch any sentence that will condemn us." Browne thus anointed the traveling press core with a name they gladly assumed, and the dozen remaining reporters took to satirically wearing badges printed with the initials "A.E.H.D." (Argus-Eyed Demons of Hell).[31]

While the reportage could be faulted as superficial, the editorial coverage deliberately portrayed the march as a subject for both ridicule and disparagement, led by an inveterate crank and a mystic agitator. Over the march's five-week duration, the relentless editorial coverage was virtually unanimous in its condemnation of the march. The *Boston Daily Globe* said that the march represented "the wildest flight of a visionary theorist" and that it did not "believe there are enough fools in the country to constitute a very considerable army for the fun to be had in an overland march." The *Toledo Blade* suggested that Coxey rob a bank to pay for the excursion. The *St. Paul Globe* portrayed Coxey as a marginal nuisance and his tramp followers as lazy, prone to crime, and a threat to innocent people. The *Atlanta Constitution* saw the march as a mob invasion with an all-too-eerie resemblance to the French Revolution. The *Milwaukee Journal* was certain this little army of occupation would find its way to jail or quickly out of town with little if any attention paid to it. The *Chicago Daily Tribune* suggested that "in the 'On to Washington Farce' now playing to small audiences in Eastern Ohio, Mr. J. S. Coxey is the leading comedian and Mr. Carl Browne is unquestionably the heavy villain."[32]

Not only was the editorial coverage almost unanimously negative, but the front pages often contained brief trailers that reinforced their editorial point of view. Coxey's March became a ripe target for these clever and suggestive epigrams that were typically sprinkled throughout newspapers during this period. For example the *Boston Globe* suggested that should Coxey run for president in 1896, he could at least count on the votes of those marching with him, assuming, of course, that any were still alive. The *Los Angeles Times* invoked an oft-used analogy, noting that the departure of the march resembled that of a departing circus parade. The *Chicago Tribune* suggested that while indeed Coxey might live in history, history would dismiss Browne, "that apostle of humbug and reincarnation."[33]

Meanwhile, if these scathing editorials and pithy epigrams were not enough to diminish the Commonweal, the editors doubled down with their derisive headlines. This only further served to brand the march as simultaneously freakish, dangerous, and ridiculous. "Dreams He Sees an Army: Then Coxey Awakens and Sees Fifty Tramps," proclaimed the *New York Times* on the eve of the march's departure. Headlines such as "Taken as a Joke," "The Crazy Coxey Crusade," or "Pranky Boys at Play" suggested to readers a less-than-serious endeavor. Other headlines questioned Coxey's sanity, shouting "Candidate for an Asylum" while others, such as "Carl Browne, the Clown," questioned Browne's credibility. As the march progressed, headlines became more anxious and prompted officials to react. "Troops Are Called Out," "Guarding the Treasury," "Officials on the Alert," and "Blood Flows from Coxeyism" were the sort of headlines that simply added to the suspense being generated as the armies approached Washington, further severing the march from its peaceful purpose.[34]

The march fared little better in many of the established magazines of the day. The conservative *Harper's Weekly*, enjoying a healthy circulation and touting itself as "the journal of civilization," predictably compared Coxey to Don Quixote and Browne to his Sancho. With its traditional Republican orientation, *Harper's* saw the movement as potentially dangerous but in the end likely to do no harm:

> These worthies have no doubt at all that when they surround the Capitol and blow their blast the walls will straight way topple, as they did in Jericho years ago, and that the proud and arrogant legislators will fall all over themselves in their haste to do the bidding of the common people. "And if they don't," says Mr. Coxey, with eyes uplifted, "God help us!"

A few weeks later, in its May 5 editorial, *Harper's* scoffed at Coxey and cast doubt on the character of those in the march. Without presenting any hard evidence, it asserted that the army contained "a liberal sprinkling of adventurers and criminals." It suggested that, while the criminal element appeared to be a minority, it eroded the moral fabric of the rest, allowing the "lawless and fanatical elements to take command."[35]

Even those journals that might seem to have provided a more sympathetic view of the march proved equally critical. For example, the Democratic *Leslie's Weekly* described the march as "Coxey's Folly" and predicted that it would end as a "ridiculous failure." Similarly, *Pomeroy's Advance Thought*, a monthly magazine started by journalist and greenback advocate Marcus Pomeroy, could not refrain from being critical of the Coxey endeavor, though it chose more substantive grounds, criticizing the issuance of bonds that drew no interest. "To give such bonds out to men who would work at road making would be to give out such paper as was given out by the Continental Congress and the Southern Confederacy ... paper that was not legal tender and therefore not money," the voice of greenback advocacy warned.[36]

Other prominent populist-oriented publications also turned on the Coxey movement. In Coxey's time the Chautauqua Society had become a forum for those in rural America to connect with urban culture and stay abreast of intellectual developments through attendance at events featuring famous authors, artists, and musicians. The eventual Democrat-Populist candidate for president in 1896, William Jennings Bryan, became one of its star attractions. Yet, as predisposed as they might be toward Coxey's populist views, the *Chautauquan's* May editorial viewed the Coxey episode as a predictable "exhibition of social crankism" and warned that it represented a threat to order. "Their whole tendency is in the direction of social disorder," it warned, presenting the marchers as industrial radicals and anarchists. Likewise, E. L. Godkin, who as editor of the *Nation* supported the gold standard, spared no amount of vitriol for the movement, noting that "the Coxeyites are Populists of the lowest grade." As a Mugwump he criticized his Republican Party for spoiling the workingman with protective tariffs. "Coxeyism" to Godkin was simply "a filthy eruption" of the same protectionist thinking; that is, that the unemployed could turn to Washington for relief with little justification for their type of protest.[37]

It seemed that, regardless of the publication, the substantive messages that Coxey and Browne sought to convey became distorted, if not altogether ignored in the avalanche of daily human-interest reportage, scurrilous headlines, and damning editorial "spin." Coxey's Good Roads program as a remedy for unemployment was largely ignored, and Browne's millennial optimism was drowned out. Yet beneath the veneer of distorting headlines and editorial banter, the press turned the nation's attention to the sympathetic characters who comprised the march and who were receiving such a warm welcome from the thousands of onlookers who flocked to the sides of the roads. The mocking headlines and condescending labels affixed to this humble procession of unemployed understandably annoyed Coxey and Browne. Yet as an unintended consequence of the massive attention the march received, the press was at the same time humanizing the ill-understood phenomenon of unemployment. Perhaps they were doing more to project the cause of the march than the authors of this spectacle realized.

"The Cause of What We Follow"

Without the benefit of readership surveys or sophisticated media diagnostics, unknown at the turn of the nineteenth century, we can only speculate as to why the Coxey story became so appealing as an ongoing serial drama. However, we do know that it made the front pages of virtually every major newspaper for more than a month. The daily episodes of the humble unemployed plodding toward their nation's capital resonated in a depression-torn nation. Perhaps for some the deprecating editorial coverage, the mocking headlines, and the reportage of the routine simply provided an entertaining confirmation of their condescending view of the unemployed. However, others may have snatched up the latest edition filled with Coxey stories for the same reason that people flocked to the sides of the road to cheer it along. As Dennis told Baker, "It is not superficial or noisy action that really makes the best news; it is the meaning that underlies the suffering or the happiness of everyday life." Whether agreeing with Coxey or not, a separate narrative emerged from the steady determination and daily forward progress of the Commonweal. It was one that defied the very stereotype of the tramp. With its hopeful tenacity and engaging humanity, the march not only drew thousands to cheer it from the roadsides, but it connected with a national readership of millions across America.[38]

Indeed, despite Browne's casting him as a "demon," as the march unfolded, and at Dennis's urging, Baker made a concerted effort to engage the marchers in conversation to learn more about them as individuals. Baker recognized that conducting formal interviews would prove futile. So instead, he engaged the recruits in casual conversation as they marched from one town to the next. Baker would strike up familiar conversations, asking the marchers about their homes, families, and their inability to rent land or find a job. From these discussions he sensed why, at almost every point along the march route, the men received warm welcomes. He observed that to present the marchers as "bums, tramps and vagabonds was a complete misrepresentation." He wrote, "The public would not be cheering the army and feeding it voluntarily without recognition, however vague, that the conditions in the country warranted some such explosion."[39]

Baker and his colleagues sensed the warmth of the reception in hamlets from New Galilee, Ohio, to Grantsville, Maryland. "The army is meeting with a surprisingly warm reception at all these little towns," Baker wrote. As the army proceeded toward Pittsburgh on April 3, every little town and hamlet—Kenwood, New Brighton, Rochester, Baden, and Economy— seemed to find their own ways to show their allegiance to the men and their cause. "Greeted by Thousands," extolled a headline in faraway St. Paul, Minnesota. Workingmen from Aliquippa joined the march in Conway and walked with it for a few miles in support. In Economy the engaging mayor welcomed the marchers, serving a lunch on a bank surrounded by budding apple trees that had begun to turn green in the early spring. The citizens of Economy also outdid themselves, supplying some hundred pounds of delicious ham, twenty bushel baskets of freshly baked bread, and two soapboxes full of boiled eggs. After lunch there were more cheering crowds greeting the marchers as they passed through Fair Oaks, Leetsdale, Shields, Edgeworth, and Quaker Valley. Baker described, "At Rochester all the factory girls at the glassworks came out to cheer." Throughout the day this outpouring of enthusiasm spurred the marchers along. Browne described it as "a continuous ovation" from its beginning to its end. Readers from Boston to San Francisco read these accounts and could, if they chose, be part of the sympathetic outpouring.[40]

Indeed, the growing size and enthusiasm of these crowds as the march neared Pittsburgh provided one of its most compelling episodes. Just two years before, a strike at the Carnegie Steelworks in Homestead had ended in bloodshed. Striking workers at the mammoth operation resisted Henry Clay Frick's efforts to lock them out. When the promising young Democratic governor, Robert E. Pattison, hesitated to use the state's militia to bring order, Frick brought in Pinkertons. In the end a dozen people died in the violence, and Homestead became one of the largest and bloodiest labor actions in a period of frequent and intense labor unrest. The emotional legacy of this event still ran high as Coxey marched his men down the Monongahela Valley to within sight of the Homestead Works. Coxey recognized the symbolism of the moment. Not only was Hugh O'Donnell, a prominent leader in the strike, now one of the embedded reporters, but Frick's nephew joined Coxey's ranks in a symbolic act of defiance.[41]

Taken collectively, the demons' accounts of the march through the Monongahela Valley, again remarkably consistent in content and form, paint a composite picture of enthusiastic support from local residents for the cause of the unemployed. To this point the march had spent its time meandering through rural villages. But as it entered the Beaver Valley of Pennsylvania, the news accounts all reported growing crowds flocking to the roadsides. People would run out of their houses and cheer the march as it passed. Baker suggested that it seemed as if somehow all thirty thousand people in the valley wanted to push the marchers toward Washington. Sparks reported "wagon loads of people coming to town long before standard bearer Jasper Johnson's flagpole showed over the crest of the hill." As the procession made its way into Beaver Falls, one woman asked a reticent Coxey to kiss her baby. Colorfully dressed bicycle men, always visible in support of Coxey's plan, escorted the parade into town. The newfangled electric cars filled with passengers waved and shouted encouragement. Each of the demons' news accounts of April 2 reported a festive mood permeating this industrial valley where local residents had collected an estimated five tons of food.[42]

In virtually every way imaginable, Coxey's Army connected to this region heavily populated with union men who worked in the nearby steel mills. Noting the outpouring of sympathy for the Commonweal's cause, the *Pittsburgh Press* remarked, "There is existing between workingmen an affinity that on such occasions as this makes them all of a kin." The army, which now numbered some 270 men, would soon swell to about twice that size as it moved through this industrial valley, though many who joined marched for only a few miles. Sparks summarized the entry into this industrial region of Pennsylvania as "A Great Day for Coxey."[43]

In the 1880s Pittsburgh had become a vibrant center for industrial growth. Poised between three rivers and situated in the heart of coal country, the city became the hub of the nation's burgeoning steel industry. The city's population would double between 1880 and 1900. Homestead, itself a sleepy hamlet with a population of 592 in 1880, grew thirty times after Carnegie purchased the operation in 1883. Indeed, throughout the region iron- and steelworks were springing up everywhere, and the related industrial growth spilled out over the entire Monongahela Valley, including the myriad of coal mines and coke operations that fed the iron-and-steel industrial infrastructure. Other industries also began to emerge, including new and impressive glassworks industries, among others.[44]

As Coxey neared Homestead, the very sight of his army of the unemployed reverberated. As the *Boston Globe* reported, "No man whose sympathies are with the working class could say a word against Coxey." As they marched on April 3, the crowds grew larger and even more boisterous than the day before in the Beaver Valley. Newspapers had touted the event for days, and now newsboys on the streets were feverishly hawking their papers by shouting, "Coxey! Coxey!" Even local bakers had the word "Coxey" emblematically decorated in the frosting on their cakes in window displays, and schools closed for the approaching ensemble.[45]

In their reports the newsmen captured how the police tried to change the march's planned route, hoping they might detour it away from areas near Pittsburgh known to be sympathetic to Coxey. Regardless, the crowds found their way. In fact, the road along the Monongahela River's side became packed with onlookers wearing red, white, and blue Coxey badges. Streaming forward to see this spectacle of the unemployed as it went by, the crowds delivered what seemed a continuing ovation. At points along the way people were estimated lined up some forty deep. Sparks described the frenzy this way: "All the other receptions pale into insignificance beside this one." All along the route the marchers were greeted with banners and songs and everywhere cheers.[46]

As the dispatches from that day described in vivid detail, the march proceeded up the New Brighton Road near Allegheny toward the Homestead Works. Police wearing helmets tried to hold back the surging crowds. By noon the traffic came to a virtual standstill. Union men, including the iron molders, boilermakers, seamstresses, and cooks, all joined the procession for the final mile. Baker's account of the triumphant entry into Pittsburgh is captured in this paragraph near the end of his long dispatch on April 3:

> From the beginning to end the march was an ovation as Browne delights to designate it. Every window was full of hearts, the housetops were covered with spectators, and even the telegraph poles and lamp posts bore a human burden. Occasionally a woman would rush from the crowd grasp the General's hand and murmur "God Bless You."

From virtually every window people were yelling "Coxey!" As the march moved steadily closer to the city center, the crowds simply overwhelmed the police force, and the dust clouds from the mob at times became blinding. It was all that one Captain Murphy could do when the marchers reached the Allegheny baseball field to close the gates against the oncoming crush of humanity.[47]

After spending April 4 in the makeshift encampment in Allegheny, the marchers now proceeded in their march through this center of industry with its sympathetic workingmen and families. The accounts consistently placed the numbers greeting them at an estimated one hundred thousand. Local union organizers, populist sympathizers, and Coxey Club members all turned out and recruited their fellow citizens in a massive show of labor support. The Keystone Drum Corps now accompanied the march, still displaying the usual procession, including its flag bearer, Johnson, at the lead, with Oklahoma Sam, Browne, and Jesse Coxey all on horseback, riding alongside the men, followed by Coxey in his phaeton, with the reporters trailing the procession. As they moved along the crowded streets in the industrial neighborhoods where the working men at the Jones and Laughlin Steelworks lived, hundreds of men sympathetically fell in line behind Coxey's soldiers of peace. At one point on this festive day, an estimated two thousand men joined the marching ranks in the shadows of the legendary Homestead Steelworks.[48]

Departing Pittsburgh and heading toward McKeesport and on to Washington, the Coxey spectacle would again journey through smaller towns and more sparsely populated rural areas. Though decidedly less momentous than the march through Pittsburgh, each daily episode nonetheless continued to occupy a prominent place on the front pages of America's newspapers. Reporters like Baker began to have a sense for what their stories were doing to enlarge this spectacle. Baker would muse how he gradually came to understand the power of the press. "Here was I all unconsciously, a part of it. What was I doing with my share of that power?" Baker asked himself rhetorically.[49]

When the march reached Hagerstown, Maryland, in its last week, the mayor held a dinner in honor of the dozen reporters who had remained with it since Massillon. The reporters, as footsore and weary as the marchers themselves, had not only accomplished the march but told its story by dispatching their stories without fail. As one reporter insightfully remarked, "We are the cause of the very thing we follow." In his diary of the march, A. M. Nicoll readily acknowledged that even though the marchers were seldom friendly to the accompanying reporters, they did recognize that when the press was absent, their story could not be conveyed. As a story in the faraway *Los Angeles Times* concluded, simply by reporting the colorful and entertaining facts, the press had enlarged what it also belittled.[50]

CHAPTER FIVE

"Coxey Is Coming"

"These poor fellows are beggars, and so are the millionaires.
The government helps the one, but refuses to help the other."[1]

Governor James Hogg (D-TX)

AS THE REPORTERS WERE gathering in Hagerstown for the dinner hosted by Mayor Keedy, seventy miles away in Washington, DC, anticipation mounted over the arrival of the Commonweal. A lone protester camped out in front of the White House on April 25 was reported to be the first indication that the Coxey forces were entering the city. President Cleveland's cabinet convened to discuss the possibility of an armed insurrection. The president's men had earlier dispatched Secret Service agents to follow the march, and now a cavalry unit was headed toward Hagerstown to intercept the oncoming invasion of industrials. Based on telegrams Browne reportedly had recently received, one hundred thousand unemployed marchers would soon descend on the city. The press tried to reassure its readers that a large force of the military was available within the District. "If the artillery at Washington barracks, the cavalry at Fort Myer, and the marines at the navy yard are not sufficient, strong reinforcements are near at hand at Fort McHenry, Md., Fort Monroe, Va., and Governor's Island NY.," the *Evening Star* reassured its readers. The chief of the Capitol police meanwhile tried to calm the House sergeant at arms that no harm would come to the Capitol. Yet all the military-like preparations made tensions run even higher.[2]

From Hagerstown it was another seventy miles to Washington. But the arrival at the Capitol, which had seemed ludicrous a month before, now seemed well within reach. While the press coverage had unnerved federal and city officials, in the poor neighborhoods of the nation's capital the disenfranchised and the jobless saw in the approaching Commonweal a reason for hope. For weeks in advance of its arrival, word that African Americans played a prominent role in the Commonweal had captured the attention of Washington's growing black community. The leading black newspaper each Saturday heralded, "Coxey Is Coming!" on the masthead of its newspaper. Now what had seemed only a distant hope weeks before was about to become reality.[3]

As a town dedicated to government rather than industry, Washington was largely spared the worst effects of the depression. Building construction did slow, the government lost revenues, and the naval ordnance works laid off a thousand employees. However, the cadre of federal government employees continued to grow. Factory closings were typically in the industrial northeast, not in the District. As the *Atlanta Constitution* reported, "Washington has been less affected, perhaps, by the Panic in financial circles than any other city." While millions were out of work across the country, government employees continued to receive their salaries paid in gold coin.[4]

Washington, DC, seemed still a genteel city, charmed by a growing intelligentsia and a "slow pace of life that left its people time to enjoy it." One visiting British writer commented, "It looks a sort of place where nobody has to work for his living, or at any rate, not hard." The District even had become a fashionable warm-weather winter haven for the newly rich. This new "aristocracy of the parvenus," as Mark Twain described them, was largely comprised of self-made "bonanza kings," often from west of the Mississippi, who had struck it rich in mining, ranching, or railroads. Many of this era's nouveau riches found Washington a most attractive city and chose to spend their winters or early retirement in newly erected mansions in Georgetown, Kalorama, and the northwest suburbs. However, their ostentatious incursion pushed the resident black population, many living at subsistence levels, further away from the city center.[5]

Indeed the idea of Coxey's approaching "industrial army" seemed at odds with Washington's identity as a government town. The city's influx of German, Greek, Chinese, Italian, and other immigrants was far smaller (about 8 percent of the population) than that of northern industrial cities, and they tended to be more skilled and entrepreneurial. Meanwhile, in the thirty years following the Civil War, the number of government employees had doubled to some twenty-one thousand. Thus as America's industrial base formed to the north, Washington had little firsthand familiarity with either the waves of immigrants it attracted or the country's nascent labor movement. After the Civil War Washington's leaders clumsily tried to create an industrial base modeled on the northeast, but plans for transforming Washington into an industrial center or a trade gateway to the South floundered. When Coxey entered the city, Washington's industrial economy consisted mainly of beer making, power generation, and print shops. It also had a munitions factory at the Navy Yard. As the District commissioners stated clearly in a warning to Coxey, "The national capital is chiefly devoted to the public business."[6]

A Deaf Ear

At the Capitol, where Coxey soon hoped to arrive, the public's business increasingly centered on the repeal of the McKinley tariff. Despite the loud protestations of the Silver Convention the summer before, the 53rd Congress had already repealed the Sherman Silver Purchase Act. So it now focused its attention on high tariffs as yet another cause of the depression. Generally speaking, the Republicans predictably voted on the side of government actions like high tariffs, which supported corporate interests. Anglo-Saxon Protestants from the northeast constituted the demographic core of the late nineteenth-century Republican Party, and their constituencies were comprised of northern industrial interests that benefited from protection. By contrast, the late nineteenth-century version of the Democratic Party touted itself as a friend of the everyday workingman. President Cleveland decried the scourge of concentrated industrial power in the form of trusts and monopolies. His Democratic colleagues, drawing much of their support from urban ethnic minorities and white southerners, remained a party wedded to notions of Jeffersonian small government and state's rights. They sought to keep the government out of the marketplace. This included repealing the McKinley tariff, since Democrats, for the most part, thought that high tariffs raised consumer prices.[7]

Regardless of their differences on tariffs, neither party conceived of direct federal intervention to create jobs by funding public works. When members from the Populist Party advocated for specific job-creating measures, their pleas fell on deaf ears. Populist Congressman John Davis of Kansas confirmed that of the five thousand measures offered in the 53rd Congress, only his party members introduced bills specifically aimed at alleviating the conditions of the unemployed. "Mr. Speaker, the Populist bills are nearly all emergency measures made necessary by the distress of the time," Davis proclaimed on the floor of the House. As Benjamin Flower, sympathetic editor of the progressive journal *Arena*, lamented, the Congress seemed entirely willing to spend "millions for armories and the military instruction of the young, but not one cent to furnish employment to able-bodied industry in its struggle to escape the terrible alternatives of stealing or starving . . . such seems to be the theory of government in the United States today." Specific measures to aid the poor, or provide jobs for the unemployed, were unheard of, and relief remained in the hands of private charities and a few local governments.[8]

Davis himself offered several emergency measures to help the poor, elderly, and unemployed. He also offered his own variation of the Coxey plan, allowing for a government fund large enough to create the establishment of a five-hundred-thousand-man "industrial army" for public works. Davis declared, "I take the ground that it is better to employ men than to starve and shoot them; and that it is better to furnish the people money to do business with, paid out for useful purposes, than it is to decrease the money and increase the taxes." Yet, though unemployment grew and the year 1894 marked the single worst period of the Depression, not a single congressional floor vote addressed any public-works measures. As Flower concluded, "The bitter cry for work, which went up from ocean to ocean, fell unheeded so far as the national government was concerned." Flower advocated a Coxey-like public-works program to reconstruct levees along the Mississippi River and found the indifference of the federal government to undertaking such initiatives simply inexplicable.[9]

Like Davis, Kansas Populist Senator Peffer also offered a bill calling on the federal government to spend some $63 million to be dispensed to the states to relieve the conditions of the poor. Peffer thought that every poor man needed a home and every elderly person should have a pension, just like those given to many soldiers who had fought for the Republic in the Civil War. Peffer also offered Coxey's Good Roads measure the week before the march left Massillon. However, recognizing the prevailing mood in Congress, he acknowledged that it was more out of courtesy than with any illusion of passage. Predictably then, though Coxey was insistent that the bills pass within two weeks of his arrival, the House bill languished in committee, and the Senate bill was actually voted down in the Committee on Education and Labor well before Coxey made it out of Pennsylvania. The idea that the federal government should have any role in helping the unemployed remained highly unpopular.[10]

The Populists' Dilemma

As Coxey approached Washington, Congress remained preoccupied with tariff repeal, and it remained mired in Senate debate. The repeal of the McKinley tariff that the House passed in February had been loaded with over six hundred Senate amendments and continued to be the subject of both industry and labor opposition. Northeastern labor groups, who associated protection with their jobs, lobbied to maintain higher tariffs. In fact, just two weeks before the arrival of Coxey's Army, over two thousand members of the Workingmen's Protective Tariff League came by train from Philadelphia to protest the passage of repeal. In the tariff debate regionalism and economic interest trumped party affiliation.[11]

While many laborers in industries such as tin plate and wool saw protection as key to keeping their jobs, for those millions already out of work, the whole debate seemed less relevant than the immediacy of finding new work. In its earlier preoccupation with repealing the Sherman Silver Act, and then the McKinley tariff, the 53rd Congress seemed to be looking backward rather than forward. The members turned a deaf ear to the needs of the unemployed about to arrive on their doorstep. Perhaps, as Colorado Silver Republican Senator Henry Teller acknowledged, Congress might do well to heed the message of the approaching industrials. "I think I may say here without contradiction that wherever they have gone in the towns, in the rural districts, everywhere they have had the sympathy and support of the people of those communities." Yet Coxey's support at the grassroots did not translate into congressional action.[12]

Even the fourteen Populists in Congress could not agree to lend their full endorsement. Before Coxey left Massillon, Nevada Populist Senator William Stewart implored him not to march. Though Stewart sympathized with Coxey's cause, he passionately defended the ballot as the only means to exercise the people's voice in a democracy:

> The ides of November are approaching. An opportunity for the people to strike for liberty will again be presented. The old parties, which have surrendered the rights of the people to the rule of concentrated capital, will ask for renewal of their lease of power at the ballot box. Every movement of the people to obtain relief outside of the forms of law will be denounced as anarchy.

Stewart thought the march itself "sheer folly," though he reassured Coxey in his letter that he personally sympathized with the cause of the unemployed. He just thought Coxey's Army would do better if its recruits simply expressed themselves at the ballot box in November, rather than on the steps of the Capitol in May.[13]

Other Populists in Congress wanted to insure that Coxey's arrival at the doorstep of Congress was as welcoming as those the Commonweal had encountered along its journey. On April 19 the long-bearded Peffer rose on the Senate floor to defend a resolution he had offered the day before.

It proposed a welcoming committee of nine senators accompanied by the vice president to officially greet Coxey as he came up the Capitol steps. As innocuous as the measure seemed, Peffer immediately found himself in a floor debate with senators who feared a violent outcome when the march arrived. Democratic Senators Francis Cockrell of Missouri and Charles Faulkner of West Virginia rose to challenge the rights of "Coxey's army" to parade without a permit, a requirement that the two contended was universally applied in every community nationwide. Democratic Senator George Vest of Missouri also rose to note that as a matter of fact the resolution was wholly unnecessary since the Constitution already protected the "law abiding" and their right to peacefully assemble. Massachusetts Republican Senator George Hoar questioned why Coxey's men were called an "army" and noted, "When those armies take their fight with Satan they do not make it by personal conference with him."[14]

Peffer tried to turn the fears of impending violence back on his opponents. The Kansas Populist warned, "I think we are on the verge of trouble, and unless we are wise and manage our own course prudently, we may have occasion in the near future to regret it." Thus the prairie Populist suggested that the threats being made from those in "authority" might prompt the very violence they sought to avoid. "Why should the police be preparing to arrest these marchers arriving in peace and carrying religious banners?" he asked rhetorically. On April 23 Peffer called for a vote on his resolution, but it failed 26–17. Forty-one senators were not even present to vote, though all four Populist senators voted yes. Even the skeptical Stewart decided that such a committee might enhance the opportunity for the decorum he sought.[15]

By the evening of April 25, in the wake of the defeat of Peffer's welcoming resolution, Populists from both the House and Senate decided that they needed to caucus and come to a unified position on Coxey. However, after two and a half hours behind closed doors, they could not agree even among themselves on whether or how to endorse the Coxey movement. Some seemed concerned that Coxey's "petition on boots" had attracted a criminal element and thus might end in violence. They also worried that the march might set back Populist electoral prospects in November. While they sought to refrain from publicly criticizing their fellow Populist, they remained nervous about what might occur once Coxey's men reached the city and how the whole event might overshadow their own efforts to advance the cause of the unemployed.[16]

Yet on the very day after the failed Populist caucus (April 26), Nebraska Populist Senator William Allen decided to offer yet another resolution, this one asking Congress to make no distinction among any petitioners, regardless of how they chose to present their petitions. Allen's resolution stated:

> That under the Constitution of the United States of America citizens of the United States, regardless of their rank or station in life, have an undoubted and unquestionable right to peaceably assemble and petition the government for redress of their grievances at any place within the United States where they do not create a breach of the peace, menace or endanger persons of property, or disturb the transaction of the public business or the free use of streets and highways by the public.

Yet, again, the opposition was strong and bipartisan. Colorado Republican Senator Edward Wolcott reflected the prevalent disdain when he noted that the approaching industrials, if they could not find jobs, would certainly find a helping hand from their fellow man. The solution to the question of the unemployed, Wolcott conveniently concluded, "will not come by wandering bands visiting Washington; it will come through the beneficence of mankind." Seconding the prevalent attitude, Senator Vest saw no reason why these "industrials" could not find work in the communities where they lived. Meanwhile, over in the House of Representatives, Democratic Pennsylvania Congressman William Hines offered a plan that the government provide $10,000 to put Coxey's men to work when they arrived, improving roads in the District:

> I'll venture the prediction that less than $500 of the appropriation will be expended. The army will get out of town so fast that all the rest of the money will be covered back into the Treasury. In fact, if such a resolution had been passed a week ago it would have resulted before this in the disbandment not only of Coxey's forces, but all the collateral branches as well.

Hines sarcastically concluded that the very offer would illuminate that these tramps did not really want work but just a handout.[17]

An Anxious Capital

Though Congress might turn a deaf ear to the pleas of the unemployed, the specter of "industrial armies" advancing eastward toward Washington captured the capital's attention. Washington's newspapers began reporting outbreaks of violence associated with the copycat Coxey armies in the far west. The week before Coxey arrived, Washington readers awoke to reports of bloodshed near Billings, Montana, as federal marshals fired on a train stolen by the renegade industrials. A front-page *Post* headline read, "Two Deputies and One of the Commonwealers Shot." In Vancouver, Washington, heavily armed soldiers were reported protecting railroad property. In Terre Haute, Indiana, an industrial army seized a train. Meanwhile, the *Post* quoted the leader of another army of industrials camped in Council Bluffs, Iowa, as saying, "All revolutions have received a baptism of blood and I don't expect this one to be an exception to the rule."[18]

Coxey and Browne fueled the anxieties in the capital by dispatching an advance man to Washington to prepare for the arrival and to entice new recruits to join. Colonel A. E. Redstone, who knew Browne from their labor protest days together in San Francisco, had moved to Washington where he allegedly practiced patent law. A skilled organizer, Redstone began producing a small newspaper called the *National Tocsin* and used it as a way to publicize the arrival of Coxey's Army and attract locals to the cause. Redstone tried to reassure the District's residents that although one hundred thousand demonstrators would soon be in Washington, the march would be peaceful and its leaders would maintain a sense of "order and decency." He tried to calm fears by suggesting that the army would arrive in a peaceful Christian spirit. It was, after all, entitled "The Commonweal of Christ." Yet with each public statement, Redstone's reassurance only fueled Washington's growing anxiety by drawing attention to the whole affair.[19]

Even before they left Massillon, the impending arrival of armies of the unemployed had caused the Secret Service to begin monitoring Coxey's plans. By the time the march reached Pennsylvania, Secret Service agents posing as new recruits had infiltrated Coxey's group. After a few days marching along, they dutifully reported that Coxey's men were clearly marching because they wanted jobs. However, this initial impression did not lead the Secret Service to let down its guard. Matthew F. Griffin, one of the impersonators who embedded himself in the march, noted in an account written in 1926, that although "looking like Coxey's Army" would later become a sarcastic slang phrase intimating an almost comic disorganization, in its time officials treated the event very seriously. "Every bit of news that came from Massillon in the week preceding the March to Washington was eagerly read," Griffin observed. Because the final parade route was thought to pass near the Treasury Building, some agents speculated that the real aim of these tramps was to raid this prominent symbol of the plutocracy. In response, the Treasury Department deployed fifty-five additional carbines and twenty revolvers to its seventy-man security guard. Indeed the threats being reported by the

Service led to the very first incidence of actual physical protection for the president and the first family.[20]

While President and Mrs. Cleveland took leisurely, evening carriage rides through the city, preparations at the White House intensified. On April 22 the president convened a daylong conference with the District of Columbia's chief of police, Major William Moore, and members of the cabinet to discuss the growing threat. Reports circulated that Cleveland's Secretary of War, Daniel S. Lamont, had ordered troops stationed at Fort Meyer to stop the Commonweal should it approach from the west, while marines stationed in the nearby Navy Yard went through riot drills in preparation for Coxey's arrival. Bands of cavalrymen patrolled Washington's outlying neighborhoods preparing to meet the invasion. The District commissioners, who typically represented the interests of Washington's business and professional constituency, issued a forceful April 23 proclamation about the approaching "criminals and evil doers." They noted that "no possible good can come of such a gathering, and with no proper preparations or means of subsistence, suffering and ultimate disorder will certainly ensue." While the District commissioners were issuing their proclamation on the threat posed "to peace and good order," the House of Representative's sergeant at arms was meeting with the chief of the Capitol police. The two officials agreed to use armed force only as a last resort but also decided they would prohibit the marchers from loitering on the Capitol grounds or entering buildings.[21]

As Washington's anxieties increased, President Cleveland, whose formidable and often stern formal manner belied a more jovial personality, attempted to appear outwardly calm. But the actions by the administration revealed its increasing level of concern. With Coxey's Army coming nearer, the precautions escalated. On April 25 Attorney General Richard Olney, following meetings of the cabinet called by the president, ordered federal troops to prevent the western armies from commandeering trains. As the *Chicago Tribune* editorialized, "It is not surprising that the motley 'armies' known as the 'Commonweal,' tramping, begging, or stealing rides from various parts of the country to Washington as the common center, have occasioned considerable anxiety on the part of the authorities of the District of Columbia and Maryland." Officials even erected what was referred to as "Fort Thurber" on the White House grounds. Henry Thurber, Cleveland's personal secretary, ordered the special shelter be erected where extra guards could be on the lookout for the suspicious criminals and anarchists rumored to be entering the District.[22]

The District's superintendent of police, William G. Moore, acknowledged major preparations to confront the Coxeyites. In a newspaper interview on April 26, he sought on the one hand to reassure District residents. He observed that he had already deputized an additional two hundred officers to handle any potential danger. On the other hand, in the same interview he made the alarming claim that many criminals had already entered the city in advance of Coxey, hoping for a riot. Moore, with his fortified police force, cited an obscure 1882 "Act to Regulate the Grounds" as his basis to use force if necessary. He could also rely on other ordinances that allowed the police ample authority to take care of Mr. Coxey and his cohorts. As Coxey would soon discover, District police would have no hesitation about enforcing the most trivial ordinances. City lawyers supported the superintendent and affirmed that Coxey could be arrested just as any other citizen, despite his prominence as a businessman.[23]

As the fortification and preparation grew ever more intense, the *Boston Daily Globe* reported to its readers, "The rest of the country has not the least conception of the state of nervousness which prevails in Washington at this time." Meanwhile, the *Washington Post* tried to reassure its anxious local readers by detailing how the District National Guard, under the leadership of Brigadier General Albert Ordway, had commenced emergency drills in preparation for the arrival. Ordway carefully planned and charted the capital's defense against the "invading armies." He had earlier published a detailed manual explaining how to respond to various types of civil disturbances, cautioning that these kinds of premeditated protests challenged conventional military techniques. While spontaneous outbreaks of group violence as occurred during other episodes of labor protest could be managed well by armed force, Ordway cautioned that premeditated, carefully planned protests like Coxey's proved far more challenging to contain.[24]

Coxey's own rhetoric did nothing to calm the situation. When reporters suggested that police would block their entrance to the Capitol building, Coxey tersely replied, "Wait until we get there." Reporters asked if the protesters would resort to force if denied entrance to the Capitol grounds. Coxey shrugged, fueling even more speculation that violence might break out. Moreover, Coxey indicated that the men were prepared to stay the summer if necessary to make their point. If they did not receive legal recourse from Congress or the courts, Coxey hinted, revolution might ensue. "I do not advocate revolution, nor do I desire it, but it will be irresistible and it will be the greatest revolution of history, if the American people are thoroughly aroused," he warned.[25]

The Color Line

Yet, if government officials and the nouveau riche in the wealthy suburbs suddenly felt anxious over the impending arrival of Coxey's Army, Washington's sizable and growing African American community welcomed its anticipated arrival. Following the Civil War an influx of twenty-three thousand new black residents from tidewater Maryland and eastern Virginia had swelled the District's black population to some seventy-five thousand. In the decade of the 1890s, blacks represented almost one-third of Washington's population, and by the end of the decade, Washington would have the largest black population of any city in the United States. Nonetheless, in an economically and socially divided Gilded Age America, the white retreat from black equality continued unabated. Despite enjoying a significant share of government employment, Washington's black population, no different than elsewhere north and south, remained separate and disenfranchised.[26]

As Coxey's Army advanced, post-reconstruction America continued its full-scale retreat from implementing the equality amendments to the Constitution. Instead, Jim Crow laws placed the nation on a downward trajectory that would culminate in the Supreme Court's affirmation of the legitimacy of "separate but equal" in the 1896 decision of *Plessy v. Ferguson*. Since President Hayes's removal of the last federal troops from the South in 1876, this steady retreat from the vision of racial equality under the guise of "accommodation" became the most politically expedient course. The steady retreat from the earlier commitments of Reconstruction led to a dark period throughout the South, where over 90 percent of the black population resided. In the period from 1891 to 1901, over one hundred persons were recorded as having been lynched each year, and the records were far from inclusive. At its peak in 1892, 155 black men were killed by unruly mobs that treated the very act of hanging itself as a spectacle. Lynching became theater with attendant advertising, speeches, souvenirs, and sadistic forms of audience participation. If crowds flocked to the side of the roads to cheer the spectacle of Coxey's industrial army in a way that reinforced their identification with the common workingman, in this same period many white Americans connected with the spectacle of lynching, in a destructive act of asserted superiority.[27]

In Washington, though the relationship between the races during Reconstruction had briefly moved in the direction of greater social and political equality, any progress made quickly deteriorated following the demise of the Freedmen's Bureau in 1872. When the Supreme Court in August 1883 overturned the Civil Rights Act of 1875, many of the city's black residents feared a return to slavery. Moreover, while the Panic of 1893 largely spared Washington's growing cadre of government workers, it impacted the black community much more severely than its white counterpart. Of the sixteen thousand Washingtonians without any means of support as a result of the failing economy, the majority were black. A study that examined the nineteen thousand Washingtonians living in alleys found three-quarters of them to be African Americans.[28]

The poor were at the core of late nineteenth-century Populist politics, but the disproportionate numbers of African Americans in poverty posed a dilemma, particularly in the Populist Southern strongholds. Populist overtures to the black population may be viewed as calling on their better angels, where the demand for economic justice trumped racial injustice. However, the more objective analysis seems to suggest that concerted efforts to seek black support were done simply as a matter of pragmatic politics—to gain political leverage and amass more votes. Indeed, the two organizations at the core of the Peoples Party—the Farmers' Alliances in the south and nascent labor unions in the north—often sought ways to include African Americans for politically expedient purposes. Poverty and unemployment snared all races in their vice. And though on the one hand the natural tendency for laboring whites, whether on the farm or in the factory, was to see blacks as unwanted and inferior competitors, in their struggle for fairer treatment the two often found it a political convenience to become grudging allies. When, for example, Georgia's Populist Representative Tom Watson made an appeal for unity with Black Farmer alliances, or the United Mine Workers accepted black miner Richard L. Davis in the ranks of its executive council, it did not necessarily signal a fundamental change in racial attitudes but that political expedience often was a deciding factor in the complicated quilt of racial relations. The bridges built between Populists and the disenfranchised black community, even if erected on the need for the all-white Southern Farmer Alliance to broaden its political base, seem notable in light of the pervasive racial discrimination of the period. When Congressman Tom Watson saved one of his ardent black supporters from a lynch mob, he observed, "You are made to hate each other because upon that hatred is rested the keystone of the arch of financial despotism which enslaves you both." It was Watson's acknowledgment of the fragile Populist political future based on the shared political fate of poor whites and blacks.[29]

Coxey and Browne openly defied these politically motivated Populist overtures for racial unity. Rather, they set out to include "the Negro" by design, not expedience. Given the prevailing attitudes, there was no good practical reason to include blacks in the march. Yet, without diversity, Coxey and Browne concluded, the Commonweal would defy its own name. Indeed, Theosophy stressed the need for racial tolerance. Having undergone this religious conversion since his inflammatory racist days with Kearney, Browne now stressed that the march should be proud of its "cosmopolitan" hue. "We want every nationality represented," Browne said in a voice reflecting his newly acquired spirit of tolerance. Browne personally recruited his friend Honoré Jaxson, a Native American from Canada. Yet, the Commonweal was particularly notable for the number of African Americans in its ranks.[30]

What garnered most attention was the Commonweal's African American flag bearer, Jasper Johnson, a recruit from Buckhannon, West Virginia. He was described in the reporter's accounts as possessing a droll face, and in keeping with the period's racial stereotyping, as being as "black as the ace of spades." Johnson's mascot dog, "Bunker Hill," could usually be found tied at night to the same American flag he carried during the day. Johnson would be temporarily drummed out of the march when he decided to offer himself as a display for a dime store museum owner. Yet, he proudly carried the flag heading the procession out of Massillon and then again in the triumphant final leg down Pennsylvania Avenue. Such an overt and public demonstration of integration in the spring of 1894 boldly challenged the prevailing racial mores of the day. So too did the reality of black and white men sharing the same space in camps all along the route. Just as the space between black and white grew larger throughout America, the men in the Commonweal marched together, ate together, and slept side by side in the same camps.[31]

Further pushing the color line, the Commonweal's glee club consisted of four other African Americans. It routinely sang an array of Southern songs to the accompaniment of a guitar, violin, and cornet. Another singer, referred to by the press as "the negro," but who was known among the other marchers as Professor C. B. Freeman, sang to the accompaniment of a hastily assembled "brass band" of sorts. Promoted as "the loudest singer in the world," he would often sing solo for hours or lead the men in a dozen or so songs that were set to the music of popular songs. Freeman's spontaneous singing was reported to be so loud that it attracted onlookers who would come from blocks away to hear him up close. His voice struck one reporter as resembling the sounds of a calliope. During the preparation phase in Massillon, some observers accused Freeman of spending more time singing songs than in helping to gather up the supplies needed for an almost four-hundred-mile march. Freeman wore a tattered brown derby hat, with his toes popping out of his shoes, and with his banjo wrapped in dirty green billiard cloth. He brought with him another African American friend, identified only as a "Jew harp player," who was so excited to be part of the spectacle that he offered to do whatever it took even if it meant "shining the General's [Coxey's] boots." Freeman told reporters that he left a wife and six children behind because he felt the calling to be a part of the historic journey.[32]

In a nation where segregation remained the norm, Coxey's March boldly and openly integrated blacks and whites. They were seen together on the road and at every campsite. Not surprisingly, therefore, word about what was going on in this march spread rapidly through the African American congregations, and leaders of black churches enthusiastically advertised its arrival. In Washington, as the black community sought greater social and economic justice, the African American churches served as the forum where blacks could meet to engage in discussing how best to influence a white-dominated political process. During the Depression this same network of politically active black churches formed "benevolent and Missionary societies" to help rescue the most destitute from the grips of the Depression. Indeed, throughout the march, areas with large black populations produced significant turnouts to greet it, and Washington would be no different. Baker noted the extent of the "negro" turnout around Frederick, Maryland. He wrote that Coxey and Browne "make no distinction between them ["the negroes"] and their white companions," and "this fact has made all the Negro population friends."[33]

Throughout this period the black community in Washington remained active politically. Though often divided among itself on tactics, the tradition of black political activism that spurred Congress to grant emancipation to slaves in the District in April 1862 continued, as blacks in Washington publicly demanded equal treatment. In making their demands, black Washingtonians typically used petitions, protests, and demonstrations to make their point as forcefully as needed to draw attention to their unequal status. As one reminder to the white community, up until 1891, blacks in Washington festively celebrated emancipation with their own large parade. Their 1884 celebration stretched more than a mile with some six thousand people present, representing persons of every class. The leaders of the black community thus clearly understood the power of the sort of spectacle that Coxey employed, and they were prepared to welcome it with open hearts.[34]

Word of the march's integration spread rapidly through the grapevine of African American churches and the black press, and Coxey's daily progress became a source of interest in black communities nationwide. In contrast to established white churches, which saw it as exuding weakness, the leaders of black churches supported the march and advertised its arrival. In areas with established black populations along the route, there could typically be found large turnouts of African Americans. Baker wrote, "They always come and stand along the whitewashed fences and cheer lustily." Baker was struck by the fact that not only were a number of "Negroes" integrated into the Army, but also that as word spread that Coxey and Browne treated all the men the same, those African Americans who came to the roadside "had a warm feeling for the commonweal."[35]

The African American newspaper the *Washington Bee* began advertising "Coxey Is Coming" at the top of its masthead the very week after the march departed Massillon. Then, just as the *Bee* had proclaimed, Coxey came to Washington, promoting his own rescue plan for the disenfranchised and downtrodden, who quietly were bearing the brunt of this economic calamity. Suddenly, this integrated procession was in full view for all to see as they arrived at Brightwood Riding Park, some seven miles from the Capitol on April 29. After five weeks and some four hundred miles, the weary marchers now came to a welcome rest. Here they would gather themselves to prepare their final triumphant march down Pennsylvania Avenue. Though the men remained small in number, thousands of people lined the streets and cheered them enthusiastically as they came from Rockville toward Silver Spring and then across the District line.[36]

Struck by the size of the turnout as they entered Brightwood, Coxey's men tried their best to approximate military order by marching in a column of twos. With the exception of the new recruits, they appeared to be understandably tired and footsore. The army had grown as it approached Washington, and one observer described the procession as "three hundred and fifty miserably-dressed, woebegone, grumbling, out-of-the-elbows and run-down-at-the-heels-specimens." As Skinner remarked in his dispatch that day, "They had bore the brunt of mud and storms and cold. They were the most unique and inexplicable aggregation ever brought together." Yet many kindred souls in Washington could well relate to these weary and disheveled troops carrying their tattered banners with their millennial messages that pointed to a brighter future. For the District's poor and downtrodden, the Commonweal's arrival marked a triumph of hope in a spring of despair.[37]

Permission to Speak

Whether hopeful, fearful, or simply anxious, Washington now seemed to hang on Coxey's every word. In the final days of the march from Hagerstown to Fredericksburg to Rockville, the press attention, which had captivated the nation, now mesmerized Washington. As this spectacle made its final approach along the "Great Road" on April 29, a storm during the night turned the dirt road into "red, wet and sticky" mud, making it hard for the marchers to keep double file. At the Silver Spring train station they were met by a contingent of workmen from Philadelphia led by Christopher Columbus Jones wearing a stovepipe hat as a sarcastic impersonation of the Gilded Age's elite. A cavalry corps dispatched from Washington also arrived, a conspicuous sign of the growing apprehension of Washington officials. However, as the Commonweal reached the intersection of Great and Blair Roads, they were met by the usual contingent of enthusiastic bicyclists.[38]

During the final journey down the Frederick Pike from Rockville, thousands of people cheered from each side of the road. The *Washington Post* reported, "A great crowd filed down the old Rockville turnpike, with cheering and music and waving hats." By this time the marchers were well accustomed to this sort of positive reception. Just as Senator Teller had noted in his earlier floor speech, this sparse assembly of tramping men seemed to engender goodwill at almost every stop during its thirty-five-day journey to Washington. As they reached the outskirts of Washington, the previously all-male brigade now added its first female—the fiery, if diminutive, Populist Annie Diggs from Kansas, a good friend of Coxey's. He greatly admired her commitment to the antimonopolist cause. Yet he and Browne were so sensitive to the criticism of the march as a slovenly collection of tramps that they took no additional risks by inviting any accusations of moral laxity that might arise if women and men marched together and camped with one another.[39]

Diggs understood her role. Just the week before Coxey's arrival, some two thousand Coxey sympathizers packed Coxey's makeshift headquarters at Washington's Rechabite Hall, even spilling out into the streets, to hear "our Little Annie," as she was known to her Populist admirers in Kansas, rail against the government's insensitivity toward the unemployed. "One million persons are starving in this country today and yet when the country rises to beg them the men up here at the Capitol with lucrative positions are not doing anything to help the unemployed of the country," she said. When she was finished with her rousing oration on behalf of her friend Coxey, a voice from the audience yelled, "Three cheers for the little woman from Kansas," after which there was applause, stomping of feet, and the pounding of canes on the wood floor.[40]

Heralding the arrival, streetcars soon overflowed with people eager to make their way to Brightwood Park to see these new celebrities that the press had created over the last five weeks. Coxey chose to camp on the out-skirts of town after an earlier effort to camp at Woodley Park near President Cleveland's summer home fell through. Eight thousand people would now visit Brightwood over the next thirty-six hours. All day on April 30 a steady stream of spectators clogged the Brightwood road from Washington, kicking up thick clouds of dust. Skinner reported that it seemed "every horse and wheel vehicle in the city had been pressed into service." He wrote, "The sight of so much splendor on wheels was really imposing." Even the street rail, which arrived a half-mile from the track, was overwhelmed with traffic.[41]

While many who came were undoubtedly simply curious, one press report characterized those flocking to the site as mostly from "the working class," Washington's forgotten. Those who came witnessed sallow-faced men, some eating chunks of bread, while others stretched out under weather-beaten tents, using their coats for pillows. After walking four hundred miles the men appeared "weary, footsore, and generally dilapidated." Though in a Pittsburgh paper one enterprising shoe seller was already advertising the "long wearing and rugged Coxey Shoe," the marchers were actually short on shoes. One of them wore a rubber boot on one foot, with the other covered in canvas.[42]

Many of those arriving to see the army's encampment took seats in the riding track's grandstand. The infield was filled with carriages with women shading themselves under their parasols. Coxey decided to speak and mounted an impromptu podium in front of the track's stands. Almost shouting to be heard, he began with his usual Populist denunciation of the monopolists. He then urged Congress to pass his Good Roads legislation, which he believed would put four million unemployed Americans back to work. "Twenty million people are hungry and can't wait two years to eat. Four million people have been idle for nine months. That's what Grover Cleveland has cost this country," Coxey shouted. Cheers echoed through the park. Coxey went on defiantly, saying that he and his men were prepared to endure the entire summer to see his legislation passed.[43]

In giving ample play to his final rallying speech, the press finally acknowledged what Coxey had been saying at almost every stop. Yet even with the scant attention his words received over the course of the five weeks, the imagery of the unemployed in their essential humanness, parading before the nation, seemed to resonate more than any words. Democratic Governor James Hogg of Texas, who himself spoke out against lynching and other forms of violence against blacks, praised the Coxey troupe for its discipline, noting in an interview that they were "honest in their efforts." In an interview he noted that the poor unemployed, in asking the government for help, were no different than the well-heeled millionaires with their teams of lobbyists asking government for special favors:

> The only difference between the two is that the poor man has only his empty stomach and his weakened and emaciated frame to represent as arguments and justification for the granting of his requests and the millionaire has his barrels of money. The money is more powerful, and consequently is more convincing to the lawmakers. These poor fellows are beggars, and so are the millionaires. The government helps the one but refuses to help the other.

Echoing these same sentiments, a gathering of workingmen back in Pittsburgh, on the heels of Coxey's visit, passed a resolution endorsing the Commonweal and noted, "If the government can coin money for the banker to loan, it can coin money to give to idle labor and pay them direct from the Treasury."[44]

As Coxey left Brightwood Park and rode the trolley to the Capitol to begin making arrangements for the final parade to the Capitol, the feelings of warmth toward him were on full display. Many on the trolley hopped off when he did and followed him as he walked right into the halls of Congress. There he seemed to be recognized by virtually everyone, including young pages busily seeking his autograph. At 4:00 p.m. the Senate had just adjourned for the afternoon, and as he waited for the sergeant at arms to appear, Coxey was greeted by passing senators who just wanted to shake his hand. As word spread that Coxey was in the Capitol, clerks and staff members thronged to see him, and he began signing autographs again for an impromptu crowd of some two hundred or so of the curious who gathered in the hallways.[45]

However, the meeting with the Senate sergeant at arms, Colonel R. S. Bright, did not go as well. Police Superintendent Moore had warned Coxey earlier in the afternoon that he would not be allowed to speak, and Bright now confirmed this. Bright said that even though he was not responsible for the law that prevented trespass on the Capitol grounds, he would enforce it. Coxey made it clear that he not only intended to speak from the Capitol steps but asserted that the Constitution trumped any city ordinance, police regulation, or congressional grounds rule that forbade such assemblies on the Capitol lawn. Asked what he intended to do when the police interfered, Coxey defiantly stated, "The Constitution was written before any police regulations. If they come in conflict with the Constitution they are void." Coxey seemed outwardly confident that the police would not impede the peaceful assemblage of the Commonweal. "Does not the Constitution guarantee the right to peaceably assemble and petition Congress?" he rhetorically asked the assembled reporters.[46]

After his discouraging meeting with Bright, Coxey proceeded to meet with District officials to apprise them of the parade route and to obtain the necessary permit to march through Washington. Coxey outlined the route for Superintendent Moore and the District commissioners. Coxey indeed received a permit for the parade, though Moore remained disturbed by Coxey's continued insistence on speaking on the Capitol grounds. During the meeting Moore and the District commissioners not only threatened to revoke the parade permit when they heard about Coxey's intention to speak but also raised issues about the sanitary conditions of a vacant lot at Second and M streets as the site where the marchers would eventually camp at the end of the day. When the commissioners seemed intent on knowing just how long the army could be expected to stay in the District, Coxey smiled and said, "Until Congress will enact the desired legislation."[47]

As evening approached and with the final leg of the march just hours away, Coxey still hoped to receive permission to give his speech. So he first, though unsuccessfully, sought out Vice President Adlai Stevenson. Then he searched for Speaker Charles Crisp, the only other official that Colonel Bright told him could waive the restriction allowing him to give his speech. Coxey finally found the Speaker at 11:00 p.m. However, when Coxey gave Crisp a preview of the speech, the Speaker promptly told Coxey he could not approve it. Thus, the day ended with Coxey still without official permission to enter the Capitol grounds. Prepared speech in hand, he returned to the National Hotel to join his wife, infant son, Legal Tender, and daughter, Mamie. He delightfully discovered that Mamie and her mother had been more successful in their rounds in Washington this day. They had succeeded in selecting the wardrobe that Mamie needed for her prominent role in the final parade as the "Goddess of Peace."[48]

Final Steps

After a long day of seeking approvals, Coxey awoke late on May 1, 1894. It was a year since the Chicago Exposition opened and nine months since Coxey and Browne met at the Bimetallic Convention and began planning how they would celebrate International Labor Day on behalf of the unemployed. The day was warm with a gentle spring breeze, and the crowds were already forming on the route Coxey had announced. As the morning wore on, the crowds would swell by some estimates to as many as thirty thousand, with African Americans an estimated half of those watching. Now, with Coxey being accompanied by his wife and Legal Tender, his phaeton took its place at the rear of the procession of an estimated six hundred marchers, perhaps more. In addition to the core of 122 or so who had made the entire march, the Philadelphia contingent swelled the ranks, as did other sympathizers and those simply wanting to revel in the moment by marching along. The police also assembled in full force. According to Skinner's dispatch, "Since the days of the [Civil] war the Capitol and other buildings have not been guarded as they are now." Policemen reportedly slept at their posts on the Capitol grounds and the march route. In all, with over two hundred new policemen sworn in overnight, some six hundred officers patrolled the city. Many of those were ominously mounted on horseback.[49]

As the procession formed to depart its temporary Brightwood quarters, the men were provided with "war clubs of peace." These staves were about four feet in length, and each had a white banner at the end that fluttered in the breeze. Carl Browne, whose sleep at the Randall House the night before had been interrupted by a fire, rallied the men with a speech, reminding them that "the eyes of the world are on you and you must conduct yourselves accordingly." The men were then put through a drill, with Browne giving the command "Gloria Peace," and the men responding by waving their peace sticks in the air three times and shouting in response. As planned, Mamie Coxey was mounted upon a white horse decorated with red and yellow trappings. Dressed as the Goddess of Peace, according to Baker's dispatch, she "wore a long white skirt, white gloves and a brimless cap trimmed with blue from which a single gold star shone, her only ornament. A wealth of blonde hair flowed loosely down her shoulders. Her delicate face was flushed with excitement and her fingers toyed nervously with the bridle." Browne with his typical Conestoga cowboy attire now fell into line behind her on his magnificent Percheron stallion. He carried one of his own peace banners. The communes fell into their assigned places in alphabetical order, with the newly arrived Philadelphia contingent led by stovepipe-hatted Christopher Columbus Jones at the rear. Leading the procession was the brass band, immediately followed by the black standard-bearer Johnson, who would lead the rest of the marchers to the Capitol.[50]

Due to Coxey's tardiness, Carl Browne gave the order to march sometime well after 10:00 a.m., and the parade proceeded down the dusty 14th Street corridor. Jesse Coxey wore a mixed gray-and-blue uniform, symbolically depicting the reconciliation of North and South. He too was mounted on a magnificent stallion and would later relay orders to the men from his father. Populist supporter Diggs, who had greeted the men at Rockville, rode in an open carriage with her family. Little Legal Tender Coxey, draped in white embroidered flannel, was in the open carriage with the Coxeys. The marchers tried to keep formation in their communes.[51]

The core of Coxey's Army that had made it from Massillon took particular time in preparing themselves. Though the banners and wagons appeared the worse for the journey, the men tried hard to keep up appearances. As Baker reported, "The army itself looked better than it had for many a day. Most of the men spent hours in getting ready for the great occasion." As they marched peaceably, the crowds grew in number and enthusiasm. Ironically, given Browne's past association with the anti-Chinese sandlot protests two decades before, the marchers found themselves warmly greeted as they passed by the Chinese diplomatic quarters. The delegation's women waved "gaily colored handkerchiefs" from the embassy windows above. Meanwhile, four mounted policeman provided an escort for the parade. As the army turned onto Pennsylvania Avenue, the crowds became so thick that they nearly choked the procession, and more mounted police were summoned to carve a path. Oklahoma Sam, who as usual was riding his pony backwards in the saddle, actually helped the police in parting the increasing numbers who lined the streets.. As they approached the east side of the Capitol, the crowds grew even more frenzied, and some even tried to jump in the carriage with the Coxeys. At this point Mrs. Coxey handed Legal Tender over to a nurse for safekeeping.[52]

As they made the turn from Pennsylvania Avenue onto New Jersey, Baker described the scene now as approaching one of near pandemonium. "Several thousand persons lined the terraces, the plaza and every available foot of space on the grass plat. The fronts of neighboring buildings were crowded and the hotel at the corner presented windows and doors full of sight seers." As they made it to the B Street entrance, it became impossible to ride any longer. Browne dismounted his stallion and entered into the crowds that now occupied the east front of the Capitol. Coxey stepped from his phaeton and then turned and kissed his wife, a gesture that brought more cheers from the admiring audience. While Browne was able to leap the small retaining wall onto the Capitol grounds, Coxey tripped and was nearly trampled by those well-wishers now chasing after Browne toward the Capitol steps. The crowd surged forward and simply ignored the "Keep off the Grass" signs. Browne made it to the corner of the steps before one of the mounted policeman, now wielding his club, tried to grab him. Browne flailed, swinging back wildly.

He was reportedly punched several times by the police who accosted him. With clothing torn and bloodied, and a necklace made by his deceased wife broken and in pieces on the ground, Browne found himself suddenly under arrest.[53]

In the chaos now ensuing, flag bearer Johnson tried to come to Browne's rescue. But the police turned on him with special fury, and he was so bloodied that he had to be taken to the hospital. The *Bee*, in its report of the day, decried the harsh treatment of Johnson. In a bitter rebuke of the District's white chief of police, the paper noted that he admitted to being more afraid of the "colored people than he was of Coxey's Army." The *Bee* reported, "Finding the Negro the less offensive [than the rest of white marchers] they [the police] clubbed him." The *Bee's* critique of police conduct at the Capitol concluded with the following rebuke: "The scene was disgraceful and the act cowardly on the part of some of those brutal and pusillanimous officers of the police force." The entire event, the paper concluded, tested not only the endurance but also the motivation of this army—tests that it passed. To the *Bee* writers the response of the officials in Washington served as ample evidence of the harshness of the times.[54]

Meanwhile, Coxey coming to his feet after nearly being trampled, respectfully asked a policeman to be ushered toward the Capitol steps. The officer obliged, and Baker artfully described how "the two wormed their way through the mob like sparrows through a wheat field." As they approached, the Secret Service kept the Cleveland White House well apprised, describing with instantaneous dispatches the final moments:

> Coxey went to the steps of the East Portico and went up about five steps. Lieutenant Kelly and other police officers met Coxey and informed him he could make no speech. Coxey said he wished to enter a protest. The officers said "you can take no action here of any kind." Coxey said he wished to read a program. The officers told him, "It cannot be read here." Coxey showed no inclination to yield and the officers hustled him off the steps into the middle of the plaza in front of the Capitol. He made no physical resistance but protested all the while and the crowd gathered and obstructed the way but seemed moved by curiosity only. No one was struck. Coxey was not formally put under arrest.

In contrast to the dispassionate Secret Service dispatch, Skinner's contemporaneous account, telegraphed immediately to meet the *Massillon Evening Independent's* deadline, captured the chaos of the moment:

> Coxey and Browne are walking up to the Capitol. Every inch of space seems to be occupied. There seems to be a stampede and people say that the police are using clubs. Coxey has been arrested. He just passed me, very white, in the center of one hundred policemen. Tens of thousands of people are following and yelling. The excitement is beyond anything the mind can conceive, yet no ugliness is manifested. The police are in entire control. . . . In clearing the Capitol steps clubs were freely used. . . . Browne got severely clubbed.

Skinner's account and the others from various eyewitnesses, though they differed in detail, all paint a picture of confusion and chaos in the moments when the march finally reached the Capitol.[55]

Baker also provided a detailed account of Coxey's attempt to speak. He noted that Coxey proceeded up the central steps of the Capitol and was greeted there by a Captain Garden of the congressional police and a Lieutenant Kelly of the District police. When Captain Garden asked Coxey his intentions, Coxey indicated that he wished to speak. When Garden told him that he would not be allowed to do so, Coxey reached into his lapel for the speech he had been long preparing. At this point the officers firmly took him by the arms and escorted him firmly back down the steps. Coxey was placed back into his phaeton, and those from the army who were still half assembled in their communes outside the Capitol grounds now retreated peaceably to their new campgrounds at 2nd and M streets.[56]

The next day the immediate verdicts on Coxey's humiliation at the Capitol were severe. Derisive headlines across America trumpeted stories about the final parade up Pennsylvania Avenue. The *Boston Globe* declared, "General Coxey's Waterloo," the *Washington Post*, "Climax of Folly," and the *Chicago Tribune*, "Coxey Farce Ends." Cleveland biographer Allen Nevins noted that "Coxey's movement passed rapidly through the phases of a great radical crusade, an itinerant catchpenny show, and a fiasco." In its wrap-up of the events of May 1, *Harper's* editors gave a similarly bleak rendition of the events, noting that "the crowds that had gathered from all parts of the city to enjoy a dramatic scene were returning in swarms to their homes, most of them having seen nothing whatever." In the May 2 *Chicago Daily Tribune* Sparks pronounced:

> Coxey's play, "The Commonweal of Christ," is over. The drop has been rung down and the iron curtain of oblivion is falling. It will never rise again upon the same characters for Coxey has had enough. Today has been seen a failure so dismal that it is pitiable rather than ridiculous.

Indeed the march ended as anticlimax, and at its conclusion its industrial remnants retreated to a malodorous vacant lot near a garbage site at First and L Streets. The curtain thus fell on the five-week-old spectacle. Baker wrote in the aftermath, "As for the *Commonweal*, it vanished in thin air." Yet, in the years that would follow, Coxey's dedication to the cause of the unemployed did not.[57]

The Crusade Continued

"To him must come some sense of satisfaction of having lived to see the government adopt his plan of putting the unemployed to work on public projects."[1]

1949 WHBC radio tribute to Coxey

AFTER THE FINAL MELEE on Capitol Hill, Coxey sat quietly in his small, barren jail cell. The successful Gilded Age businessman wrote to a prominent attorney back in his hometown of Massillon, acknowledging the good mattress and nice feather pillow that Mrs. Coxey had brought him so he could sleep more comfortably. He noted how, though "imprisoned for an idea," he found himself "just as busy in jail as outside of it." In their shared cell Carl Browne still nursed some wounds from the brutal clubbing at the hands of District policemen. He welcomed Baker, his newfound reporter friend, who came to return Browne's broken necklace retrieved from the Capitol grounds. With blood still matted into his long hair from the fracas, Browne told Baker, "You're the only friend I've got left in the world." The two would remain in touch in the coming years. In his memoirs Baker would note that Browne wrote to him frequently, signing always, "The Pen is Mightier than the Sword."[2]

Having walked some four hundred miles from Massillon to reach Washington, Baker was now glad to be boarding the train back to Chicago. He wrote to his father that he was just "terribly tired of the whole infernal business." In short, he admitted, he did not have anything more left to say about the march. He departed from Washington in frustration. However, the soon-to-be famous muckraker and ultimate confidant to President Woodrow Wilson would later reflect on his defining journalistic experience. Years later Baker recalled the Commonweal's triumphal procession through Pittsburgh and wondered whether there had ever been anything quite like it before. He had enjoyed the camaraderie of the marchers and disagreed with those who took a condescending attitude toward them:

To call them an army of "bums, tramps and vagabonds," as some of the commentators were doing, was a complete misrepresentation. A considerable proportion were genuine farmers and workingmen whose only offense was the fact that they could not buy or rent land—having no money—or find a job at which they could earn a living.

And yet, Baker mused, it was as if Coxey and Browne believed in "magic—the magic power centered in Washington." He concluded, "So far as I could see the power at Washington had scarcely fluttered an eyelid."[3]

Though Baker accurately assessed official Washington's indifference to Coxey's cause, he and the other reporters had clearly opened the public's eyes to the essential humanity of the unemployed. Though in the years immediately following the march governments would remain slow to act, Coxey and his industrial army had generated momentum toward a broader understanding of an inconvenient truth of industrial society. Three years after the march, when Walter Wyckoff began publishing a series of articles about his own eighteen-month tramping experience for *Scribner's Magazine*, it was reviewed not only with acclaim but also with sympathy toward its tramp protagonists. Wyckoff's work occupied a prominent space in an already growing tramp literature. In an April 3, 1898, *Chicago Tribune* page-long review, Louis De Foe noted the enormous physical and mental hardships endured by what Wyckoff referred to as the "army of the unemployed." De Foe concluded that, though Wyckoff had encountered compassion for his assumed jobless condition, there were few government or private initiatives designed to help alleviate it.[4]

Indeed, governments remained slow to acknowledge this new challenge. One exception, however, was the emergence of so-called job exchanges. Initially, most of the early clearinghouses were operated privately. But they quickly became subject to manipulation and profiteering. Thus, increasingly state governments entered the fray, interestingly beginning with Coxey's home state of Ohio in 1891. By the time America entered World War I, half the states had their own state-run employee exchanges. In the chaotic job market that existed in Gilded Age America, these new mechanisms served to match the jobless with local employers. Far less expensive than public-works programs, these bureaus gained strength from union support. Union bosses saw these state exchanges, many of which they helped to staff, as a way of gaining greater control over the labor pool, an avenue to recruit new members, and a check on the nefarious activities of private exchanges.[5]

However, when the Immigration Act of 1907 established a federal exchange in the Department of Commerce and Labor, union attitudes pivoted. Suddenly the federal government seemed to be taking the side of immigrants, placing them in jobs that union members themselves could fill. At a conference at the end of President Theodore Roosevelt's last term, John Mitchell, former head of the United Mine Workers, told outgoing Labor Secretary Oscar Straus, that thanks to the federal exchange, "too often the man who arrived in this country yesterday got a job, while the man who has spent much of his life in this country was waiting in the streets." Sam Gompers, president of the AFL joined in the criticism. Thus, the most critical constituency in support of federal involvement to help the unemployed was not at all content with Washington's first significant attempt to address the problem.[6]

As controversy swirled over the federal presence in job exchanges, Coxey continued to relentlessly pursue his own bold plan for public works. Bypassing Roosevelt's cabinet, he took his idea directly to the president himself. Actually the president had expressed an interest in Coxey's idea, which seemed much like his own proposal to put the unemployed back to work by constructing a network of waterways. Coxey, who had returned to Washington on his own several times since the march, met the president at the White House on February 27, 1908. While the two found they could agree on a large federal role in building public works, Coxey disagreed with Roosevelt's proposal that construction be financed with federally issued, interest-bearing bonds. Likewise, Roosevelt seemed puzzled by Coxey's non-interest bond proposal. As it turned out, the president's idea gained little more traction with Congress than had Coxey's Good Roads plan. Nonetheless, in the decade following Coxey's March, now at last there seemed some gradual recognition at the highest level that the federal government must play some role in helping the unemployed. Moreover, a newly formed American Association of Labor Legislation, comprised of those from academia, government, business, and labor, became a forceful lobby on behalf of the jobless.[7]

Coxey would remain indefatigable throughout his life in his efforts to engage government on behalf of the unemployed. Two years after he met with Roosevelt, Coxey tried to place a referendum on the ballot in Ohio, allowing his home state to issue interest-free bonds to raise money to pay workers, buy road-building equipment, and retain contractors to construct a network of roads. In this attempt Coxey confronted the reality of popular skepticism toward public works as a means for putting the jobless to work. He failed to obtain the requisite number of signatures to put the measure up for a vote.[8]

At the same time, and with little fanfare, the still operative Good Roads movement, finding itself under new leadership, was continuing to mount its own understated campaign for a greater federal presence in road building. A Department of Agriculture bureaucrat named Logan Page, who served as director of the Bureau of Public Roads (successor to the Office of Road Inquiry), was instrumental in establishing the American Association of State Highway Officials. This network of state officials would soon prove instrumental in enacting the first Federal Aid Road Act in 1916, which put $75 million (again well short of Coxey's plan) in federal money to be matched by states in constructing roads. Though US entry into World War I would interrupt the modest progress toward federal funding of a national system of roads, the first steps toward Coxey's grander vision were falling into place, even as he continued to espouse his much bolder plan.[9]

Also, during the First World War, the United States Employment Service was established in the Department of Labor. Though less about measuring and alleviating unemployment than it was about making sure there were no labor shortages in critical war industries, this new department would nonetheless create the precedent of a federal office dedicated to jobs. As the war wound down, an independent Labor Policies Board encouraged the idea of local investment in public works to assimilate returning soldiers in the work force. And, within the Departments of Commerce and Labor, the methods for identifying more accurately the numbers of unemployed, though still inexact, were providing more accurate assessments. In 1915 the Bureau of Labor Statistics began to publish the *Monthly Labor Review*, which compiled the best employment measurements available, even though it was conducted on an industry-by-industry and locality-by-locality basis. By 1926 the survey had grown to some ten thousand businesses in fifty-four industries covering about three million workers, which allowed for an even more accurate estimate of national unemployment. Thus, even as Coxey's legislation and other similar bills would continue to flounder in Congress, important seeds were being planted for the realization of his vision for the unemployed.[10]

Yet progress came slowly. Even in the immediate aftermath of the great stock market crash on October 24, 1929, the issue of the unemployed continued to flummox government officials. In this, the worst economy since Coxey marched, the legions of unemployed queuing at breadlines and selling apples now captured center stage. President Hoover immediately turned to Colonel Arthur Woods, the "Grand Marshal of Relief Efforts," to identify options for dealing with the surging mass of jobless. Yet Woods was the very same man whom President Warren Harding had appointed a decade earlier during the brief economic downturn in 1920–1921. And again, despite the severity of the economic collapse, Woods seemed content to follow the same time-worn strategy. "The principal part of our work is cooperating with local organizations," said Woods. The "Relief Tsar" repeatedly praised the "extraordinarily vigorous" local relief efforts going on around the country.[11]

With the continued feeble federal response, perhaps Coxey felt it was again time to ratchet up public attention for his own grand plan. He bypassed Woods and went directly to Hoover's secretary of commerce, Robert Lamont, one of the engineers who had designed the Chicago Colombian Exposition where Coxey's March figuratively began some thirty-seven years before. With the economic situation deteriorating daily, Coxey thought, those in the federal government might finally turn a receptive ear to his plan. But in his meeting with the secretary on October 21, 1930, Coxey again experienced the usual polite dismissal.[12]

As the extent of the Great Depression now began to touch every American, newspaper stories recounted how the nation had come through a similar depression in the 1890s. These same stories would remind readers about how Coxey, now in his late seventies, had led a march of the unemployed to Washington. Yet, with the Hoover administration failing to assert any bold federal remedy, the legacy of Coxey's March would not remain confined to quaint memories conjured by newspaper articles. Instead it served as an inspiration for yet another march on Washington, similar in many respects to its predecessor. On January 7, 1932, almost twenty thousand unemployed arrived in Washington demanding some $5 billion in emergency spending for public works to end the depression. Though their message was similar to Coxey's, this army of unemployed arrived in the capital not on foot but riding in a caravan of buses and trucks from Pittsburgh.

Father James R. Cox, a priest long devoted to eradicating unemployment and hunger in his Pittsburgh parish, led this delegation of unemployed to the capital. Immediately upon hearing about Cox's plan, a sympathetic Coxey eagerly telegrammed that his "spirit was marching with them." Like Coxey before him, concerned with the potential perception that this demonstration would turn violent, Cox staged a reverent visit of the jobless to Arlington Cemetery, where they paid their respects. Yet, unlike Coxey's Army, Cox's troops did not march up Pennsylvania Avenue. Rather, their state's Republican senator, James Davis, who had served as Hoover's labor secretary, skillfully negotiated a meeting between the president and the priest. On January 7, as the marchers waited patiently in carefully designated areas, Cox told the president that he feared violence if something was not done soon to alleviate the hardships of the unemployed. Though Hoover's treasury secretary, the Pittsburgh native Andrew Mellon, had quietly asked that the buses transporting the unemployed be given free gas at Gulf stations he owned along the route, the president himself seemed far less obliging. He perfunctorily told Father Cox, "I am glad to receive you as the representative of Pennsylvania's unemployed. I have intense sympathy for your difficulties." Then the president claimed some half a billion was already committed by his administration to address the unemployment issue—his diplomatic way of dismissing Cox's request for ten times that amount. Cox's army of unemployed would eventually leave Washington no more satisfied than Coxey's had over three decades earlier.[13]

Meanwhile, back in Massillon, Coxey continued to spend his own money furthering the cause. In the decades following his march, he expanded his own business and created more jobs at his now-extensive network of quarries and ranches. By 1932 Coxey's business empire included a steel-casting plant in Mt. Vernon, Ohio, coal mines in Flushing, Ohio, zinc mines near Joplin, Missouri, and gold and silver reserves in eastern Nevada. Though he endured a brief period in receivership, it did not take long for his business acumen to again make his growing business empire profitable. Witnessing firsthand Coxey's own remarkable success as they began to suffer from the depression, the voters in Massillon decided in November 1931 to turn to this successful local businessman and native son to be their mayor. It was the only election Coxey would win in seventeen separate campaigns for office, including everything from state legislator to president. Coincidentally, he and Father Cox were both candidates in the 1932 presidential campaign, though Cox would withdraw and throw the support of his "Hunger Party" to Franklin Roosevelt.[14]

For both of these reformers, and for the now-growing number of crusaders for the cause of the unemployed, Roosevelt's victory in the 1932 election was welcome news. Coxey would waste no time, as he had with each preceding president since the march, in again trying to promote his idea for jobs creation. The election gave Coxey the renewed hope that his plan might finally be realized, and he wrote the president on November 15, presumptuously instructing him, "This is one thing I hope that you will get to understand clearly ... that it is not necessary to have the stamp of government placed upon gold as a means of exchange to be used in canceling debts." Little did he know in December, following Roosevelt's landslide, and as he left Massillon on an eight-hundred-mile journey to present his ideas to the president–elect in Warm Springs, Georgia, that the nation was finally on the cusp of a massive "public-works revolution." On December 4, Coxey waited patiently as the governor of Kansas, Harry Hines Woodring, soon to become Roosevelt's secretary of war, presented his ideas for "farm relief" to the newly elected president. The week before, the *New York Times* had succinctly characterized the economic situation, predicting the coming winter would be one "of greater suffering than any in modern times."[15]

With the depression growing worse and with Roosevelt's election, the politics of the nation seemed finally ready to connect with the challenges presented by the growing ranks of unemployed. It had been thirty-eight years since Coxey, aided and abetted by a dozen intrepid reporters, cast a new light on the unemployment problem. Then, he had carried in his breast pocket a speech that he was barred from giving, which said:

> We have come here through toil and weary march, through storms and tempests, over mountains and amid the trials of poverty and distress at the doors of Congress in the name of Him whose banners we bear, in the name of Him who pleaded for the poor and the oppressed, that they should heed the voice of the distress and despair that is now coming up from every section of our country, that they should consider the conditions of the unemployed of our land and enact such laws as will give them employment, bring happier conditions to the people and the smile of contentment to our citizens.

With far more farms foreclosed and factories shuttered in 1932 than in 1894, much more was needed than programs that relied on individual philanthropy or strapped local relief budgets. The Roosevelt administration proved up to the task. Under Roosevelt's Public Works Administration (1933), Coxey would see the federal government finally assume ownership of a massive public-works program designed to put the jobless back to work. Before he died in 1951 at the age of ninety-seven, he would also see President Truman sign into law the Full Employment Act (1946), laying the responsibilities for full employment and unemployment relief squarely with the federal government.[16]

At the outset of the march that made him famous, Jacob Coxey noted, "That while we reaffirm our faith in the Omaha Platform ... as progressive men we have the right to advance over the lines." His crusade for jobs in 1894 and in the ensuing years not only crossed well-drawn lines but in its boldness seemed both ludicrous, yet also oddly endearing. Whether stubbornly cranky or amazingly clairvoyant, Coxey's March can be seen as more than a populist protest emblematic of an era. The "industrials" whom Coxey recruited marched in full view of a rapidly changing nation and by their sheer dignified presence revealed that the unemployed were not inferior intellectually, morally, or spiritually. Nor in this new economy were they going away. For five weeks they became the story that focused America's attention. In a transitional era this event cascaded into history, setting precedents for other causes, while laying important groundwork to realize its own—the engagement of the federal government in addressing unemployment. The cause seems just as relevant today in a new information economy as it was in the new industrial economy of the Gilded Age, when Coxey began his crusade for the unemployed.[17]

Notes

Notes to Introduction

1. Henry Vincent, *The Story of the Commonweal* (Chicago: W. B. Conkey, 1894), 50.

2. Shirley Plumer Austin, "The Downfall of Coxeyism," *Chautauquan* 18, no. 4 (July 1894): 448–52. The causes of the 1893–1897 depression, including the railroad bubble are well described in Richard White, *Railroaded: The Transcontinentals and the Making of Modern America* (New York: W. W. Norton, 2011), 370–413; also, for ripple effects of rail collapse, see Douglas Steeples and David O. Whitten, *Democracy in Desperation: The Depression of 1893* (Westport, CT: Greenwood Press, 1998), 1–41; Charles Hoffman, *The Depression of the Nineties: An Economic History* (Westport, CT: Greenwood Press, 1970), 54–71.

3. Austin, "Downfall of Coxeyism," 448–52; Junius Henri Browne, "Succor for the Unemployed," *Harper's Weekly* 38 (January 6, 1894): 10.

4. America was both industrializing and incorporating at an unprecedented pace in the Gilded Age. Alan Trachtenberg notes, "By 1904, for example, about three hundred industrial corporations had won control of over more than two fifths of all manufacturing in the country, affecting operations of about four fifths of the nation's industries"; see Alan Trachtenberg, *The Incorporation of America: Culture and Society in the Gilded Age* (New York: Hill & Wang, 1982), 4. An accurate national estimate of the total unemployed was difficult since no official government figures existed. Samuel Gompers estimated the unemployment at three million. In his account of the Panic, Frank B. Latham estimates four million; see Frank Brown Latham *The Panic of 1893: A Time of Strikes, Riots, Hobo Camps, Coxey's "Army," Starvation, Withering Droughts, and Fears of Revolution* (New York: F. Watts, 1971), 4. See also Hoffman, *Depression of the Nineties*, 109–10; Hoffman estimates that at its worst in the winter of 1893–1894, unemployment hovered at about 2.5 million, 97–110; *Statistical Abstract of the United States* (Washington: Government Printing Office, 1895), https://archive.org/details/statisticalabstr015457mbp.

5. Catherine Reef, *Poverty in America* (New York: Facts on File, 2007), xv; Udo Sautter, *Three Cheers for the Unemployed: Government and Unemployment before the New Deal* (Cambridge: Cambridge University Press, 2001), 14–46. See John A. Garraty, *Unemployment in History: Economic Thought and Public Policy* (New York: Harper & Row, 1978), 109n12.

6. A complicated taxonomy of the poor arose out of reform efforts in the Gilded Age. A survey of late nineteenth-century public attitudes toward the homeless can be found in Kenneth L. Kusmer, *Down and Out and on the Road: The Homeless in American History* (New York: Oxford University Press, 2002); see in particular his discussion of the "worthy poor," 73–97. See also Nels Anderson, *On Hobos and Homelessness* (Chicago: University of Chicago Press, 1998), and Paul T. Rigenbach, *Tramps and Reformers 1873–1916* (Westport, CT: Greenwood Press, 1973), for excellent descriptions of tramp culture.

7. Andrew Carnegie, *The Gospel of Wealth* (New York: Century Company, 1901), 4; Richard Hofstadter, *Social Darwinism in American Thought* (Boston: Beacon Press, 1944), 210.

8. Embrey Bernard Howson, *Jacob Sechler Coxey: A Biography of a Monetary Reformer* (New York: Arno Press, 1982), 115–17, 120; Coxey, HBC Radio Story #98, "General Jacob S. Coxey's 95th Birthday," Jacob Sechler Coxey Sr. Papers, Massillon Museum, Massillon, OH, 3; "Pennvenvon Window Glass Plant," *Pittsburgh People* 2, no. 3 (March 1941): 4.

9. Guy McNeill Wells of the *Cleveland Press* and a Cleveland correspondent to the *Wall Street Journal*, untitled article about Coxey dated June 30, 1934, which appears in Jacob Coxey's papers at the Massillon Museum in Massillon, Ohio; Coxey, HBC Radio Story # 98; "Pennvenvon Window Glass Plant," 4.

10. Jacob Sechler Coxey, "The Coxey Plan," Jacob Sechler Coxey Papers, Massillon Museum, Massillon, OH, 48–51. This volume also contains the transcript of Coxey's appearance before the Ways and Means Committee on January 8, 1895, 19–44. Regarding the testimony Coxey provided in 1895 where he states the plan would result in $1.50 an hour wage, he earlier referred to $1.25 an hour in 1891 when he was interviewed by his local newspaper; see "Farewell to Poverty," *Massillon Evening Independent*, December 20, 1891. The text of the plan also appears in several different places in the J. S. Coxey archives housed in the Massillon Museum; e.g., the *Preamble of the Constitution and By-Laws of the Coxey Non-Interest Bearing Bond Club National Organization* contains "The Coxey Non-Interest Bond Bill" and "The Coxey Good Roads Bill"; as for the plan's price tag, though no precise records exist of federal budget size in 1894, it is estimated to have been approximately $450 million; see http://www. usgovernmentspending.com/fed_spending_1894USmn. (That Coxey's plan exceeded the 1894 federal budget was corroborated by David Gibbons, Professional Staff Member to House Appropriations Committee; United States House of Representatives at the request of the author on February 23, 2009.)

11. "The Pulpit View," *Washington Post*, April 23, 1894; Frank Leonard, "Helping the Unemployed in the Nineteenth Century: The Case of the American Tramp," *Social Service Review* 40, no. 4 (December 1966): 429–34; Herbert Gutman, "The Workers' Search for Power: Labor in the Gilded Age," in *Power and Culture: Essays on the American Working Class*, ed. Ira Berlin (New York: New Press, 1987), 86–87; "Ohio's Don Quixote," *Chicago Tribune*, February 5, 1894; "Coxey and Lodge," *Harper's Weekly* 38, no. 1952 (May 19, 1894): 458.

12. Lucy G. Barber, *Marching on Washington: The Forging of an American Political Tradition* (Berkley: University of California Press, 2002), 11–44; Three Senate Populists and Eleven in House; see http://www.senate.gov/history/partydiv.htm and http://history.house.gov/Congressional-Overview/Profiles/53rd/.

13. Michael S. Sweeney, "The Desire for the Sensational," *Journalism History* 23, no. 3 (Autumn 1997): 114.

14. Vivian Graff Rosenberg, *Turn of the Century American Journalist, Home-Spun Philosopher: Ray Stannard Baker* (published by author, 1977), 69; see also Robert C. Bannister, *Ray Stannard Baker: The Mind and Thought of a Progressive* (New Haven, CT: Yale University Press, 1966), 47.

15. Mark Pittenger, *Class Unknown: Undercover Investigations of American Work from the Progressive Era to the Present* (New York: New York University Press, 2012), 14–15; Todd DePastino, *Citizen Hobo: How a Century of Homelessness Shaped America* (Chicago: University of Chicago Press, 2003), 5–15; David Bender, *American Abyss: Savagery and Civilization in the Age of Industry* (Ithaca, NY: Cornell University Press, 2009), 154–57. For a map showing numbers and approximate routes of the nine (perhaps more) industrial armies moving from points west, see Schwantes, "Routes of the Armies of the Commonweal," 8–9. Geographically, Kelly's departed from San Francisco, Frye's from Los Angeles, and Jones's from Philadelphia, but there were at least five others and perhaps as many as fifteen leaders who tried to organize and join Coxey. The *Raleigh News Observer* reported the following tally and progress on April 24: "General Kelly's 1,000 men; Neola, Iowa; General Frye's 1,000 Terre Haute, Indiana; General Frye's second division, 800 men, McCleansboro, Illinois; General Grayson 1,000 men Plattville, Colorado; General Galcin 200 men, Loveland Ohio; Sergeant Randall, 500 men Chicago; 100 men at Little Falls, Minnesota; 300 men at Butte, Montana; 100 men at Monmouth, Illinois; 100 men at Ottumwa, Iowa; Captain Sullivan, 1,000 men, Chicago; 150 men at Anderson, Indiana; and General Aubrey, 700 men, Indianapolis, Indiana."

16. Vincent, who marched with Coxey as far as McKeesport, Pennsylvania, published *The Story of the Commonweal* to help raise money for the other industrial armies that Coxey spawned; Vincent, *Story of the Commonweal of Christ*, 48. Vincent was a member of the Populist group the Videttes, who allegedly plotted an anarchist dynamite explosion in Coffeyville, Kansas, in 1888. However, he became better known for his crusading journalism. He served as the editor of a populist paper in Kansas known as the *Non-Conformist*. He dedicated his journalism to restoring a "republican" America that valued the producer and placed the larger community in front of narrower self-interest. When Vincent met Coxey in Chicago, he was a reporter for the *Chicago Express*. Soon he would found the *Chicago Searchlight*, which became a bellwether, populist reform newspaper. Peter H. Argesinger, *Populism: Its Rise and Fall* (Lawrence: Kansas University Press, 1992), 1–3, discusses how as "populism" gradually entered the language, other terms that referred to this producer unrest also competed for attention. For example, long-bearded Populist Kansas senator William A. Peffer, an advocate of Coxey's right to demonstrate and who introduced his Good Roads legislation, was alternately referred to not only as a Populist but also as a "Pefferite." "Pefferism" in its time could be used interchangeably with "Populism,"

just as "Coxeyism" entered the language in 1894 as a way of describing the ideas embodied in Coxey's March. Charles Postel, *The Populist Vision* (New York: Oxford University Press, 2007), 22, succinctly makes the demarcation between *populism* as a constant in our political dialogue and the specific institutionalization of a Populist Party. Indeed Lawrence Goodwyn, in *Democratic Promise: The Populist Moment in America* (New York: Oxford University Press, 1976), 51, notes that the term "populism" itself was not coined until 1892. He notes that though during the period 1886–1887 the "organizational methods and ideological basis of American populism were fashioned, it would not be until 1892 that it acquired a distinctive name—'Populism'"; Donald McMurry, *Coxey's Army: A Study of the Industrial Army Movement of 1894* (Seattle: University of Washington Press, 1929), 260–85, in which McMurry discusses the "Meaning of the Movement."

17. Richard Hofstadter, *Age of Reform*, 165. Populism itself posed problems for the consensus historian Hofstadter, who chose to see the movement as expressing the "'soft' side of agrarianism." Norman Pollack, *The Populist Response to Industrial America* (Cambridge, MA: Harvard University Press, 1962), 41–68; Pollack's account depicts the Populists as reconciled to industrialization and thus trying to develop their own sophisticated response. Pollack goes well beyond the farm gate in his examination of the populist groundswell against a corporate economy; Goodwyn, *Democratic Promise*, 52–65, 307–11; Carlos Schwantes, *Coxey's Army: An American Odyssey* (Moscow: University of Idaho Press, 1985), ix–x; Benjamin F. Alexander, *Coxey's Army: Popular Protest in the Gilded Age* (Baltimore, MD: Johns Hopkins University Press, 2015), 4.

18. Postel in *The Populist Vision* makes the case that Populists in the late nineteenth-century United States embraced modernity with broad and bold plans, like Coxey's, and that their vision of a "Cooperative Commonwealth" competed with the ascendant corporate form of economic organization. As Postel notes at 288, "The Populists wanted an active government to ensure fair access to the benefits of modernity." Vincent, *Story of the Commonweal*, 15.

Notes to Chapter One

1. The quote from Mayor Harrison appears in slightly different versions in "Freedom of Silver," *Chicago Daily Tribune*, August 2, 1893, and "Down to Work," *Los Angeles Times*, August 2, 1893 (from which the quote here is taken).

2. Donald L. Miller, *The City of the Century: The Epic of Chicago and the Making of America* (New York: Simon & Schuster, 1991), 488; Erik Larson, *The Devil in the White City: A Saga of Magic and Murder at the Fair That Changed America* (New York: Vintage Books, 2003), 4, 27–29, 235–38; Trachtenberg, *Incorporation of America*, 208–34.

3. While an estimated 27 million people paid admission to the fair, that total does not reveal how many were multiple admissions. At the same time, free passes were also issued to large numbers. For this reason James Gilbert suggests that fewer than half the 27 million actually came. But since the entire US population was about 54 million, this still represents a significant number. Moreover, the cost in an era where $500 a year represented a working wage, could be as much as $55 without train fare, according to James Gilbert, *Perfect Cities: Chicago's Utopias of 1893* (Chicago: University of Chicago Press, 1991), 121. Donald L. Miller suggests that "American families mortgaged their farms and houses and borrowed money on their life insurance or trimmed their Christmas budgets to save up for a summer week in Chicago, Donald Miller, *City of the Century*, 488. See also H. W. Brands, *The Reckless Decade: America in the 1890s* (Chicago: University of Chicago Press, 1995), 42–45; Carl S. Smith, *Urban Disorder and the Shape of Belief: The Great Chicago Fire, the Haymarket Bomb, and the Model Town of Pullman* (Chicago: University of Chicago Press, 1995), 112; Gilbert, *Perfect Cities*, 126; John E. Semonche, *Ray Stannard Baker* (Chapel Hill: University of North Carolina Press, 1969), 52–53.

4. Larson, *Devil in the White City*, 4, 27–29, 235–38; see also "History of Kelly's Local Agent." Carl Browne, *When Coxey's "Army" Marcht* (San Francisco, CA: n.p., 1944); Thomas J. Schlereth, *Victorian America: Transformations in Everyday Life, 1876–1915* (New York: HarperCollins, 1994), 172–75; Brands, *Reckless Decade*, 42–45; Carl Smith, *Urban Disorder*, 112; W. T. Stead, "Coxeyism, a Character Sketch," *American Review of Reviews* (July 1894), 49. Semonche, *Ray Stannard Baker*, 52–53; William F. Stead, *Chicago Today, or the Labour War in America* (London: Review of Reviews Office, 1894), 7; William F. Stead, *If Christ Came to Chicago: A Plea for the Union of All Who Love in the Service of All Who Suffer* (Chicago: Laird & Lee, 1894) 140; William G. McLoughlin, *Revivals, Awakenings, and Reform: An Essay on Religion and Social Change in America, 1607–1977* (Chicago: University of Chicago Press, 1978),

152; Samuel Rezneck, "Unemployment, Unrest and Relief in the United States during the Depression of 1893–97," *Journal of Political Economy* 61, no. 4 (1953): 327, 329–332. Rezneck (332) points out this view toward public works at the time: "Benjamin Flowers, the utopian editor of the *Arena*, protested in 1894 that many worth-while projects, such as roads and the Mississippi levees, might have saved the day, but for the fact that 'gold is more precious in the eyes of our legislators than independent, self-respecting citizenship.... Millions for armories and the military instruction of the young, but not one cent to furnish employment to able bodied industry in its struggle to escape the terrible alternatives of stealing or starving—such seems to be the theory of government in the United States today.'"

5. "Scenes on the Street," *Atlanta Constitution*, May 6, 1893; "A Panicky Day," *Los Angeles Times*, May 5, 1893; "Verging on Monopoly," *New York Times*, December 27, 1891; Steeples and Whitten, *Democracy in Desperation*, 33.

6. Steeples and Whitten, *Democracy in Desperation*, 19–23; Lawrence Goodwyn, *The Populist Moment: A Short History of the Agrarian Revolt in America* (New York: Oxford University Press, 1978), 23–24.

7. Mitchell Bard, "Ideology and Depression Politics I: Grover Cleveland (1893–97)," *Presidential Studies Quarterly* 15, no. 1 (January 1, 1985): 77–88.

8. Goodwyn, *Democratic Promise*, 26–39. The precise number of business failures is broken down as 15,242 businesses, 119 railroads, and 642 bank failures in Steeples and Whitten, *Democracy in Desperation*, 34–37; these two authors provide the most sophisticated analysis of the causes of the crisis. They factor the strength of business cycles and the downturn, particularly in the agricultural sector beginning in the late 1880s and eschew more contemporary accounts, notably W. Jett Lauck's 1907 analysis, which emphasized the run on gold caused by the Sherman Act (1890), the loss of confidence in Britain, and the general European economic downturn beginning in 1890; see W. Jett Lauck, *The Causes of the Panic of 1893* (Boston: Houghton, Mifflin, 1907), 97–109; Junius Browne, "Succor," 10; Matthew Algeo, *The President Is a Sick Man: Wherein the Supposedly Virtuous Grover Cleveland Survives a Secret Surgery at Sea and Vilifies the Courageous Newspaperman Who Dared Expose the Truth* (Chicago: Chicago Review Press, 2011), 83–84.

9. "A Silver Convention Called," *New York Times*, July 5, 1893; "The Bimetallic Convention," *Los Angeles Times*, August 2, 1893; "Bimetallic League," *Baltimore Sun*, August 2, 1893.

10. Milton Friedman, "The Crime of 1873," *Journal of Political Economy* 98, no. 16 (December 1990): 1159–93; Richard Franklin Bensel, *The Political Economy of American Industrialization, 1877–1910* (New York: Cambridge University Press, 2000), 155, 370–71, 1355; Walter Nugent, "Comments on Wyatt Wells, 'Rhetoric of the Standards: The Debate over Gold and Silver in the 1890s,'" *Journal of the Gilded Age and Progressive Era* 14, no. 1 (2015): 69–76.

11. Michael O'Malley, *Face Value* (Chicago: University of Chicago Press, 2012), 86–94; Matthew Hild, *Greenbackers, Knights of Labor, and Populists* (Athens: University of Georgia Press, 2007), 20–24; Irwin Unger, *The Greenback Era: A Social and Political History of American Finance, 1865–1879* (Princeton, NJ: Princeton University Press, 1964), 249–321; Bruce G. Carruthers and Sarah Babb, "The Color of Money and the Nature of Value: Greenbacks and Gold in Postbellum America," *American Journal of Sociology* 101, no. 6 (May 1, 1996):1556–91; Gretchen Ritter, *Goldbugs and Greenbacks: The Antimonopoly Tradition and the Politics of Finance in America* (Cambridge: Cambridge University Press, 1997), 38–39, 62–109. When Congress passed the Resumption Act in 1875, it allowed a four-year hiatus until greenbacks could be exchanged for gold. This allowed an ample period for speculators to drive up the price of greenbacks and made the entire redemption process more expensive. Speculators could buy greenbacks cheaply, betting on the fact that they could convert them at face value—or at least something approximating full worth. As these moneymen bought up greenbacks for this purpose, the money supply further contracted. Meanwhile Congress also demonetized silver in 1873 ("The Crime of 1873"), further exacerbating the speculative fevers and to the delight of bankers on Wall Street, causing the remaining greenbacks to rise precipitously in the four years before they could be redeemed. Thus, by 1880 when the Resumption Act was fully in place, the amount of money per capita was calculated to be a mere $19.36, in marked contrast to the $30.35 per capita at the end of the Civil War.

12. Steeples and Whitten, *Democracy in Desperation*, 14–23, 42–60, 87; Thomas A. Clinch, *Urban Populism and Free Silver in Montana: A Narrative of Ideology in Political Action* (Missoula: University of Montana Press, 1970), 82–87. Michael McGerr notes in *A Fierce Discontent: The Rise and Fall of the Progressive Movement in America, 1870–1920* (New York: Oxford University Press, 2003), 7: "In a land of some 76 million people, the 'Upper Ten' were no more than a tiny minority; a mere sliver of the nation." The term derived from British terminology used to describe the very richest in English society;

see Licht, *Industrializing America* (Baltimore, MD: Johns Hopkins University Press, 1995), 183, and discussion of income disparity, where the top 1 percent owned 51 percent of all property. "Currency and Capital," *Harper's Weekly* 38 (1906): 614.

13. "Warner Makes a Statement," *New York Times*, July 28, 1893; General A. J. Warner, *Opening Address to the Silver Convention Delivered August 1, 1893* (Washington, DC: Geo. R. Gray, Printer, 1893); "Freedom of Silver," *Chicago Daily Tribune*, August 2, 1893; "Make Their Plea," *Chicago Daily Tribune*, August 3, 1893; Howson, *Coxey*, 77–103; Richard H. Timberlake Jr., "Repeal of Silver Monetization in the Late Nineteenth Century," *Journal of Money, Credit and Banking* 10, no. 1 (February 1, 1978): 42; Unger, *Greenback Era*, 249–85; Wells, "Rhetoric," 50.

14. "Champions of Silver," *Baltimore Sun*, August 3, 1893.

15. See next note regarding the origins of the term "Populism"; "Closing Scenes," *Los Angeles Times*, August 3, 1893.

16. Postel, *Populist Vision*, 12–13. "Populism" can be used as a term to describe a constant in politics; that is, the assertion of those seeking greater equality with the elites, or it can be used in the specific historical context of the late nineteenth century and the movement that led to the formation of the People's Party. Postel described the eclectic nature of the party: "The precise configuration of the coalition varied at the state level, but the orders tended to fall into discrete categories: farmers' associations; labor organizations; women's groups; and an array of nonconformists, including urban radicals, tax and currency reformers, prohibitionists, middle-class utopians, spiritual innovators, and miscellaneous iconoclasts." John Donald Hicks, *The Populist Revolt: A History of the Farmers' Alliance and the People's Party* (Lincoln: University of Nebraska Press, 1961), 299. Richard White, *Railroaded*, 332–35, speaks of the Farmers Alliance and Knights of Labor recognizing "the imitation of corporations as the first step toward eliminating corporate abuse and power."

17. Carnegie, *Gospel of Wealth*, 3.

18. Howson, *Coxey*, 15–16, 85–90; Russel B. Nye, *A Baker's Dozen: Thirteen Unusual Americans* (East Lansing: Michigan State University Press, 1956), 209–10; see, in particular, the challenges to unpacking Coxey's early life as detailed in note 1 to chapter 1 in Howson's biography of Coxey.

19. Howson, *Coxey*, 115–16; William H. Lewis, "General Jacob S. Coxey," *Glass Cutter* 20, no. 9 (March, 1955): 5.

20. Howson, *Coxey*, 115–17; Jean Strouse, *Morgan: American Financier* (New York: HarperCollins, 2000), 215–16.

21. Howson, *Coxey*, 87. For a comprehensive narrative on business reformers in the era, see Gerald Berk, *Alternative Tracks: The Constitution of American Industrial Order, 1865–1917* (Baltimore, MD: Johns Hopkins University Press, 1994).

22. Unger, *Greenback Era*, 55, 97–99; Ralph Ross Ricker, *The Greenback-Labor Movement in Pennsylvania* (Bellefonte, PA: Pennsylvania Heritage, 1966), 24–25; Edward Kellogg, *A New Monetary System: The Only Means of Securing the Respective Rights of Labor and Property, and of Protecting the Public from Financial Revulsions* (New York: Rudd & Carleton, 1861), 34; Henry Charles Carey, *Principles of Political Economy* (Philadelphia: Carey, Lea & Blanchard, 1837), 140; Rossiter W. Raymond, *Peter Cooper* (New York: Houghton, Mifflin, 1901), 100–101. Richard H. Timberlake, *Monetary Policy in the United States: An Intellectual and Institutional History* (Chicago: University of Chicago Press, 1978), 129–45. Yet another Pennsylvania iron man and Kellogg disciple, Alexander Campbell, toward the conclusion of the Civil War called for an end to the National Banks, for the Treasury to issue legal tender, and for federally issued bonds at 3 percent to be interchangeable or "incontrovertible" with federal greenbacks. So influential were his ideas that they came to be known as "Campbellism" and came to dominate the labor reform movement of the late 1860s; see Unger, *Greenback Era*, 98–102. Due to Carey's early hand in the Industrial League, and its heavy concentration in Pennsylvania, it quickly transformed itself and became known simply as the Pennsylvania Industrial League.

23. Sweeney, "Sensational," 115. Sweeney confirmed what this researcher learned from archivists at the Massillon Museum, that Coxey and Browne's papers stored at Coxey's Paul's Station home burned in a house fire in 1894. In the correspondence and papers available from other sources, we gain insight into the march but little about the wellsprings for Coxey's or Browne's ideas; Nye, *Baker's Dozen*, 210. Irwin Unger, "Business Men and Specie Resumption," *Political Science Quarterly* 74, no. 1 (March 1, 1959): 53.

24. Unger, *Greenback Era*, 79–85; Chester McA. Destler, "The Origin and Character of the Pendleton Plan," *Mississippi Valley Historical Review* 24, no. 2 (1937): 171–84; Unger, *Greenback Era*, 79–85; Destler, "Pendleton Plan," 171–84; Robert Dixon Sawrey, *Dubious Victory: The Reconstruction Debate in Ohio* (Lexington: University of Kentucky Press, 1992), 107–9.

25. Howson, *Coxey*, 119 (in particular see 156n15 for a well-documented accounting of Coxey's wage system compared with contemporary national averages). Coxey's wages at his quarries ranged from $1.35 an hour to $2.75. For quote from Guy McNeill Wells, see June 30, 1924, untitled excerpt by Guy McNeill Wells, financial editor of the *Cleveland Press* and Cleveland correspondent to the *Wall Street Journal* in unfiled materials from Jacob Coxey's papers at Massillon Museum, Massillon, OH.

26. Brown, *Coxey*, 4; Vincent, *Story of the Commonweal*, 112; "Stewart and Bryan Speak," *Chicago Daily Tribune*, August 2, 1893; "To Shout for Silver," *Chicago Daily Tribune*, July 30, 1893; Shirley Plummer Austin, "Coxey's Commonweal Army," *Chautauquan* 19 (July 1894): 332.

27. Nell Irvin Painter, *Standing at Armageddon: The United States 1877–1919* (New York: W. W. Norton, 1987), 48–49; James Green, *Death in the Haymarket* (New York: Random House, 2006), 288–89.

28. The *Chicago Daily Tribune* referred to Browne as "a cowboy from California in a buckskin suit." See "Freedom of Silver," *Chicago Daily Tribune*, August 2, 1893. Browne speaks in his autobiographical treatment of the march of having been recruited for the Chicago Exposition's Wild West Show. Browne, *When Coxey's "Army" Marcht*, 4. See also Ray Allen Billington, *Frederick Jackson Turner: Historian, Scholar, Teacher* (New York: Oxford University Press, 1973), 126–28.

29. Ray Stannard Baker, *American Chronicle: The Autobiography of Ray Stannard Baker* (New York: C. Scribner's Sons, 1945), 20. A description of Ignatius Donnelly appears in Hicks, *Populist Revolt*, 162–64; Vincent, *Story of the Commonweal*, 109–11; "Make Their Plea," *Chicago Daily Tribune*, August 3, 1893; Austin, "Coxey's Commonweal Army," 332; Browne, *When Coxey's "Army" Marcht*, 4.

30. As previously described in note 23, a fire at Coxey's home in the fall of 1894 destroyed many of his and Browne's personal papers associated with the march. The remaining Coxey papers, largely housed at the Massillon Museum in Massillon, Ohio, do not provide much in the way of insight into what Browne and Coxey discussed during their chance meeting in Chicago at the Bimetallic Convention. Yet the intensity of those discussions is confirmed by Coxey's invitation to Browne to continue their discussions by coming to live with him at his home in Massillon. As Browne noted in his own biography, written with the assistance of William McDevitt and published in May 1914, "The Idea of the 'March' originated in Chicago."

31. Vincent, *Story of the Commonweal*, 109–11; Browne, *When Coxey's "Army" Marcht*, 4; Nye, *Baker's Dozen*, 212. "Make Their Plea," *Chicago Daily Tribune*, August 3, 1893; Austin, "Coxey's Commonweal Army," 332.

32. Vincent, *Story of the Commonweal*, 109–11; Doyce B. Nunis, Denis Kearney, and J. Bryce, "The Demagogue and the Demographer: Correspondence of Denis Kearney and Lord Bryce," *Pacific Historical Review* 36, no. 3 (1967): 269–88. At the height of the San Francisco sandlot violence, on July 23, 1877, a crowd that officials in San Francisco labeled as "hoodlums and vagrants," went on a violent binge through Chinatown, causing some $10,000 in damage, burning stores, smashing windows, and taking lives. Later that October, undeterred by the omnipresent show of force by so-called Committees of Vigilance, Kearney led an unruly crowd up Knob Hill in San Francisco to the doorstep of the mansion of Charles Crocker, chief architect of the Central Pacific Railroad. Fearing that the houses of some of San Francisco's most wealthy patrons might be destroyed, officials deployed troops in the neighborhood, while three US naval vessels loomed offshore, theoretically serving warning to Kearney; see "The Workingmen's Party of California, 1877–1882," *California Historical Quarterly* 55, no. 1 (April 1, 1976): 58–73; Browne, *When Coxey's "Army" Marcht*, 26–27; Vincent, *Story of the Commonweal*, 109–13; Ralph Kauer, "The Workingmen's Party of California," *Pacific Historical Review* 13, no. 3 (1944): 278–79; "Cooling Off," *Boston Globe*, July 28, 1877.

33. "Illinois Steel Works to Close," *Chicago Daily Tribune*, August 26, 1894; Carl Smith, *Urban Disorder*, 233; Larson, *Devil in the White City*, 4, 27–29, 235–38.

34. Schwantes, *Coxey's Army*, 12; "Bounced," *Los Angeles Times*, September 6, 1893; "How to Aid the Unemployed," *Chicago Daily Tribune*, December 5, 1893; "Asked Not to March," *Chicago Daily Tribune*, August 25, 1893; "Will Demand Bread," *Chicago Daily Tribune*, August 16, 1893; "Attack on a Store," *Chicago Daily Tribune*, August 29, 1893. Browne had experienced earlier difficulties with the law. His checkered journalistic reputation in California became the subject of legal challenges filed by fellow journalists, who attacked him for filing libelous stories. Thus, at the very moment that Browne was haranguing the plutocracy on the shores of Lake Michigan, the *Los Angeles Times* was running an editorial describing him as a "long haired, bearskin coated freak of nature who calls himself an artist." "Editorial Notes," *Mendocino Dispatch Democrat*, December 15, 1893; see also "Bounced," *Los Angeles Times*, September 6, 1893, and "Article 1–No Title," *Los Angeles Times*, September 7, 1893. Earlier editorial criticism of Browne in *Los Angeles Times*, August 14, 1888, arose when Browne was

accused by the editor of the *San Francisco Weekly Star* of being a lackey for the railroads and a fraud as a representative of the United Labor Party. Later in 1890 articles again appeared citing Browne's judicial woes. Accused of trying to extort money from Willie Childs in return for suppressing an article in Browne's self-published, *The Cactus*, Browne was ultimately acquitted in an 1890 trial; see "Acquitted," *Los Angeles Times*, October 13, 1890. See also "A Blackmailer," *Los Angeles Times*, October 12, 1888. See also McMurry, *Coxey's Army*, 30n1 and 189n2.

35. "Bounced," *Los Angeles Times*, September 6, 1893, and "Article 1–No Title," *Los Angeles Times*, September 7, 1893.

36. Carl Smith, *Urban Disorder*, 233; "Census of the Poor," *Chicago Daily Tribune*, December 14, 1893.

37. "If They Had No Cash," *Chicago Daily Tribune*, December 10, 1893.

38. *Twentieth Century Farmer* 1, no. 2 (April 1894): 3 in Jacob S. Coxey Sr., Papers, Massillon Museum, Massillon, OH.

Notes to Chapter Two

1. Browne, "Bulletin Number 3," February 28, 1894, J. S. Coxey Good Roads Association, Jacob Sechler Coxey Sr. Papers, Massillon Museum, Massillon, OH. See articles accompanying "Twenty Five Tramps Find Their Way to Massillon," *Chicago Tribune*, March 23, 1894; "Pennsylvania Will Ask Ohio Tramps to Stay at Home," *Washington Post*, March 19, 1894; "Coxey's Army Soon to March," *New York Times*, March 23, 1894.

2. Osman C. Hooper, "The Coxey Movement in Ohio," *Ohio Archaeological and Historical Quarterly* 9 (Columbus: Fred J. Heer, 1901), 155; "Army Growing," *Boston Daily Globe*, April 6, 1894; "Coxey's Army Order," *Chicago Daily Tribune*, March 5, 1894; reference to organizing the march in communes occurs in "Organization of the Army of Peace," *Chicago Daily Tribune*, February 10, 1894.

3. See Browne, "Bulletin Number 3"; Shirley Plumer Austin, "Downfall of Coxeyism," 448–50. Austin gives an in-depth analysis of the backgrounds of many of those in Coxey's Army. W. T. Stead, "Coxeyism," 51, cites an analysis done by University of Chicago professor Isaac A. Hourwich of General Randall's Army, which formed in Chicago: "Of 262 industrials, 181 were skilled mechanics representing 70 trades; 74 were unskilled, and 7 were tradesmen.... They averaged seven years of school life; 26 had attended high schools, businesses and professional colleges, academies and universities. Of 115 questioned, only 2 were badly educated." The term "tramp" dated to the Civil War and, as Kenneth L. Kusmer traces its evolution, became a popular term to describe wandering unemployed who often used America's growing rail system to move from town to town; see also a Commonweal roster of those marching by occupation and home in Coxey Papers, box 3, Massillon Museum, Massillon, OH; see Kusmer, *Down and Out*, 35–56; and "Tramps Are Ready," *Chicago Daily Tribune*, March 17, 1894; Sweeney, "Sensational"; Nye, "Jacob Coxey," in *Baker's Dozen*, 221. The *Boston Daily Globe*, April 11, 1894, also observed, "Tramps constitute about two fifths of the force, while the remainder are mainly roving workingmen of different trades who state that they are willing to desert at any time for good positions."

4. Austin, "Downfall of Coxeyism," 449–52.

5. "Severe Treatment for Tramps," *New York Times*, March 20, 1889. William Goodwin Moody and J. Laurence Laughlin, "Workingmen's Grievances," *North American Review* 138, no. 330 (May 1894): 505.

6. Moody and Laughlin, "Workingmen's Grievances," 505; DePastino, *Citizen Hobo*, 3–29.

7. David Montgomery, "Wage Labor, Bondage, and Citizenship in Nineteenth-Century America," *International Labor and Working-Class History* 48 (October 1, 1995): 19; Ralph Waldo Emerson, *Self Reliance and Other Essays* (Mineola, NY: Dover, 1993), 33.

8. DePastino, *Citizen Hobo*, 5–15; Bender, *American Abyss*, 154–57; Pittenger, *Class Unknown*, 14–15; "Professor Wyckoff," *Daily Chicago Tribune*, February 10, 1899.

9. Moody and Laughlin, "Workingmen's Grievances," 505.

10. Leonard, "Helping the Unemployed," 430, notes that Wayland stated this in "The Tramp Question," in *Proceedings of the National Conference of Charities and Correction*, 1877, 112; Michael B. Katz, *In the Shadow of the Poorhouse: A Social History of Welfare in America* (New York: Basic Books, 1986), 4–7; Andrew Carnegie, *The Autobiography of Andrew Carnegie* (Boston: Houghton Mifflin, 1920), 339.

11. Roswell D. Hitchcock, *Socialism* (New York: Anson D. F. Randolph, 1879), 10, 86–95.

12. Garraty, *Unemployment in History*, 108–9; Sautter, *Three Cheers*, 18–20.

13. The earliest references to the term "unemployment" from the seventeenth century are in the context of unused resources or time wasted. Later, classical economists including Smith, Malthus,

and Ricardo referred tangentially to joblessness but typically as a byproduct of what they referred to as "overproduction." In addition to Sautter's, *Three Cheers*, which discusses the evolution of the term, a 1917 doctoral dissertation at Columbia by Frederick C. Mills, "Contemporary Theories of Unemployment and Unemployment Relief" (PhD diss., Columbia University, 1917), discusses the attitudes of Adam Smith, David Ricardo, and Thomas Malthus toward the jobless phenomenon. The Google Books Ngram (https://books.google.com/ngrams) measurement for the word "unemployed" shows that the first real rise in use (based on the books it samples) occurs in 1890; see also etymology of the word "unemployed" in the Oxford English Dictionary, www.oed.com:

While some reference to "unemployed" as in jobless, this use only gradually took hold in 1880's. Thus the reference:

2.

a. Not engaged in any work or occupation; idle; spec. temporarily out of work.

1667   Milton *Paradise Lost* iv. 617   Other Creatures all day long Rove idle unemploid, and less need rest.

1677   A. Yarranton *England's Improvem.* I. 61   Admit there be in England and Wales a hundred thousand poor people unemployed [*sic*].

1740   C. Cibber Apol. *Life C. Cibber* vii. 133   I remember him three times, for some Years, unemploy'd [*sic*] in any Theatre.

1824   L. M. Hawkins *Annaline* I. 40   Being unemployed they amused themselves and others with conjectures.

1862   J. Ruskin *Unto this Last* iii. 100   The vexed question of the destinies of the unemployed workmen.

1887   St. James's Gaz. 22 Dec. 4/1   Persons who are unemployed because they are unemployable.

See also Kusmer, *Down and Out*, 102–3; Sautter, *Three Cheers*, 14–42; Kenneth Lapides, "Marx's Doctrine of Wage Labor," *Science and Society* 66, no. 2 (Summer 2002): 256–63.

14. Steeples and Whitten, *Democracy in Desperation*, 50; Rezneck, "Unemployment, Unrest," 327. By all accounts, at its depths this four-year depression would leave an estimated three to four million Americans without jobs. At least one in every four men eligible to work could not find a job. An accurate national estimate of the total unemployed is difficult since no official government figures exist. Samuel Gompers estimated the unemployment at three million. In his account of the Panic, Frank B. Latham estimates four million, see Latham, *Panic of 1893*, 4. An excellent contemporary compendium of state-by-state information is contained in Carlos C. Closson, "The Unemployed in American Cities," *Quarterly Journal of Economics* 8, no. 2 (January 1, 1894): 168–217. See also Hoffman, *Depression of the Nineties*, 109–10, who estimates that at its worst in the winter of 1893–1894, unemployment hovered at about 2.5 million; Joseph Goldberg and William T. Moye, *The First Hundred Years of the Bureau of Labor Statistics, 1884–1994* (Washington DC: Government Printing Office, 1984), 3–5.

15. Closson, "Unemployed," 168–217; Hoffman, *Depression of the Nineties*, 97–112; Sautter, *Three Cheers*, 3–44; Michael Katz, *In the Shadows*, 152–54.

16. Reef, *Poverty in America*, vv; Sautter, *Three Cheers*, 14–46. See Garraty, *Unemployment in History*, 109n12; David R. Dewey, "Irregularity of Employment," *Publications of the American Economic Association* 9, no. 5/6 (October–December 1894): 53–67.

17. Leonard, "Helping the Unemployed," 431–32. For US Census Data, see http://www.census. gov/dataviz/visualizations/005/, "The number and size of U.S. cities increased dramatically between 1790 and 1890 as the country's population grew and became increasingly urban. By 1890, people living in cities of 100,000 or more made up a larger proportion of all urban dwellers. This reflected a shift from a rural, agrarian society to one focused on industrial production, especially in the Northeast and around the Great Lakes."

18. Leah Hannah Feder, *Unemployment Relief in Periods of Depression* (New York: Russell Sage Foundation, 1936), 18–36; Andrew Carnegie, "The Advantages of Poverty," in *Gospel of Wealth*, ed. Edward C. Kirkland (Cambridge, MA: Harvard University Press, 1965), 64; Priscilla Ferguson Clement, "Nineteenth Century Welfare Policy Programs and Poor Women: Philadelphia as a Case Study," *Feminist Studies* 18, no. 1 (Spring 1992): 35–58.

19. Michael Katz, *In the Shadows*, 3–59.

20. Sidney Fine, *Laissez Faire and the General Welfare State: A Study of Conflict in American Thought, 1865–1901* (Ann Arbor: University of Michigan Press, 1964), 118–25; Benjamin Franklin, *Memoirs*, vol. 2 (New York: Harper & Sons, 1839), 85; Ron Chernow, *Titan* (New York: Vintage Books, 1998), 54–55.

21. Michael Katz, *In the Shadows*, 68–83.

22. Feder, *Unemployment Relief*, 18–36; Melvin G. Holli, *Reform in Detroit: Hazen S. Pingree and Urban Politics* (New York: Oxford University Press, 1969), 56–73.

23. Feder, *Unemployment Relief*, 186–88.

24. Ibid.

25. "Farewell to Poverty," *Massillon Evening Independent*, December 30, 1891; see "Coxey at the Capitol," in Coxey, "Coxey Plan." Howson, *Coxey*, 118–19; 23 *Congressional Record*, March 29, 1892: 2632. Congressman John George Warwick's biographical information is available at http://www.thomas. gov and at http://bioguide.congress.gov/scripts/biodisplay.pl?index=W000169, *Biographical Directory of the United States Congress*; Margy Vogt, *Towpath to Towpath: A History of Massillon, Ohio* (Massillon, OH: Bates Printing, 2002), 68–69.

26. Skinner, "Coxey Folly," 227; Introduced in the Senate on March 19, 1894, by Kansas Populist Party Senator Peffer and in the House by California Congressman Thomas J. Geary, who was an acquaintance of Carl Browne. The identical Good Roads bills as introduced appear in appendix 1 of *The Cause and the Cure*, statement by Mr. J. S. Coxey of Massillon, Ohio, on the Currency Question Before the Subcommittee of Ways and Means, January 5, 1895, Ray Stannard Baker Papers, Library of Congress, Washington, DC.

27. Coxey, "Coxey Plan," 28. This volume also contains the transcript of Coxey's appearance before the Ways and Means Committee on January 8, 1895, 19–44. Regarding the testimony Coxey provided in 1895, where he stated the plan would result in $1.50 an hour wage, he earlier referred to $1.25 an hour in 1891, when he was interviewed by his local newspaper; see "Farewell to Poverty," *Massillon Evening Independent*, December 20, 1891.

28. Nicholas Dungan, *Gallatin: American's Swiss Founding Father* (New York: New York University Press, 2010), 78; Thomas Brownfield Searight, *The Old Pike: A History of the National Road* (Uniontown, PA: published by author, 1894), 111; Vincent, *Story of the Commonweal*, 91; William G. Hilles, "The Good Roads Movement in the United States" (Master's thesis, Duke University, 1958), 19; Painter, *Standing at Armageddon*, 38. See extensive accounts of railroad influence in the Gilded Age, including how the Illinois Central transformed central Illinois in Jack Beatty, *The Age of Betrayal: The Triumph of Money In America, 1865–1900* (New York: Knopf, 2007), 34–36. According to Maurice G. Baxter, *Henry Clay and the American System* (Lexington: University Press of Kentucky, 2004), 47, Clay was forceful in his advocacy of a "chain of turnpike roads and canals from Passamaquoddy to New Orleans, and other similar roads intersecting the mountains, to facilitate intercourse between all parts of the country and to bind and connect us together." President Madison went so far in his annual messages to Congress in 1815 and 1816 to propose that even a Constitutional amendment might be in order to develop such a system of national roads. See also Schwantes, *Coxey's Army*, 65. Schwantes summarizes the impact of the railroads that had essentially bypassed the idea for roads linking farmers with markets that Coxey ably pursued; referring to the rail's views of rural America: "This was a primitive and isolated land, bypassed by the railroads and thus by the mainstream of American history since the Civil War." As Richard White suggests in *Railroaded*, 140–74, the railroads were far more effective in exploiting this space for profit and charging farmers outlandish rates than they were interested in efficiently linking farmer to market.

29. Searight, *Old Pike*, 111.

30. Ibid.; Jonathan Gilmer Speed, "Common Highways," *Atlanta Constitution*, November 20, 1892.

31. Contemporary accounts of Albert A. Pope's life are found in Norris Galphin Osborn, *Men of Mark in Connecticut: Ideals of American Life Told in Biographies and Autobiographies of Eminent Living Americans*, vol. 3 (Hartford, CT: W. R. Goodspeed, 1907), 207–9; and *The Historical Register* (New York: Edwin C. Hill, 1919), 75–77. See also Philip P. Mason, "The League of American Wheelmen" (PhD diss., University of Michigan, 1957), 65; Owen D. Gutfreund, *Twentieth-Century Sprawl: Highways and the Reshaping of the American Landscape* (New York: Oxford University Press, 2004), 9–17; Ninon Neckar, "With the League of American Wheelmen at Washington," *Outing and the Wheelmen* 4, no. 6 (September 1884): 425; also per the railroads' engagement, see "Good Roads Movement," *Milwaukee Sentinel*, April 10, 1894.

32. Mason, "League of American Wheelmen," 65; Jonathan Gilmer Speed, "Country Roads and Highways," *Lippincott's Monthly Magazine* 48 (September 1891): 355; see "Country Road Question," *Chicago Daily Tribune*, March 28, 1882; and "The Pasadena Road," *Los Angeles Times*, May 27, 1882.

33. Country Gentleman, "American Roads," *New England Farmer and Horticulture Register* 39, no. 16 (April 19, 1884): 1; "Country Roads," *American Farmer* 3, no. 19 (October 1, 1843): 270; "Country

Roads," *Ohio Farmer* 68, no. 21 (November 21, 1885): 328; "The Farm," *Michigan Farmer (1843–1908)* 18, no. 24 (June 13, 1887): 2.

34. "Social, Economic and Educational," *Ohio Farmer* 83, no. 7 (February 16, 1893): 132; "Road Improvement," *Ohio Farmer* 83, no. 4 (January 26, 1893): 63; A. T. M'Kelvy, "Swinging Round the Circle," *Ohio Farmer* 83, no. 5 (February 2, 1893): 82.

35. "At Work for Good Roads," *New York Times*, November 20, 1892; *National League for Good Roads* 1, no. 1 (November 1892): 7; Norman Bolotin and Christine Laing, *The World's Columbian Exposition* (Washington, DC: Preservation Press, 1992), 3.

36. 23 *Congressional Record*, July 5, 1892: 5765; "From 1890 to 1892 James R. Dunn, also from Massillon, served as President of the LAW. Dunn, who stirred controversy with his rules governing bicycle racing expenses, spoke eloquently on the need for Good Roads and lobbied tirelessly on their behalf. And though there is no evidence Coxey knew Dunn, it is hard to believe that in a town of just over ten thousand, Dunn's notoriety escaped Coxey's attention, or vice versa; Dunn spoke to an overflow crowd at the Grand Opera House, where he "poured into the ears of the vast assemblage before him sound doctrine on the subject of road improvement"; see Chris Wheeler, "Outing for May," *Outing* 18, no. 2 (May 1891): 137–41; Howson, *Coxey*, 118–19; and Vogt, *Towpath to Towpath*, 223. Vogt places Massillon's population circa 1890 at 10,092; see also Richard F. Weingroff, *Portrait of a General: General Roy Stone: Special Agent and Engineer for Road Inquiry, Office of Road Inquiry, Department of Agriculture, October 3, 1893–October 23, 1899* (Washington DC: Federal Highway Administration, 1993), 2 (see http://www.fhwa.dot.gov/infrastructure/stone.cfm).

37. 23 Congressional Record, July 27, 1892: 6846.

38. "The Message and Documents of Two Houses of Congress Beginning in the third session of the 53rd Congress," Report of the Secretary of Agriculture (Washington, DC: Government Printing Office, 1895), 62; Jonathan Gilmer Speed, "Common Highways"; Hilles, "Good Roads Movement," 51; 23 Congressional Record, July 29, 1892: 6941; "At Work for Good Roads," *New York Times*, November 20, 1892; "To Improve the Roads," *New York Times*, March 4, 1893; Albert A. Pope, "An Industrial Revolution by Good Roads," *Forum* (March 1892): 115–19; Albert A. Pope, "Vox Populi: How to Raise Money to Improve Roads," *Daily Picayune*, October 18, 1893.

39. National League for Good Roads, *National League for Good Roads* 1, no. 1 (November 1892): 7; Bolotin and Laing, *Columbian Exposition*, 3; *Morning Oregonian*, November 15, 1892; "Catalogue of Books on Good Roads," *New York Times*, February 2, 1893; "To Improve the Roads," *New York Times*, November 20, 1892; Pope, "Industrial Revolution," 115–19; see Mason, "League of American Wheelmen," 86, who discusses legislative efforts at uniform road bills in Massachusetts, Indiana, Illinois, Pennsylvania, Ohio, and Virginia; and also Sidney Aronson, "The Sociology of the Bicycle," *Social Forces* 33, no. 3 (March 1, 1952): 310.

40. See chapter 4, note. 11, in Hilles: "Norton to Stone," n.d. cited by George R. Chatburn, *Highways and Highway Transportation* (New York: 1923), 138; Coxey's plan was endorsed by the Ohio's People's Party as a way to create jobs without upkeep fees; "Extract from Ohio People's Party Platform," *Coxey Good Roads and Non-Interest Bearing Bond Library: Cause and Cure* (Massillon: Clay Block, 1895) 1, no. 2 (March 1895): 28–30. Indeed Coxey's Good Roads scheme not only put people back to work but put people to work "on something that was not up for sale," the platform noted.

Notes to Chapter Three

1. "Coxey Is Coming," *Washington Bee*, April 28, 1894.

2. Vincent, *Story of the Commonweal*, 50–51; Barber, *Marching on Washington*, 5–9; W. T. Stead, "Coxeyism," 47.

3. Baz Kershaw, "Curiosity or Contempt: On Spectacle, the Human and Activism," *Theater Journal* 55, no. 4 (December 1, 2003): 595. Alfred F. Young, *The Shoemaker and the Tea Party: Memory and the American Revolution* (Boston: Beacon Press, 1999), 102–5; Daniel A. Cohen, "Passing the Torch: Boston Firemen, 'Tea Party' Patriots, and the Burning of the Charlestown Convent," *Journal of the Early Republic* 24, no. 4 (December 1, 2004): 534–40.

4. William Beik, "The Culture of Protest in Seventeenth-Century French Towns," *Social History* 15, no. 1 (January 1990): 19–20; Susan G. Davis, "Strike Parades and the Politics of Representing Class in Antebellum Philadelphia," *Drama Review* 29, no. 3 (October 1, 1985):106–7.

5. "The Coal Miner's Strike in Pennsylvania—A Mob of Strikers in Wilkes Barre," *New York Times*, July 23, 1868; Isaac Aaronovich Hourwich, *Immigration and Labor: The Economic Aspects of European Immigration to the United States* (New York: B. W. Huebsch, 1922), 450; Montgomery, "Wage Labor," 12. The question remains as to whether Coxey and Browne were consciously influenced by any of these historical precedents. Henry Vincent not only attributed the idea to Polk, and he compared Coxey neither to the Chartists nor to the Blanketeers but to the Irishman Jack Cade who led a peaceful fifteenth-century protest of Kent peasants against Henry VI; see Henry Vincent, *The Story of the Commonweal* (Chicago: W. B. Conkey Company, 1894), 39–48.

6. "The March to Washington," *Emporia Gazette*, April 26, 1894; see reference also to a Captain Reno in Stan Edward Hoig, *Fort Reno and the Indian Territory Frontier* (Fayetteville: University of Arkansas Press, 2000), 150; and further reference to David N. Heizer in "David N. Heizer Former Official of G.A.R. Dead," *Chicago Daily Tribune*, March 28, 1932; see "Early Barton County History," by D. N. Heizer, http://kslib.info/businessdirectoryii.aspx?bid=1591 and http://genealogytrails.com/kan/barton/bartonhistory22.html. Heizer's own reputation seems intact. A leading agriculturalist, Heizer also held several public offices when he resided in Colorado earlier in his life, including jobs as a census taker and registrar. "A Magnificent Faith," *Massillon Evening Independent*, January 27, 1894; see Coxey, "Bulletin Number One: Coxey Good Roads Association of the U.S."; Vincent, *Story of the Commonweal*, 46–47; Sweeney, "Sensational," 117. To further confuse the lineage for the idea, Coxey, at the age of 87, claimed that the idea came from a reporter from the *Massillon Evening Independent*, undoubtedly Robert Skinner.

7. See Browne, When *Coxey's "Army" Marcht*, 5; subsequent historians of the march (notably McMurry, *Coxey's Army*, 38–40, and Schwantes, *Coxey's Army*, 32) view Browne as the originator of the idea and the leading force in its design and execution.

8. "A Labour Leader," *Boston Daily Globe*, July 8, 1878; "The Hoodlum's King," *Washington Post*, July 8, 1878; "King Kearney," *Boston Daily Globe*, July 23, 1878; Dennis Kearney, *Speeches of Dennis Kearney* (New York: Jesse Haney, 1878) 6, 26–29; "Kearney at the Capital," *Boston Daily Globe*, August 30, 1878. Coxey would march two years after the Homestead Strike of 1892 and in the midst of the Depression of 1893–1897. Moreover, many of the attributes and characteristics of Coxey's own march would seem to reveal just how much Browne may have borrowed from Kearney's experience. These include Kearney's incessant criticism of the press. Kearney once referred to the reporters covering his visit as "these villainous serpents, these shiny imps of hell," imagery Browne would use in 1894 when he described the reporters who covered Coxey's Army as the "Argus Eyed Demons from Hell."

9. Vincent, *Commonweal*, 109–12; "Coxey's Idle Army," *Boston Daily Globe*, March 20, 1894; W. T. Stead, "Coxeyism," 47–57; "Telegraphic Notes of Support," *Chicago Daily Tribune*," July 7, 1893. See reference to the $7,000 horse that Browne rode in "General Coxey on New Crusade," *New York Times*, February 3, 1924; also "Trotters Sold at Auction," *New York Times*, February 24, 1893; "Ohio's Don Quixote," *Chicago Daily Tribune*, February 5, 1894; Homer E. Socolofsky, "Jacob Coxey: Ohio's Fairly Respectable Populist," *Kansas Quarterly* 1, no. 4 (Fall 1969): 63; Henry Demarest Lloyd, "The Populists in St. Louis," in George Brown Tindall, ed., *The Populist Reader: Selections from the Works of American Populist Leaders* (New York: Harper & Row, 1966), 221. Browne makes other claims in his reminiscence of the march (*When Coxey's "Army" Marcht*), which are contradicted by the facts. For example, he claims that as a result of his lobbying the AFL-CIO adopted Coxey's Good Roads plan as part of its platform. It was not a part of the platform but rather one of hundreds of resolutions adopted separately. See *Report of the Proceedings of the Thirteenth Annual Convention of the American Federation of Labor*, December 11–19, 1893, Resolution 106, 47; Vincent, *Story of the Commonweal*, 49; Robert Skinner in the February 7, 1894, *Massillon Evening Independent* actually quotes Polk and his idea to "deliver a petition with boots on"; Vincent himself actually thought the idea might have originally belonged to Leonidas Polk, the onetime president of the Farmers Alliance. Vincent, active in populist circles for some two decades, noted that Polk first suggested the idea of delivering a "living petition" to Congress, or as he also said, "one with boots on," though the Kansas Populist readily acknowledged it doubtful that Coxey or Browne had ever heard of Polk's idea as they began hatching their own plans.

10. "Coxey's Men," *St. Paul Daily News*, March 20, 1894; see also "Join Coxey's Army," *Chicago Daily News*, March 23, 1894; and "Says Coxey Is Sane and Patriotic," *Chicago Daily Tribune*, March 24, 1894; Ray Stannard Baker, "Coxey and His Commonweal," *Tourney* (May 1894): 117. "Schemes for Relief," *Chicago Daily Tribune*, December 17, 1893; Baker, *American Chronicle*, 6; "General News from New York," *Chicago Daily Tribune*, February 9, 1894; and "Coxey's Idle Army, *Boston Daily Globe*,

March 20, 1894; "Peace Army Growing," *Chicago Record,* March 16, 1894; "Editorial Comments," *Atlanta Constitution,* May 4, 1894.

11. Joscelyn Godwin, *The Theosophical Enlightenment* (Albany: State University of New York, 1994), 227–28, 277–307, 325–29; Madame Blavatsky and H. P. Blavatsky, "Recent Progress in Theosophy," *North American Review* 151, no. 405 (1890): 173–86; "Idea of Theosophy," *Chicago Daily Tribune,* September 18, 1893; Michael Barkun, "Coxey's Army as a Millennial Movement," *Religion* 18, no. 4 (October 1988): 376. Browne unabashedly claimed to be in part the reincarnated Greek orator "Callisthenes," as well as part Christ (Browne incorrectly cited Callisthenes, the historian. It appears likely that Browne meant to compare himself with Demosthenes, the famous speaker). Browne simply extended the transcendental aspects of Theosophy to conceive his own particular reincarnation theory. In explaining his views to Robert Skinner of the *Massillon Evening Independent,* Browne noted, "As all the chemical elements of a human being, as science proves, go back into their various reservoirs of nature at the death of a person, and thus are used over and over again in the birth of other persons, why not the *soul matter* be used over again." Not to be outdone, the suddenly converted Coxey claimed he possessed part of Andrew Jackson's soul, undoubtedly the Populist part (see Robert Skinner, "Reformers and Theosophists," *Massillon Evening Independent,* February 20, 1894).

12. E. T. Hargrove, "Progress of Theosophy in the United States," *North American Review* 162, no. 475 (June 1, 1896): 698–704; Shirley Plummer Austin, "Coxey's Commonweal Army," 333; Baker, "Coxey and His Commonweal," 117; "General Order No. 1," *Massillon Evening Independent,* March 22, 1894; Osman C. Hooper, "Coxey Movement," 158–59; Robert Skinner, "Reformers and Theosophists," *Massillon Evening Independent,* February 20, 1894; Browne, "Bulletin Number 3."

13. W. T. Stead, "Coxeyism," 54; McMurry, *Coxey's Army,* 68–71; Hooper, "Coxey Movement," 160; Browne, *When Coxey's "Army" Marcht,* 6.

14. Godwin, *Theosophical Enlightenment,* 227–28, 277–307, 325–29; Blavatsky and Blavatsky, "Recent Progress," 173–86; "Mrs. Besant to Discuss Theosophy," *Chicago Daily Tribune,* September 14, 1893; Barkun, "Coxey's Army," 377. See also Godwin, *Theosophical Enlightenment,* 227–28, 277–307, 325–29; Frederic J. Baumgartner, *Longing for the End: A History of Millennialism in Western Civilization* (New York: Palgrave Macmillan, 2001), 110; Bruce F. Campbell, *Ancient Wisdom Revived: A History of the Theosophical Movement* (Berkley: University of California Press, 1980), 58–60; "All Kinds of Theosophy," *Washington Post,* September 10, 1893. While it enjoyed a sudden notoriety in Chicago that summer, as a religion Theosophy had long roots dating back at least to a self-taught German shoemaker named Jakob Boehme. In the early seventeenth century he conceived his worldview that the human soul contained within it the divine and that it was possible to gain mystical union with the supernatural. His writings lay at the foundation of the founding of the London Theosophical Society (1783) and, a century later, the founding in the United States of the Theosophical Society of New York (1875) in the Irving Place parlor of Russian émigré Helena Blavatsky. Blavatsky herself acknowledged, "Scarcely the most optimistic among the society's organizers dreamt of such success as has rewarded their labors." The *Washington Post* noted flourishing Theosophy chapters throughout Europe and Asia, as well as seventy-five in the United States. Though Blavatsky died two years prior to this world religious gathering in Chicago, the Theosophical Society boasted branches throughout the world. This growth coupled with the religion's Asian and transcendental flavor may be one reason that organizers of the "Parliament" provided them with two full days of exposure at the Exposition.

15. Louis Menand, *The Metaphysical Club: A Story of Ideas in America* (New York: Farrar, Strauss & Giroux, 2001), 82–92.

16. Keith Thompson, *The Political Ideas of the Utopian Socialists* (London: Fran Cass & Co., 1982), 129; Julia Franklin, ed., *Selections from the Works of Fourier* (London: S. Sonnenshein, 1901), 179–80. Indeed even those close to the march, including Vincent, referred to the men collectively as an "industrial army."

17. Vincent, *Story of the Commonweal,* 12; Edward Bellamy, *Looking Backward 2000–1887,* (Boston: Ticknor, 1888) 76; Trachtenberg, *Incorporation of America,* 38–52; Steven Trimble and Donald E. Winters, "Editor's Page: Warnings from the Past: 'Caesar's Column' and 'Nineteen-Eighty Four,'" *Minnesota History,* 49, no. 3 (October 1, 1984): 112. These authors discuss how an alternative dystopian view countered the notion of inevitable technological ascent toward a modern utopia, by projecting their own pessimistic vision of how the struggle between man and machine would end. Donnelly's dystopian *Caesar's Column* concludes with the image of a mass grave that survives in a burning New York City. In this dramatic climax the ordinary citizens of the twentieth century find themselves captive

to exploitive corporate oligarchs who control everything and have created a dysfunctional society marked by "its poverty, its misery, its sin, its injustice, its scramble for gold." John F. Kasson, *Civilizing the Machine: Technology and Republican Values in America, 1776-1900* (New York: Macmillan, 1976), 186. Kasson notes the twelve-year period between 1888 and 1900 as "the heyday of American utopian novels and treatises," during which at least 160 such works were published; Albert William Levi, "Edward Bellamy: Utopian," *Ethics* 55, no. 2 (January 1, 1945): 142; John Hope Franklin, "Edward Bellamy and the Nationalist Movement," *New England Quarterly* 11, no. 4 (December 1, 1938): 754.

18. Browne, "Bulletin Number 3." For copies of the two cartoons, see box 71, Ray Stannard Baker Papers, Library of Congress.

19. Vincent, *Story of the Commonweal,* 110; Hooper, "Coxey Movement," 167-68; "Peace Army Growing," *Chicago Record,* March 16, 1894; Baker, *American Chronicle,* 20; "To Sing for the Army," *Chicago Record,* March 21, 1894.

20. Depictions of Browne's many murals and drawings that adorned the wagons and banners of the Commonweal can be found in boxes 23 and 71 in the Papers of Ray Stannard Baker at the Library of Congress.

21. Miles Orville, *The Real Thing* (Chapel Hill; University of North Carolina Press), 104-9.

22. Jackson Lears, *Fables of Abundance* (New York: Basic Books, 1994), 107-13; Kershaw, "Curiosity or Contempt," 594; James Trier, "Guy Debord's 'The Society of the Spectacle,'" *Journal of Adolescent and Adult Literacy* 51, no. 1 (September 2007): 69. The term "spectacle" took on a Marxian connotation after publication of Guy Debord's, *The Society of the Spectacle* (London: Rebel Press, 1967). Debord suggested that as advertising increasingly took hold throughout the twentieth century, the spectacular itself became "commodified." Distinctions between "the real" and "the imagery of the real" blurred. Coxey's March fits the broadest definitions of what Guy Debord defined as a twentieth-century spectacle, since it possessed its own separateness and autonomy and its own coherent language. In the vernacular of Debord it was a representation of the realities being lived but also "everything life lacks." In Debord's world of the spectacular, "individuals consume a world fabricated by others rather than producing their own." Similarly, though hardly a commodification of the commercial, Coxey's spectacle commodified producer plight so familiar to millions beyond just those unemployed; "Coxey at the Capitol"; Coxey, "Coxey Plan," 48-53.

23. Orville, *The Real Thing,* 20-22, 34-36.

24. Philip M. Katz, *From Appomattox to Montmartre: Americans and the Paris Commune* (Cambridge, MA: Harvard University Press, 1998), 4-25. Katz traces the connectivity of the American labor movement and the French Commune. Gustave Paul Clusert, the Minister of War in this French worker revolution in the spring of 1871, served as a colonel in the Union Army during the American Civil War; Clusert represents one of several examples of cross-fertilization of French revolutionary and martial culture. "Organization of 'Army of Peace,'" *Chicago Daily Tribune,* February 10, 1894; the Jacob Sechler Coxey Sr. Papers at the Massillon Museum contain a roster of individuals under the banner Commonweal of Christ with J. S. Coxey listed as president, Carl Browne as chief marshal, and aides to the chief marshal including Jesse A. Coxey, Coxey's oldest son. The roster of participants is then carefully organized by communes (A, B, C, D, etc.) and housed within either the Chicago or Philadelphia Communities. In the Library of Congress Papers of Ray Stannard Baker (box 71), see February 8, 1894, letter by Carl Browne "Dear Sir and Brothers" on stationery of the Office of J. S. Coxey, in which he describes the organization of the march.

25. "Coxey's Army," *Boston Daily Advertiser,* March 19, 1894; and "General Coxey's Order," *Atlanta Constitution,* March 23, 1894; Hooper, "Coxey Movement," 162-63, quotes from the "Circular of Organization" issued by Carl Browne "So the proposed procession will be composed of groups of men numbering five (5) in each, one of whom must be selected to act as marshal—Group Marshal—be numbered in order of the date of group formation. Groups may be federated into companies or communes, of not less than thirty men (30) no more than one hundred and five (105). Communes may be federated into regiments or communities of not less than two hundred and fifteen (215) no more than ten hundred and fifty five (1055). Communities may be federated into cantons (divisions) of two or more. All communes, cantons, and communities must select five marshals, to be numbered at first, second, and so on, the same as the Group Marshals shall be designated, thus: First Group Marshal, First Commune Marshal, First Canton Marshal, First Community Marshal. Badges of designation will be furnished by Brother Coxey bearing appropriate design made by myself (Browne) upon sending certification, or when any group or organization joins the procession."

26. "Look Out for IM, Congressman," *New York Times,* January 28, 1894; "Coxey's Army Order," *Chicago Daily Tribune,* March 5, 1894; reference to organizing the march in communes occurs in "Organization of the Army of Peace," *Chicago Daily Tribune,* February 10, 1894.

27. Coxey, "Bulletin Number One."

28. For population of Massillon, see *Abstract of the Eleventh Census:* 1890 Massillon appears on page 35, population 10,092, as compared to 6,836 in 1880; see Coxey, "Bulletin Number One." Postel, *Populist Vision,* 45–69, speaks of the populist emphasis on education and the networks of sympathizers they established to rally around their various bold ideas for reform through networks similar to what Coxey established for Good Roads; "Coxey's Great Army," *Chicago Record,* March 15, 1894; "Coxey's Army Order," *Chicago Daily Tribune,* March 5, 1894.

29. "Coxey's Great Army," *Chicago Record,* March 15, 1894; "Coxey's Army Order," *Chicago Daily Tribune,* March 5, 1894. Solon C. Thayer ran for secretary of state on the Populist ticket in 1892, finishing fourth in a field of four; see William Alexander Taylor and Aubrey Clarence Taylor, *Ohio Statesman and Annals of Progress: From the Year 1788 to the Year 1900* (Columbus OH: Press at the Westphalia Co. State Printers, 1899), 113. Thayer apparently continued his political activism and was cited in "Newsman," *Massillon Evening Independent,* October 25, 1895, as a prominent Populist, and later listed as an elector for the Socialist ticket in the 1912 presidential election; see "Election Proclamation," *Lebanon Daily News,* October 25, 1912. See *Twentieth Century Farmer* 1, no. 2 (April 1894): 3, in Jacob Sechler Coxey Sr. Papers in Massillon Museum, Massillon, OH.

30. "Route of the Commonweal" in box 23 of Ray Stannard Baker Papers, Library of Congress attributes the route to J. H. Dippold, first engineer, marshal from Pittsburgh, PA. See McMurry, *Coxey's Army,* 59–60, for a description of the march's average pace and distance.

31. In an article, "Crankery Is Contagious," *Chicago Daily News,* March 14, 1894, the estimate of three million recruits appears. In an interview Coxey made the prediction of 500,000 in Washington, DC; see "Half a Million Men," *Washington Post,* March 18, 1894. Yet, at the same time others close to the march disputed these claims. An unidentified commissary loader suggested 50,000 recruits in "Coxey's Conceit," *Logansport Daily Journal,* March 13, 1894; "Encouraging for Coxey," *Galveston Daily News,* March 16, 1894, records that the sheer volume of encouraging letters received each day led Coxey to exude a growing sense of confidence. Each day the mailbags were filled with new encouragement. Harry Naughton from Homestead, Pennsylvania, promised 100 men, while Messrs. Kinbell and Gough from Millville, New Jersey, said they would meet Coxey with 1500 men when the march reached Hagerstown, Maryland. J. A. Conrad of Poplar Bluffs, Missouri, writing on behalf of a thousand of the unemployed, said they would all pay their own way to Massillon. D. S. Armstrong of Terre Haute, Indiana, wrote to say he would bring a large group of unemployed brakeman and firemen from the railroad. Rufus Henry of Stout, Ohio, said his army of two hundred and seventeen would join Coxey in Pittsburgh. John Stoof of New Castle, Pennsylvania, said he intended to join the army with a force of several hundred.

32. These letters appeared in "An Army on Paper," *Atlanta Constitution,* March 16, 1894.

33. "Peace Army Growing," *Chicago Record,* March 16, 1894; "Law Says No," *Boston Daily Globe,* March 24, 1894; "Hoaxing General Coxey," *Chicago Daily News,* March 24, 1894; "The Coxey Movement," *Massillon Evening Independent,* March 15, 1894; "The J. S. Coxey Crusade," *Massillon Evening Independent,* March 20, 1894; Baker, *American Chronicle,* 8. "Hoaxing General Coxey," *Chicago Daily Tribune,* March 24, 1894; "Will Move Tomorrow," *Chicago Record,* March 28, 1894.

34. Coxey's conflicting estimates, issued only days apart, appear in "Coxey Predicts a Large Army," *Chicago Daily Tribune,* March 12, 1894; and "Rumors Denied," *Janesville Gazette* (WI), March 14, 1894. An account of witnesses to new recruits by the rail men appears in "On Their Way to Join Coxey," *Alton Daily Telegraph* (IL), March 15, 1894.

35. "Coxey and His Army," *Milwaukee Sentinel,* March 20, 1894; and "Mail Recruits Only," *Chicago Daily News,* March 21, 1894. See reports of up to twenty thousand en route in "Exists on Paper Only," *Washington Post,* March 24, 1894; "Will Move Tomorrow," *Chicago Record,* March 28, 1894; "Coxey's 100 Recruits," *Boston Daily Globe,* March 25, 1894; see also "General Coxey," *St. Paul Daily News,* March 24, 1894; "In His Dreams He Sees an Army," *New York Times,* March 25, 1894.

36. This composite description of the march's departure is compiled from several newspaper sources including, "Moving from Massillon," *Evening Independent* (Massillon, OH), March 26, 1894; "Not Wholly a Myth," *Washington Post,* March 25, 1894; "What Coxey Wants," *Milwaukee Journal,* March 24, 1894; "To Sing for the Army," *Chicago Record,* March 21, 1894; "Will Move Tomorrow," *Chicago Record,* March 28, 1894; "On the March," *Boston Daily Globe,* March 26, 1894; "In Camp at Canton," *Chicago Daily News,* March 26, 1894; "Stewart's Advice," *Rocky Mountain News,* March 26, 1894; "Off for Washington,"

Milwaukee Journal, March 26, 1894. Other firsthand accounts include Browne, *When Coxey's "Army" Marcht*, 8–9; Baker, *American Chronicle*, 13–15; McMurry, *Coxey's Army*, 46–48; Schwantes, *Coxey's Army*, 42–48; and George A. Gipe, "Rebel in a Wing Collar," *American Heritage* 18, no. 1 (December 1966): 25. There are also within these accounts discrepancies in the numbers of men that left. Vincent, *Story of the Commonweal*, 56, puts the number at 122, and Schwantes, *Coxey's Army*, agrees (other news accounts range from 75 to 200). McMurry, *Coxey's Army*, refers to the "hundred industrials." For estimates, see also Vincent, *Story of the Commonweal*, 56; "Off for Washington," *Milwaukee Sentinel*, March 26, 1894; "On the March," *Boston Daily Globe*, March 26, 1894; "The March Begun," *Bryan (OH) Democrat*, March 28, 1894.

Notes to Chapter Four

1. W. T. Stead, "Coxeyism," 56.

2. Ray Stannard Baker, "Marching with Coxey," *Baltimore American*, May 20, 1894, says the number of reporters leaving Massillon was about forty but quickly was reduced to a core dozen; Baker, *American Chronicle*, 7; for physical descriptions of Baker, see John E. Simonche, *Ray Stannard Baker* (Chapel Hill: University of North Carolina Press, 1969), 53–54.

3. Ray Stannard Baker, *Native American: The Book of My Youth* (New York: Scribner, 1941), 149; Semonche, *Ray Stannard Baker*, 52–62; Louis Agassiz, *Geological Sketches* (Boston: Ticknor & Fields, 1866), 234. Regarding the influence of science on young reporters, see Michael Schudson, *Origins of the Ideal of Objectivity in the Professions: Studies in the History of American Journalism and American Law, 1830–1940* (New York: Garland Publishing, 1990), 168–69. Schudson notes that "many of the journalists of the 1890s and after were either trained in a scientific discipline or shared in the popular admiration for science. Baker took special interest in his science courses at Michigan Agricultural College; Lincoln Steffens did graduate work in Wilhelm Wundt's world-famous psychological laboratory."

4. Bannister, *Ray Stannard Baker*, 36–45; Baker, *American Chronicle*, 1–2; Wayne Klatt, *Chicago Journalism: A History* (Jefferson, NC: McFarland, 2009), 19–27; Sidney Kobre, *The Yellow Press and Gilded Age Journalism* (Tallahassee: Florida State University Press, 1964), 183–93.

5. Semonche, *Ray Stannard Baker*, 54–65; Baker, *Native American*, 149, 301. For a definition of "new journalism," see also Ted Curtis Smythe, *The Gilded Age Press, 1865–1900* (New York: Praeger, 2003), 71–97; Orville, *The Real Thing*, 104–9; Karen Roggenkamp, *Narrating the News* (Kent, OH: Kent State University Press, 2005), xii; Doug Underwood, *The Undeclared War between Journalism and Fiction* (New York: Palgrave McMillan, 2013), 4; Underwood describes how the term "new journalism" is also used by historians of journalism to describe a similar but later phenomenon allowing journalists the ability "to combine the best of fiction's narrative technique with the fact seeking practices of journalists"; Thomas Bernard Connery, *Journalism and Realism* (Evanston, IL: Northwestern University Press, 2011), 177–81.

6. The Massillon Museum has done an extensive project on the life and times of Robert Peet Skinner; the best biographical information about Skinner's Massillon experiences and his later diplomatic career appear on the Massillon Museum's web site http://www.massillonmuseum.org/66.

7. Skinner's articles in the *Massillon Evening Independent* are available at the Massillon Library. The first detailed story appeared on January 6; then the first front-page story on January 23. After this a steady stream of articles appears on the front page of the *Independent* through the march's departure and as Skinner accompanied the march to Washington. "Good Roads," *Massillon Evening Independent*, January 6, 1894; "A Story of Real Life," *Massillon Evening Independent*, January 23, 1894.

8. "Good Roads," *Massillon Evening Independent*, January 6, 1894; "A Story of Real Life," *Massillon Evening Independent*, January 23, 1894; "Clippings from Coxiana," *Massillon Evening Independent*, February 24, 1894.

9. Baker, *American Chronicle*, 1–8; Bannister, *Ray Stannard Baker*, 61; Nye, "Jacob Coxey," in *Baker's Dozen*, 221, 117; Sweeney, "Sensational." Telegrams from C. H. Dennis to Ray S. Baker, March 20, 28, 1894, in Ray Stannard Baker papers, Library of Congress, box 23.

10. Baker, *American Chronicle*, 7, 18–19; Connery, *Journalism and Realism*, 174–85; Matthew Goodman, *Eighty Days* (New York: Random House, 2013), 27–34; "Moving from Massillon," *Massillon Evening Independent*, March 26, 1894.

11. Vincent, *Story of the Commonweal*, 120; Ray Stannard Baker, "Marching with Coxey," *Baltimore American*, May 20, 1894; Baker, *American Chronicle*, 21.

12. Sweeney, "Sensational," 114–25; "Coxey Camps at Columbiana," *Washington Post*, March 30, 1894.

13. Sweeney, "Sensational," 114. As a crude indicator of the popularity, the search engine ProQuest Historical Newspapers as of 2015 reveals 1,204 separate articles that mention Coxey between the eve of Coxey's departure from Massillon (March 24) until he reached the Capitol steps (stories from May 2 that reported the final episode are included in this count). In that same period President Cleveland's name appears in 956 stories, 97 of which also mention Coxey. The newspapers included are the *Boston Daily Globe, Chicago Daily Tribune, Los Angeles Times, New York Times, Atlanta Constitution,* and *Washington Post.* W. T. Stead, "Coxeyism," 48.

14. Baker in "Marching with Coxey" actually listed O'Donnell as being with the *New York Press.* However that paper did not exist until 1897. O'Donnell himself noted in an article "O'Donnell on Coxey," in the *Washington Post,* May 7, 1894, that he was in fact reporting for the *Pittsburgh Dispatch.*

15. As noted in chapter 3, the "new naturalism" is a term most associated with the icon of this literary genre, William Dean Howells. His method is described by Susan Goodman and Carl Dawson, *William Dean Howells: A Writer's Life* (Berkeley: University of California Press: 2005), 119, where they discuss one of his early works, *Venetian Life:* "Here, as in later books, he plays with the boundaries between fact and fiction, the ways by which fiction can grow from observed life, however distasteful into a new reality that corresponds to an actual world." Garet Garrett, *The Driver* (New York: E. P. Dutton, 1922), 1–4. "Will Move Tomorrow," *Chicago Record,* March 6, 1894.

16. Jack London, "The March of Kelly's Army," *Cosmopolitan* 43, no. 6 (October 1907): 643–48.

17. Michael Robertson, *Stephen Crane and the Making of Modern American Literature* (New York: Columbia University Press, 1997), 76; Franklin Luther Mott, *American Journalism: A History of Newspapers in the United States through 250 Years, 1690–1940* (New York: Macmillan, 1941), 488–89; Lincoln Steffens, *The Autobiography of Lincoln Steffens* (New York: Harcourt, Brace & World, 1931), 314.

18. Stephanie C. Palmer, "Realist Magic in the Fiction of William Dean Howells," *Nineteenth-Century Literature* 57 no. 2 (2002): 210–36.

19. Mott, *American Journalism,* 437. See Nellie Bly, "Nellie Bly and Coxey's Army," *World,* May 6, 1894; *Massillon Evening Independent,* May 1, 1894; and "March Ends in Riot," *Chicago Record,* May 2, 1894. Though the *World* had already run stories about Coxey's March including about the trial of Coxey and Browne, their Sunday, May 6, edition contains a curious piece bylined by Bly, who claimed not only to have infiltrated Coxey's March but also to have led the final parade to the Capitol. "She Led the Half Starved Commonwealers on Their March into Washington Last Tuesday," trumpeted the subheadline. Bly's bylined account rendered a less than sympathetic, though self-serving account. It even begins with this lead: "I went to Washington last week and headed the Commonwealers on their march from Brightwood Driving Park to the gates of the Capitol." As the article unfolds, Bly describes what "taking the lead" meant. Since she was not riding a horse and was confined to a buggy (taxi) and what she called "her stupid cab driver," she resigned herself to being embedded in the procession. "But as usual I was in luck," she wrote, then describing how another man offered to escort her in his buggy and to take the lead if she wished. When Oklahoma Sam introduced her to Coxey, he offered her a part in the procession. Then she claimed to have boldly informed him she was going to take the lead. Her critical May 6 piece goes on to scoff at both Coxey and Browne, "as the workingman's pretended benefactors," who took advantage of the marchers for their own notoriety. "A more woe-begone [*sic*] and hapless-looking lot of men I have never seen," she observed. Yet her account takes its most self-serving twist when Bly claims it was her tip that led to the arrest of Coxey. Arriving at the Capitol, she describes approaching an officer and inquiring as to where Coxey would be speaking. When the officer emphatically indicated there would be no speech, she then remarked to him, "'Then you better go that way,' I [Bly] said pointing to the direction where the men meant to enter." Bly, after asserting she led the march, thus casts herself as central to the story of Coxey's arrest. Unlike the other firsthand accounts which speak to the violence that ensued, Bly refers almost matter-of-factly to the "gentleness [with which] the policeman handled the men and felt some regret that the New York policeman had not charge of the job." Contrast her rendition with Skinner's firsthand account on May 1, where he reports a stampede and that "the police are using clubs," or Baker's lead on May 1, "Coxey's eventful march from Massillon to the marble steps of the capitol closed today in riot and bloodshed."

20. "Tramps Flocking In," *Milwaukee Journal,* March 27, 1894; "Coxey's Little Army," *Milwaukee Sentinel,* March 27, 1894; Vincent, *Story of the Commonweal,* 61. Accounts vary as to the number of men already with or joining the army at this point. One account suggested the army numbered only ninety-eight men, the discrepancy could lie in the counting of the forty-some reporters accompanying the march, see "More Men in Line," *Boston Daily Globe,* March 28, 1894; "Coxey's Caravan," *Atchison Daily Globe,* March 28, 1894; "Army at Alliance," *Rocky Mountain News,* March 28, 1894; "Hungry, Tired

and Cold," *Bangor Daily Whig and Courier*, March 28, 1894; and "New Men for Coxey," *Chicago Daily Tribune*, March 28, 1894; "Entered in Triumph," *Chicago Record*, March 28, 1894.

21. "Coxey Still Marching On," *Atlanta Constitution*, April 13, 1894; "Afraid of the Army," *Chicago Record*, April 13, 1894;

22. "Unknown Put Out," *Chicago Record*, April 16, 1894; "Will Now Ride," *Boston Daily Globe*, April 16, 1894; "Coxey's Navy Command," *Washington Post*, April 18, 1894; "All Follow the Grub Wagon," *Chicago Daily Tribune*, April 16, 1894.

23. "Coxey Less Boastful," *Washington Post*, April 27, 1894.

24. The Great Unknown was a convenient press fiction used to enhance the drama of the story of Coxey's March. Rumors swirled around his origins, though reporters, particularly those from Chicago, knew him as alias Louis Smith, or in fact Dr. E. P. Pizarro or Bazarro (Baker notes in *American Chronicle*, 13, that both were used), who had sold medicines to Indians. Klatt, *Chicago Journalism*, 55, notes that "the Chicago press had ample precedent for developing intrigue in pseudo characters or pseudo events." For example, *Tribune* reporter John E. Wilkie gained notoriety when, in 1890, he reported the story of a boy who could climb a rope tossed into midair (later Wilkie would go on to head the secret service). The Unknown was caricatured by reporters as a "big, handsome, well-dressed man," who seemed "a strict disciplinarian, and appeared to be a born leader." Upon his arrival he promptly decided to give a speech to those assembled. But his remarks were so "incendiary" that they immediately sparked speculation that this charismatic presence was perhaps Samuel Fielden, the recently pardoned Haymarket anarchist from Chicago. To confirm his actual identity, *Chicago Daily Tribune* reporters went to 77 Peoria Street, where the Unknown's photograph was positively identified by his wife. She confirmed for the *Tribune* reporters that her husband was the "President of the National Patriotic Society for Prevention of Cruelty to Humanity," and also the manufacturer of a "blood medicine." Before revealing the Unknown's actual identity, the reporters further enhanced the mystery surrounding him by introducing a separate mysterious woman they quickly suggested to be his wife. This surrogate "Goddess of Peace," reportedly the real "Mrs. Unknown," joined the march in Alliance, Ohio, on the 2:00 p.m. train from Chicago on March 26. She reportedly registered at the Keplinger Hotel as one "Mrs. Smith," since the reporters also referred to the Unknown as Louis Smith. She wore a heavy black veil to conceal a black eye. A hotel maid sympathetically told reporters that the injury must have resulted from a blow from a small child. Those who watched her enter the hotel lobby reported that she appeared very well educated and well dressed. This fueled the speculation that she might indeed be "Mrs. Unknown," since by all accounts the Unknown himself not only was well spoken but seemed, by appearance, to be quite well-to-do; in fact, he had been rumored to have helped with financing the march. To build further suspense, the reporters also labeled the elegant Mrs. Unknown as the "Veiled Lady." The Unknown himself would later put these press monikers in placards he used to draw crowds at shows he staged following his days with Coxey's March. While reporters thus deliberately kept the identities of "The Unknown" and the "Veiled Lady" very much a mystery with their readers, Browne made it quite clear that Mrs. Unknown had to march ahead of the procession and keep her distance. Regardless of her association with "Smith," she would be treated no differently from any other aspiring female member of the Commonweal; i.e., like Coxey's own daughter she would not be allowed to join the march. See "May Be Mrs. Great Unknown," *Chicago Daily Tribune*, March 27, 1894; Baker, *American Chronicle*, 13; McMurry, *Coxey's Army*, 99; "Says Smith Is Jensen," *Chicago Daily Tribune*, April 11, 1894; "All Follow the Grub Wagon," *Chicago Daily Tribune*, April 16, 1894; "Colonel Browne Bobs Up," *Washington Post*, April 16, 1894; "Not Wholly a Myth," *Washington Post*, March 25, 1894; and "What Coxey Wants," *Milwaukee Journal*, March 24, 1894; "Coxey on the March," *Wisconsin State Register*, March 30, 1894. In "Unknown the Prince of Fakers," *Chicago Tribune*, April 17, 1894, the reputed wife of Pizzaro (though the so-called Veiled Lady also with the march at this point) was identified by the press as "reportedly" Pizzaro's wife (which throws into question exactly the identity of the "Veiled Lady"). In the article, Pizarro's two daughters positively identify a photo and discuss the business relationship that Pizzarro had with Browne selling Kickapoo Indian remedies in Chicago the summer before. They also discuss how they intended to join Coxey in his march; "She May Be Mrs. Great Unknown," *Chicago Daily Tribune*, March 27, 1894; Schwantes, *Coxey's Army*, 51–52; see also Ray Stannard Baker Papers, Box 71, for a placard advertising: "To-Night The Great Unknown, The Original Louis Smith, Jesse Coxey and the Veiled Lady of the Commonweal Movement will appear at Miller's Hall; The 'Unknown' will be speaker of the evening and give an exciting account of his wonderful trip across the mountains while in charge of Coxey's Army. Admission,—25cts. Lecture at 8 o'clock sharp."

25. Kwiat, "The Newspaper Experience: Crane, Norris, and Dreiser," *Nineteenth-Century Fiction* 8, no. 2 (1953): 101–2.

26. The transition in American journalism in the late nineteenth century is presented in its nuanced variegation by Richard L. Kaplan, *Politics and the American Press* (Cambridge: Cambridge University Press, 2002), 12–16, 77–99.

27. "Coxey Puts Up Toll," *Chicago Daily Tribune*, April 10, 1894; "Forced to Pay Toll," *Chicago Record*, April 10, 1894. Though no readership surveys existed at the time, the Coxey story was widely popular, as indicated in Note 13 to this chapter. In addition to the ProQuest metrics that previously indicated how Coxey's march was mentioned almost twice as much as President Cleveland during the march's five week duration, a separate search for articles that appeared in newspapers nationwide between the time Coxey departed Massillon (March 25) until he reached the Capitol steps (stories from May 2 that reported the final episode are included in this count) in the search engine "Chronicling America" (Library of Congress) reveals 3,004 articles where Coxey is mentioned. Similarly, Newspaper Archive results in 3,620 articles where the term Coxey is mentioned during the same five-week period.

28. "Diary of a March," *Chicago Record*, April 21, 1894; "Another Wrong," *Boston Daily*, March 29, 1894; "Coxey Visits Chicago for a Day," *Chicago Daily Tribune*, March 29, 1894; "Have Lots of Pluck," *Chicago Daily*, March 30, 1894; "Coxey Camps at Columbiana," *Washington Post*, March 30, 1894.

29. Vincent, *Story of the Commonweal*, 50; "Coxey's Army Grows," *Chicago Daily Tribune*, April 2, 1894; "Over the Muddy Hills," *Washington Post*, April 7, 1894.

30. Hugh Rockoff, "The 'Wizard of Oz' as a Monetary Allegory," *Journal of Political Economy* 98, no. 4 (August 1990): 749. Rockoff notes, "Although the March addressed serious problems, Coxey's army took on an "opera bouffe" quality." The term "Coxey's Army" makes its way into the *American Thesaurus of Slang* as a term meaning "unorganized gang" and the *Dictionary of Slang and Unconstructed English* as a "rag time army." See Lester Berney and Melvin Van Den Bark, eds., *American Thesaurus of Slang* (New York: Thomas Y. Crowell, 1942), and Eric Partridge, *A Dictionary of Slang and Unreconstructed English* (New York: Macmillan, 1970).

31. "Coxey Camps at Columbiana," *Washington Post*, March 30, 1894; Vincent, *Story of the Commonweal*, 120–21; "Coxey's Army of Tramps," *Chicago Daily Tribune*, April 7, 1894; "Coxey and His Cranks," *Washington Post*, March 18, 1894.

32. "Coxey's Idle Army," *Boston Daily Globe*, March 20, 1894; "Coxey's Cranks," *Chicago Daily Tribune*, March 16, 1894; "Editorial Notes," *Chicago Daily Tribune*, March 28, 1894. See "Coxey's Fantastical Program," *Chicago Daily Tribune*, January 28, 1894; "A Fizzle at the Start," *Washington Post*, March 15, 1894; "The Coxey Crank Movement," *Chicago Tribune*, April 2, 1894; "The Coxeyites," *Chicago Daily Tribune*, April 23, 1894.

33. "Editorial Points," *Boston Daily Globe* April 19, 1894; "A Costly Lesson," *Los Angeles Times*, March 26, 1894. "No Title," *Chicago Daily Tribune*, April 18, 1894.

34. "In Dreams He Sees an Army: Then Coxey Awakens and Sees Only Fifty Tramps," *New York Times*, March 25, 1894; "Taken as a Joke," *Chicago Daily Tribune*, March 27, 1894; "The Crazy Coxey Crusade," *Los Angeles Times*, March 28, 1894; "Pranky Boys at Play," *Chicago Daily Tribune*, April 2, 1894; "Coxey Crusade: Another Idea of Carl Browne the Clown," *Los Angeles Times*, April 13,1894; "Candidate for an Asylum," *Washington Post*, January 28, 1894; "Ohio's Don Quixote," *Chicago Daily Tribune*, February 5, 1894; "Troops Are Called Out," *North American (Philadelphia)*, April 26, 1894; "Guarding the Treasury," *Atlanta Constitution*, April 25, 1894; "Blood Flows from Coxeyism," *New York Times*, April 26, 1894; "Officials Are on the Alert," *Daily Picayune* (New Orleans, LA), April 25, 1894.

35. "The Coxey Browne Crusade," *Harper's Weekly*, 38, no. 1945 (March 31, 1894): 808; "The Army of the Commonweal," *Harper's Weekly*, 38, no. 1950 (May 5, 1894): 411.

36. Albert Bigalow Paine, *Thomas Nast: His Period and His Pictures* (New York: Macmillan, 1904), 234, describes *Leslie's Weekly* as sympathetic to both Democrats and liberal Republicans; "The Coxey Folly," *Leslie's Weekly* 84, no. 227 (April 5, 1895); "No Title," *Pomeroy's Advance Thought* (May 1894), 8; Rossiter Johnson and John Howard Brown, *The Twentieth Century Biographical Dictionary of Notable Americans* (Boston: Biographical Society, 1908), notes Benjamin Pomeroy, founder of the publication to be a devout Greenbacker.

37. The Chautauqua Society, as writers as much separated in time and perspective as Richard Hofstadter and Michael Kazin both note, was a largely rural phenomenon that sought to bring cultural and intellectual features and speakers to largely rural audiences. See "The Vanishing Hayseed," in Hofstadter, *Age of Reform*, 128n4; and Michael Kazin, *A Godly Hero: The Life of William Jennings Bryan* (New York: Alfred A. Knopf, 2006), 121–31; "Social Unrest and Disorder," *Chautauquan* 19 no. 2 (May 1894): 233; "The Coxey Problem," *Nation* 58, no. 1507 (May 17, 1894): 358: David M. Tucker, *Mugwumps: Public Moralists of the Gilded Age* (Columbia: University of Missouri Press, 1998), 101.

38. Telegrams from C. H. Dennis to Ray S. Baker, March 20 and 28, 1894, in Ray Stannard Baker Papers, Library of Congress, box 23; Vincent, *Story of the Commonweal*, 15; Baker, *American Chronicle*, 19.

39. Baker, *Native American*, 149, 301; Baker, *American Chronicle*, 7, 18–19.

40. "To March with Coxey," *Chicago Record*, April 6, 1894; "Like Gabriel's Horn," *Chicago Record*, April 3, 1894; "Greeted by Thousands," *St. Paul Daily News*, April 2, 1894; "A Great Day for Coxey," *North American*, April 2, 1894; McMurry, *Coxey's Army*, 77.

41. For discussion of Governor Pattison's conflicted role in the Homestead Strike of 1892, see Les Standiford, *Meet You in Hell: Andrew Carnegie, Henry Clay Frick, and the Bitter Partnership That Transformed America* (New York: Three River Press, 2005), 187–88, 190–92. The *New York Times* reported "Childs" to be the nephew of Frick, as did other papers, see "Coxey Has a New Commissary," *New York Times*, April 6, 1894, but Baker's account suggests that Childs was the nephew of Carnegie; see "To March with Coxey," *Chicago Record* April 6, 1894.

42. "Streak of Luck," *Boston Daily Globe*, April 2, 1894; "Coxey's Army Grows," *Chicago Daily*, April 2, 1894; "Kissed Little Peter," *Chicago Record*, April 2, 1894.

43. See McMurry, *Coxey's Army*, 77, who quotes the *Pittsburgh Press* of April 1, 1894, on the affinity of unions toward Coxey's March; "Dollars," *Los Angeles Times*, April 2, 1894; Browne, *When Coxey's "Army" Marcht*, 20. Vincent, *Story of the Commonweal*, 70; "Coxey's Army at Beaver Falls," *New York Times*, April 2, 1894. "Coxey Close to Pittsburgh," *Morning Oregonian*, April 2, 1894, 1. "Coxey's Hippodrome," *St. Paul Daily News*, April 2, 1894.

44. Edward Slavishak, *Bodies of Work* (Durham: Duke University Press, 2008), 21–26.

45. "Made Its Long March," *Chicago Daily Tribune*, April 3, 1894; "Chance to Walk," *Boston Daily Globe*, April 3, 1894.

46. "Engulfed in a Crowd," *Chicago Daily Tribune*, April 4, 1894; "Was Coxey's Big Day," *Chicago Record*, April 4, 1894; "Welcomed by Thousands," *Boston Daily Globe*, April 4, 1894; see also Vincent, *Story of the Commonweal*, 73–76; McMurry, *Coxey's Army*, 79–91; Schwantes, *Coxey's Army*, 54–57.

47. "Was Coxey's Big Day," *Chicago Record*, April 4, 1894; "Welcomed by Thousands," *Boston Daily Globe*, April 4, 1894; see also Vincent, *Story of the Commonweal*, 73–76; McMurry, *Coxey's Army*, 79–91; Schwantes, *Coxey's Army*, 54–57. "Engulfed in a Crowd," *Chicago Daily Tribune*, April 4, 1894. Baker, *American Chronicle*, 18.

48. "Afraid of His Army," *Chicago Daily Tribune*," April 7, 1894. "Coxey Wins Recruits," *Chicago Daily Tribune*, April 6, 1894; "Marched through Pittsburgh," *Atlanta Constitution*, April 6, 1894; "Coxey at Homestead," *Washington Post*, April 6, 1894; "Coxey Is Victorious," *Chicago Record*, April 6, 1894. See also McMurry, *Coxey's Army*, 89–91.

49. Baker, *American Chronicle*, 11–13.

50. Sweeney, "Sensational," 121; "Diary of the March," *Chicago Record*, April 21, 1894; untitled, *Los Angeles Times*, March 28, 1894.

Notes to Chapter Five

1. "Governor Hogg Talks," *Atlanta Constitution*, April 28, 1894.

2. "Marching with Coxey," *Baltimore American*, May 20, 1894; "As to Coxey's Army," *Washington Evening Star*, April 23, 1894; "Stopped at the White House Gates," *Washington Post*, April 23, 1894; "Guarding the Capitol," *Washington Post*, April 25, 1894; "Coxey at His Rubicon," *Washington Post*, April 23, 1894.

3. "Coxey Is Coming" appeared on the masthead of the weekly *Washington Bee*, March 31, 1894, April 7, 1894, and April 21, 1894.

4. "Fortunes to Be Made," *Washington Post*, September 6, 1894; "Industrial Depression: Various Manufacturing Enterprises Close Their Doors," *Washington Post*, December 24, 1894; "The Home of the President," *New York Times*, September 16, 1894; "A Double Twist," *Atlanta Constitution*, September 3, 1893.

5. Reverend Reynolds S. Hole, *A Little Tour of America* (Carlisle, MA: Applewood Books, 1894), 311; Constance McLaughlin Green, *Washington: Capital City* (Princeton, NJ: Princeton University Press, 1963), 100; Carl Abbott, "Dimensions of Regional Change in Washington, D.C.," *American Historical Review* 95, no. 5 (December 1, 1990): 1375–78; Zachary M. Schrag, *The Great Society Subway: A History of the Washington Metro* (Baltimore. MD: Johns Hopkins University Press, 2006), 14–15; McGerr, *Fierce Discontent*, 7; Constance McLaughlin Green, *Washington: A History of the Capital 1800-1950* (Princeton:

Princeton University Press, 1962), 5–8; Mark Twain, *The Gilded Age* (Hartford, CT: American Publishing, 1884), 295, 79–96; Kathryn Allamong Jacob, "Like Moths to a Candle: The Nouveaux Riches Flock to Washington," in *Urban Odyssey: A Multicultural History of Washington, D.C.*, ed. Francine Curro Cary (Washington: Smithsonian Institution Press, 1996), 79–96.

    6. Keith Melder, *City of Magnificent Intentions: A History of Washington D.C.* (Washington, DC: Intac, 1997), 257–60; Cary, *Urban Odyssey*, xvi–xvii; Hole, *Little Tour*, 311; Green, *Washington: Capital City*, 6–7, 100; "In Advance of Coxey," *Washington Post*, April 24, 1894.

    7. Worth Robert Miller, "The Lost World of Gilded Age Politics," *Journal of the Gilded Age and Progressive Era* 1, no. 1 (January 1, 2002), 49–67; see also Richard White, *Railroaded*, 333–34; Alyn Brodsky, *Grover Cleveland: A Study in Character* (New York: St. Martin's Press, 2000), 285–87; O. Gene Clanton, *Congressional Populism and the Crisis of the 1890s* (Lawrence: University of Kansas Press, 1998), 63–66.

    8. Gene Clanton, "Congressional Populism," in *American Populism*, ed. William F. Holmes (Lexington, MA: D.C. Heath), 115–16; 20 Congressional Record, August 27, 1894; quote of Benjamin Flower appears in Rezneck, "Unemployment, Unrest," 332.

    9. Gene Clanton, "Congressional Populism," in Holmes, *American Populism*, 115–16; for an excellent discussion of the attempts to legislate relief during the Panic of 1893 and ensuing depression, see Clanton, *Congressional Populism*, 62–72; Congressional Record, 53rd Cong., 2d Sess., August 27, 1894, appendix 1393–95; quote of Benjamin Flower appears in Samuel Rezneck, "Unemployment, Unrest," 332; Benjamin O. Flower, "Emergency Measures Which Would Have Maintained Self-Respecting Manhood," 9 *Arena* (May, 1894) 822.

    10. Congressional Record, 53rd Cong., 2d sess. (April 10, 1894), 3606.

    11. Robert V. Remini, *The House: The History of the House of Representatives* (New York: HarperCollins, 2006), 255–57; Worth Miller, "Lost World," 55; *Salem Daily News*, April 21, 1894.

    12. 26 Congressional Record, May 10, 1894, 4567–68.

    13. "Senator Stewart Writes to Coxey," *Chicago Daily Tribune*, March 26, 1894.

    14. Congressional Record, April 19, 1894, 3843; "Peffer Champions the Armies," *Chicago Daily Tribune*, April 20, 1894.

    15. Congressional Record, April 19, 1894, 3843; Congressional Record, April 23, 3960–61; interestingly, the seventeen included only one Democrat, and only five Republicans were opposed. While Republicans had spoken against this measure, they seemed more willing to provide a forum that might embarrass the Democratic administration.

    16. "Populists in Caucus," *North American* (Philadelphia), April 26, 1894; Hicks, *Coxey's Army*, 110.

    17. Congressional Record, April 26, 4105–8; "Coxey and the Senate," *Washington Post*, April 20, 1894.

    18. Industrial army movement detailed in Vincent, *Story of the Commonweal*; Schwantes, *Coxey's Army*; and McMurry, *Coxey's Army*; Simon Cordery, *Mother Jones: Raising Cain and Consciousness* (Albuquerque: University of New Mexico Press, 2010), 45–47; "Marshals Baffled," *Washington Post*, April 26, 1894; "General Kelley Is Oratorical," *Washington Post*, April 23, 1894; Green, *Washington*, 35; "In Advance of Coxey," *Washington Post*, April 24, 1894; "Marshals Baffled: Unable to Stop Progress of Stolen Train," *Washington Post*, April 26, 1894.

    19. "Coxey's Army," *Boston Daily Advertiser*, March 23, 1894; "Coxey at His Rubicon," *Washington Post*, April 23, 1894; "Not Worth Worrying About," *New York Times*, April 24, 1894; Schwantes, *Coxey's Army*, 143; "Getting Near the Capital," *Chicago Record*, April 23, 1894; Barber, *Marching on Washington*, 18; "A. E. Redstone," *Report 23*, 50th Congress 1st Sess., December 19, 1887; "Crusade of the Idle," *Washington Post*, March 18, 1894.

    20. Matthew F. Griffin, "Secret Service Memories" (Part 1), *Flynn's Weekly* 13 (March 1926): 915–16; Griffin joined the march near Pittsburgh under an alias and posing as a new recruit. Though accounts in *Flynn's Weekly* (a periodical for mystery articles) and in the detective stories entitled *Old Cap Collier with the Coxey's Army* (New York: Munro's Publishing House), 3–4, give vivid descriptions of the service's infiltration, actual correspondence from two Secret Service agents, J. W. Cribbs and S. A. Donnella, gives more accurate insight. They were dispatched to Westport, Maryland, to meet the army. Reporting to William P. Hazen, the chief of the Secret Service, they became confused by the appearance of the Unknown, whom they referred to simply as "Smith." The agents erroneously concluded that "Smith" was advancing for the march but became alarmed by Smith's inflammatory speech. Nonetheless, on April 19 Cribbs reported having become acquainted with a great number of the marchers and was convinced they simply wanted to pass Coxey's bills. On April 24, James Scanlon, another agent dispatched to follow Coxey on a trip to New York, reported that he "had met no known

Anarchists." Thus, the Secret Service reports were for the most part reassuring. Letter from William P. Hazen, Chief of the Secret Service, to John G. Carlisle, Secretary of the Treasury, April 20, 1894, Papers of President Grover Cleveland, Reel 84, Series 2, Library of Congress; Philip H. Melonson, *The Secret Service: The Hidden History of an Enigmatic Agency* (New York: Carol & Graf, 2005) 24–25.

21. "In Advance of Coxey," *Washington Post*, April 24, 1894; Allan Nevins, *Grover Cleveland: A Study in Courage* (Norwalk: Easton Press, 1932), 521; "Grover Isn't Afraid," *Chicago Daily Tribune*, April 26, 1894; Barber, *Marching on Washington*, 27; "Not Worth Worrying About," *New York Times*, April 24, 1894; "Told to Keep Out," *Chicago Daily Tribune*, April 24, 1894; Delos Franklin Wilcox, *Great Cities in America: Their Problems and Their Government* (New York: MacMillan, 1913), 30–32; "Preparing for an Emergency," *New York Times*, April 27, 1894; "Caught Napping," *Boston Daily Globe*, April 26, 1894; "Police Preparations," *Washington Post*, April 27, 1894; "Ridicule for Coxey's Movement," *Chicago Daily Tribune*, April 25, 1894.

22. Alyn Brodsky describes the duality of Cleveland's personality, alternating between a jovial and a stern side, in *Grover Cleveland*, 16; Nevins, *Grover Cleveland*, 521; "Grover Isn't Afraid," *Chicago Daily Tribune*, April 26, 1894; Socolofsky, "Jacob Coxey," 66.

23. Barber, *Marching on Washington*, 27; Schwantes, *Coxey's March*, 231; "Told to Keep Out," *Chicago Daily Tribune*, April 24, 1894; "No Place for Coxey," *Washington Post*, April 17, 1894; "Ready for Coxey," *St. Paul Daily News*, March 23, 1894.

24. "Caught Napping," *Boston Daily Globe*, April 26, 1894; "Police Preparations," *Washington Post*, April 27, 1894; "Ridicule for Coxey's Movement," *Chicago Daily Tribune*, April 25, 1894. Albert Ordway, *Drill Regulations for Street Duty: Including Lecture on Relations between Military and Civil Authority: Rights and Duties of Military Officers: and Methods of Dealing with Riots* (Washington, DC: James J. Chapman), 312–13.

25. "Capital Invaded," *Boston Daily Globe*, April 30, 1894; "Commonweal at the Capitol," *Milwaukee Sentinel*, April 30, 1894.

26. *Washington Bee*, March 31, 1894, April 7, 1894, and April 21, 1894; Abbott, "Regional Change," 1375; Lois Horton, "The Days of Jubilee: Black Migration during the Civil War and Reconstruction," in Cary, *Urban Odyssey*, 65–77; Green, *Washington: Capital City*, 70, 132; Constance McLaughlin Green, *Secret City*, 119–54.

27. The "equality amendments" describe the 13th, 14th, and 15th amendments to the Constitution, including the outlawing of slavery, equal citizenship, and the right to vote. Brands, *Reckless Decade*, 214–53; Amy Louise Wood, *Lynching and Spectacle: Witnessing Racial Violence in America, 1890–1940* (Chapel Hill: University of North Carolina Press, 2011), 19–30; Ronald Cedric White Jr., *Liberty and Justice for All: Racial Reform and the Social Gospel (1877–1925)* (Louisville, KY: John Knox Press, 2002), 10–21.

28. Kate Masur, *An Example for All the Land: Emancipation and the Struggle for Equality in Washington D.C.* (Chapel Hill: University of North Carolina Press, 2010), 198, 200; Green, *Secret City*, 119–54.

29. Robert McMath, *American Populism: A Social History, 1877–1898* (New York: Macmillan, 1993), 171–76; C. Vann Woodward, *The Strange Career of Jim Crow* (New York: Oxford University Press, 1974), 64, 80–82. In his classic analysis of a Jim Crow South, historian Woodward would write of the union of black and white Populists, "The two races had surprised each other and astonished their opponents by the harmony they achieved and the good will with which they cooperated"; Gutman, *Work, Culture and Society*, 125–72; Postel, *Populist Vision*, 197–203. The Populist's profile on racial relations was decidedly mixed. When Watson arrived in Washington as a Populist Congressman whom blacks helped elect in Georgia, he was joined by first-term Senator Marion Butler of North Carolina, a Populist senator whose fusion with white supremacist Republicans committed him to support black colonization. In the Populist Party pragmatism seemed always to triumph over principle when it came to race relations.

30. Thomas Flanagan, *Louis "David" Riel: Prophet of the New World* (Toronto: University of Toronto Press, 1996); "Peace Army Growing," *Chicago Record*, March 16, 1893; Donald B. Smith, *Honoré Jaxon: Prairie Visionary* (Regina, Saskatchewan: Coteau Books, 2007), 97–98. When he arrived, Jaxson raised eyebrows throughout Massillon with his native Metis costume. Described in press accounts as a "half breed Chicago Indian" who had spent time in an insane asylum, Jaxson actually fought during Canadian reformer Louis Riel's Red River and North-West Rebellions. He quickly became one of Coxey's favorite recruits with "his long hair, glib tongue, and buck skin half breed costume," before he left to traverse the route as a self-anointed advance man. In a little-reported episode during the march, Jaxson went out ahead of his fellow recruits. Though he lacked corroboration, he claimed to have made the trip from Massillon to Washington in eleven days and upon his arrival said it proved the physical and mental superiority of the Native American.

31. Baker, unlike McMurry, Schwantes, or Vincent, refers to Jasper Johnson as Jasper Johnson Buchanan (perhaps confusing where he was from); see "Army Is in Trouble," *Chicago Record*, March 27, 1894; Vincent, however, names him Jasper Johnson from Buckanon (not Baker's Buchanan), West Virginia; see Vincent, *Story of the Commonweal*, 56; as does Robert Skinner in his account of the departure in the *Evening Independent* of March 26, 1894.

32. "To Sing for the Army," *Chicago Record*, March 21, 1894; "Army Still Afloat," *Chicago Record*, April 18, 1894; "Bozarro Got the Collection," *Chicago Daily Tribune*, April 19, 1894; "Travelling All Night," *Washington Post*, April 19, 1894.

33. Wood, *Lynching and Spectacle*, 19–30; Ray Stannard Baker, unlike McMurry, Schwantes, or Vincent, refers to Jasper Johnson as Jasper Johnson Buchanan; see "Army Is in Trouble," *Chicago Record*, March 27, 1894; Vincent, however, names him Jasper Johnson from Buchanon (should be Buckhannon, West Virginia); see Vincent, *Story of the Commonweal*, 56; "Pulpit View of Coxey," *Washington Post*, April 23, 1894; Postel, *Populist Vision*, 257–58; Mitchell A. Kachun, *Festivals of Freedom: Memory and Meaning in African American Emancipation Celebrations, 1808–1915* (Amherst: University of Massachusetts Press, 2003), 209–32; "Met by Armed Forces," *Chicago Record*, April 24, 1894; "Coxey Is Coming," *Washington Bee*, March 31, April 7, and April 21, 1894; Kachun, *Festivals of Freedom*, 205–32.

34. Masur, *All the Land*, 7–11.

35. "Pulpit View of Coxey," *Washington Post*, April 23, 1894; Postel, *Populist Vision*, 257–58; "Met by Armed Forces," *Chicago Record*, April 24, 1894.

36. See masthead, "Coxey Is Coming," in *Washington Bee* issues: March 31, April 2, and April 7, 1894.

37. "Bivouac at Woodley," *Washington Post*, April 26, 1894; "Coxey Not Afraid of Grover," *Chicago Daily Tribune*, April 24, 1894; "Coxey at the Capitol," *Chicago Record*, April 29, 1894; Browne, *When Coxey's "Army" Marcht*, 17–18; Barber, *Marching on Washington*, 5; "Coxey's March Is Ended," *North American* (Philadelphia), April 30, 1894; "Coxey at His Goal," *Massillon Evening Independent*, April 30, 1894.

38. "Coxey Less Boastful," *Washington Post*, April 27, 1894; "Coxey and His 300," *Washington Post*, April 30, 1894; Schwantes, *Coxey's Army*, 172.

39. "Coxey and His 300," *Washington Post*, April 30, 1894; Carlos A. Schwantes, "Western Women in Coxey's Army in 1894," *Arizona and the West* 26, no. 1 (April 1, 1984): 6, 8; early on it was reported that some women dressed as men had joined Coxey's ranks, though these reports did not persist; see Schwantes, *Coxey's Army*, 126–32.

40. "Lauding Coxey's Band," *Washington Post*, April 22, 1894.

41. "Coxey's March Ended," *Massillon Evening Independent*, April 30, 1894.

42. Barber, *Marching on Washington*, 32–33. "Commonweal at the Capitol," *Milwaukee Sentinel*, April 30, 1894; "Coxey in Washington," *Emporia Gazette*, April 30, 1894; "Capital Invaded," *Boston Daily Globe*, April 30, 1894; the Coxey Shoe advertisement appears in the *Pittsburgh Commercial Gazette*, April 7, 1894.

43. Brightwood Riding Park was a commercial horse racing track; "Coxey at His Goal," *Massillon Evening Independent*, April 30 1894; "More Men in Line," *Boston Daily Globe*, March 28, 1894; Lara Otis, "Washington's Lost Race Tracks," *Washington History* 24 (2012): 145–46.

44. "Governor Hogg Talks," *Atlanta Constitution*, April 28, 1894; Postel, *Populist Vision*, 192; "Congress Denounced," *Washington Post*, May 1, 1894.

45. "Coxey Will Defy the Law," *New York Times*, May 1, 1894; "On the Capitol Steps," *Washington Post*, May 1, 1894.

46. "Coxey at His Goal," *Massillon Evening Independent*, April 30, 1894; "Coxey Will Defy the Law," *New York Times*, May 1, 1894; "Will a Riot Result?" *Massillon Evening Independent*, May 1, 1894.

47. "Will a Riot Result?" *Massillon Evening Independent*, May 1, 1894; "Mamie Coxey Has Gone," *Massillon Evening Independent*, April 30, 1894; "Coxey in Washington," *Emporia Gazette*, April 30, 1894; "On the Capitol Steps," *Washington Post*, May 1, 1894.

48. "Camp George Washington," *Standard* (Ogden, UT), May 2, 1894; "Goes to See Speaker Crisp," *Logansport Daily* (IN), May 1, 1894.

49. "On the Capitol Steps," *Washington Post*, May 1, 1894; Barber, *Marching on Washington*, 33–37; "'Gen' Coxey's Waterloo," *Boston Globe*, May 2, 1894; Coxey's speech reprinted in Coxey, "Coxey Plan," 48–51. "Will a Riot Result?" *Massillon Evening Independent*, May 1, 1894; "600 Policemen on Duty," *Washington Post*, May 1, 1894.

50. "March Ends in Riot," *Chicago Record*, May 2, 1894; "'Gen' Coxey's Waterloo," *Boston Globe*, May 2, 1894; "Climax of Folly," *Washington Post*, May 2, 1894.

51. "Climax of Folly," *Washington Post*, May 2, 1894; "March Ends in Riot," *Chicago Record*, May 2, 1894; "'Gen' Coxey's Waterloo," *Boston Globe*, May 2, 1894.

52. "March Ends in Riot," *Chicago Record*, May 2, 1894; "'Gen' Coxey's Waterloo," *Boston Globe*, May 2, 1894.

53. "March Ends in Riot," *Chicago Record*, May 2, 1894; "'Gen' Coxey's Waterloo," *Boston Globe*, May 2, 1894.

54. "The Uncrowned King and His Subjects," *Washington Bee*, May 4, 1894; "Coxey Is Coming," *Washington Bee*, April 2, 1894; *Washington Bee*, March 31, 1894; *Washington Bee*, April 7, 1894.

55. Telegram from Capitol, May 1, 1894, from the Secret Service to the Executive Mansion, see Papers of President Grover Cleveland, Reel 84, Series 2, Library of Congress; "Coxey and Browne Arrested," *Massillon Evening Independent*, May 1, 1894.

56. "March Ends in Riot," *Chicago Record*, May 2, 1894; Baker's letter to his father, written from Pennell's Grand Hotel in Fostoria, Ohio, en route back to Chicago, can be found in box 23 of Ray Stannard Baker Papers, Library of Congress.

57. "Coxey Farce Ends," *Chicago Tribune*, May 2, 1894; "General Coxey Waterloo," *Boston Daily Globe*, May 2, 1894; "Climax of Folly," *Washington Post*, May 2, 1894; Nevins, *Grover Cleveland*, 605; "Coxey in Washington," *Harper's Weekly*, May 12, 1894, 43; *Chicago Daily Tribune*, May 2, 1894; *Boston Globe*, May 2, 1894; Schwantes, *Coxey's Army*, 183. Baker's letter to his father written from Pennell's Grand Hotel in Fostoria Ohio en route back to Chicago can be found in box 23 of Ray Stannard Baker papers at Library of Congress.

Notes to Epilogue

1. On April 16, 1949, Coxey's ninety-fifth birthday, *the Massillon Evening Independent* wrote an editorial that captured the essence of the one they had run on his eighty-first birthday (1935), celebrating the New Deal's embrace of public works as a way to put the unemployed back to work. From a reprint of the transcript of the WHBC (Canton, OH) story on Coxey's ninety-fifth birthday.

2. Letter dated May 24, 1894, to F. L. Baldwin in Papers of Jacob Sechler Coxey Sr., Massillon Museum, Massillon, OH; Baldwin was a prominent attorney according to Vogt, *Towpath to Towpath*, 56, 73, 77. Baker, "Marching with Coxey," *Baltimore American*; Browne's letters to Baker appear in Wilbur Miller's *Coxey's Army Scrapbook* by Wilbur Miller at Ohio State Historical Society, Microfilm MIC72. Similarly Coxey struck up relationships with the reporters. As early as July 6, 1894, he wrote to Wilbur Miller of the *Cincinnati Enquirer*, addressing him as "Friend," and saying in an affectionate note, "'A friend in need is a friend indeed,' and you will ever be in my memory as a true friend." In later years Coxey wrote to Miller, noting how pleased he was to discover Miller's whereabouts in Syracuse since he (Coxey) tried to keep tabs on the location of all the reporters who began with the march. Coxey's April 3, 1930, letter to Miller, then living in Syracuse. Coxey notes: "I have been wondering for a long time where you were, as there are only a few left out of the 35 correspondents that started on the March 36 years ago, certainly surprised as well as being much pleased." See also Carl's Campaign Cactus in *Coxey's Army Scrapbook* by Wilbur Miller at Ohio State Historical Society, Microfilm MIC72. See also Baker, *American Chronicle*, 25.

3. Baker's letter to his father written from Pennell's Grand Hotel in Fostoria, Ohio, en route back to Chicago can be found in box 23 of Ray Stannard Baker Papers at Library of Congress; Ray Stannard Baker, *American Chronicle*, 6–36.

4. Sautter, *Three Cheers*, 38; Rigenbach, *Tramps and Reformers*, 41–42; Josiah Flynt, who would publish *Tramping with Tramps* in 1899, had already begun his examination of what it meant to be on the road and unemployed the year before Coxey marched. Louis V. De Foe, "How a Great City Rewards the Search for Honest Work," *Chicago Tribune*, April 3, 1898; see also "Mr. Wyckoff in the West," *New York Times*, November 7, 1898; "New Literature," *Boston Daily Globe*, November 7, 1898; "Lived Like a Tramp," *Baltimore Sun*, June 26, 1901; Kusmer, *Down and Out*, 169–91. In chapter 9 Kusmer surveys the wealth of late nineteenth- and early twentieth-century literature and art that explored tramping, including notable authors William Dean Howells, *A Traveller from Altruria* (1894), and Stephen Crane's "The Men in the Storm" (1894). As Kusmer notes, "Their writings did introduce new ways of viewing tramps and vagrants, and in the long run they helped to break down the stereotypes that had first emerged in the 1870s. John London in his book *The Road* adopted the view of Josiah Flynt, who in his famous *Tramping with Tramps* (1899), painted the picture of men who tramped by choice, not necessity. This was the tramp imagery that Norman Rockwell adopted in his paintings for the *Saturday Evening Post*.

It was a romanticized version "that emptied the image of the tramp of any element of class conflict or resistance." Wyckoff, by contrast, dealt with tramps as having no choice but to wander in search of the next job. His social experiment was meant to bring to light the extent of unemployment, although as he said in a speech delivered at Northwestern University, he thought skilled laborers willing to relocate could always find a job." See "Wyckoff Delivers a Lecture," *Chicago Tribune*, January 21, 1900; Louis V. De Foe, "How a Great City Rewards the Search for Honest Work," *Chicago Tribune*, April 3, 1898.

5. Sautter, *Three Cheers*, 52–62, 73–81; Coxey's home state of Ohio was one of the few states that went so far as to actually establish a state-run "labor exchange," a clearinghouse that sought to match out-of-work laborers with new employers.

6. "Labor Men Object to Federal Bureau," *New York Times*, February 12, 1909; "Council of Labor Talks of Idle Men," *Atlanta Constitution*, February 11, 1909; "The Discontent of Gompers," *New York Times*, February 12, 1909; "Straus Confers with Labor Men," February 11, 1909.

7. Howson, *Coxey*, 213–387; Howson meticulously documents Coxey's many failed political ventures against the backdrop of an impressive business-growth trajectory, save for a brief period of bankruptcy in 1904; see Howson's explanation of Coxey's difference with Roosevelt, 284–86; "Coxey Meets Roosevelt," *New York Times*, February 28, 1908; Howson makes the observation on page 299, which helps explain Coxey's reaction to Roosevelt's idea for financing waterways; Sautter, *Three Cheers*, 26–31.

8. Howson, *Coxey*, 295–300.

9. Gutfreund, *Twentieth-Century Sprawl*, 17–22; "Federal Aid Road Act 1916" (Richmond: Virginia State Highway Commission Bulletin No. 100, 1917), 11–21; Howson, *Coxey*, 295–300; Udo Sautter, "Government and Unemployment: The Use of Public Works before the New Deal," *Journal of American History* 73, no. 1 (June 1, 1996): 59–86. Coxey's bills were again offered in Congress in 1919 but with no more acclaim and certainly no more action than had occurred in 1894. Moreover, when Iowa Senator William Kenyon introduced a bill to create a $400 million emergency public-works fund, it went nowhere, despite significant support from groups as diverse as the American Federation of Labor and the Chicago Association of Commerce; for information regarding the history of the Bureau of Labor Statistics, see its web site, http://www.bls.gov/bls/history/home.htm.

10. Sautter, *Three Cheers*, 137, 150–51; Udo Sautter, "Government and Unemployment: The Use of Public Works Before the New Deal," *Journal of American History* 73, no. 1 (June 1, 1996): 65.

11. "President Selects Colonel Woods to Head Relief for Jobless," *New York Times*, October 22, 1930.

12. "Coxey and Woods Confer on Jobless," *New York Times*, October 23, 1930.

13. Donald W. Whisenhunt, *Utopian Movements and Ideas of the Great Depression: Dreams, Believers, and Madmen* (Lanham: Lexington Books, 2013) 45–67; "Cox's Army," *Time Magazine* 19, no. 3 (January 18, 1932): 12; "Jobless Caravan Headed by Priest to Beg Congress for Relief Work," *Washington Post*, January 7, 1932; "Idle Marchers Make a Plea and Depart Capital," *Washington Post*, January 8, 1932; "Jobless Marchers Appeal to Hoover," *New York Times*, January 8, 1932; "Idle Marchers Invade Capital," *Boston Globe*, January 7, 1932.

14. Howson, *Coxey*, 253, 269–70; Riley Miner, "Coxey's Army Over the Top at Last," *Massillon Evening Independent*, December 19, 1931.

15. As Carl Smith notes in his volume on the New Deal, "The terrific increase in pre-Depression spending on public construction that these programs represented, the far reaching federal efforts invested in directing this money, and the long run impact of the infrastructure itself form the components of a public works revolution." "Grave Issues Face the Lame Duck Congress," *New York Times*, November 27, 1932; letter from Jacob Coxey to Governor Franklin D. Roosevelt, dated November 15, 1932, from the Jacob Sechler Coxey Sr. archives at the Massillon Museum, Massillon, OH.

16. Coxey's speech reprinted in Coxey, "Coxey Plan," 48–51.

17. Howson, *Coxey*, 388–419; See WHBC interview with J. S. Coxey by E. T. Heald, April 16, 1949, from Jacob Sechler Coxey Sr. Papers, Massillon Museum, Massillon, OH; see November 15, 1932, letter from Jacob Coxey to Governor Franklin D. Roosevelt (president-elect), Jacob Sechler Coxey Sr. Papers, Massillon Museum, Massillon, OH. According to one account, "Franklin D. Roosevelt took office as President of the United States in 1933 and began calling in experts in every line of activity. While on one of his trips to Warm Springs, Georgia, Roosevelt called Coxey in for a conference on his ideas for the unemployment program; see Lewis, "General Jacob S. Coxey," 5.

Bibliography

Archives

Ray Stannard Baker Papers, Library of Congress, Washington, DC.
Grover Cleveland Papers (1837–1908), Library of Congress, Washington, DC.
Jacob S. Coxey Sr. Papers, Massillon Museum, Massillon, OH.
Wilbur Miller Papers, Ohio Historical Society, Columbus, OH.
Robert E. Pattison Papers (1855–1904), Pennsylvania State Archives, Harrisburg, PA.

Books

Alexander, Benjamin F. *Coxey's Army: Popular Protest in the Gilded Age*. Baltimore, MD: Johns Hopkins University Press, 2015.
Algeo, Matthew. *The President Is a Sick Man: Wherein the Supposedly Virtuous Grover Cleveland Survives a Secret Surgery at Sea and Vilifies the Courageous Newspaperman Who Dared Expose the Truth*. Chicago: Chicago Review Press, 2011.
Anderson, Nels. *On Hobos and Homelessness*. Chicago: University of Chicago Press, 1998.
Argesinger, Peter H. *Populism: Its Rise and Fall*. Lawrence: Kansas University Press, 1992.
Baker, Ray Stannard. *American Chronicle: The Autobiography of Ray Stannard Baker*. New York: C. Scribner's Sons, 1945.
———. *Native American: The Book of My Youth*. New York: Scribner, 1941.
Bannister, Robert C. *Ray Stannard Baker; The Mind and Thought of a Progressive*. New Haven, CT: Yale University Press, 1966.
Barber, Lucy G. *Marching on Washington: The Forging of an American Political Tradition*. Berkeley: University of California Press, 2002.
Baumgartner, Frederic J. *Longing for the End: A History of Millennialism in Western Civilization*. New York: Palgrave Macmillan, 2001.
Baxter, Maurice G. *Henry Clay and the American System*. Lexington: University Press of Kentucky, 2004.
Beatty, Jack. *Age of Betrayal: The Triumph of Money in America, 1865–1900*. 1st ed. New York: Knopf, 2007.
Bellamy, Edward. *Looking Backward, 2000–1887*. Boston: Ticknor, 1888.
Bender, David. *American Abyss: Savagery and Civilization in the Age of Industry*. Ithaca, NY: Cornell University Press, 2009.
Bensel, Richard Franklin. *The Political Economy of American Industrialization, 1877–1910*. New York: Cambridge University Press, 2000.
Berk, Gerald. *Alternative Tracks: The Constitution of American Industrial Order, 1865–1917*. Baltimore, MD: Johns Hopkins University Press, 1994.
Berlin, Ira, ed. *Power and Culture: Essays on the American Working Class*. New York: New Press, 1987.
Billington, Ray Allen. *Frederick Jackson Turner: Historian, Scholar, Teacher*. New York: Oxford University Press, 1973.
Bolotin, Norman, and Christine Laing. *The World's Columbian Exposition: The Chicago World's Fair of 1893*. Washington, DC: Preservation Press, 1992.
Brands, H. W. *The Reckless Decade: America in the 1890s*. Chicago: University of Chicago Press, 2002.
Brodsky, Alyn. *Grover Cleveland: A Study in Character*. New York: St. Martin's Press, 2000.
Browne, Carl. *When Coxey's "Army" Marcht on Washington, 1894*. San Francisco, CA: n.p., 1944.
Campbell, Bruce F. *Ancient Wisdom Revived: A History of the Theosophical Movement*. Berkeley: University of California Press, 1980.

Carey, Henry Charles. *The Harmony of Interests: Agricultural, Manufacturing, and Commercial.* Philadelphia: J. S. Skinner, 1851.
———. *Principles of Political Economy.* Philadelphia: Carey, Lea & Blanchard, 1837.
Carnegie, Andrew. *The Autobiography of Andrew Carnegie.* Boston, MA: Houghton Mifflin, 1920.
———. *The Gospel of Wealth.* New York: Century Company, 1901.
Cary, Francine Curro, ed. *Urban Odyssey: A Multicultural History of Washington, D.C.* Washington: Smithsonian Institution Press, 1996.
Cayton, Andrew Robert Lee. *Ohio: The History of a People.* Columbus: Ohio State University Press, 2002.
Chase, Malcolm. *Chartism: A New History.* Manchester, UK: Manchester University Press, 2007.
Clanton, O. Gene. *Congressional Populism and the Crisis of the 1890s.* Lawrence: University Press of Kansas, 1998.
———. *Populism: The Humane Preference in America, 1890–1900.* Social Movements Past and Present. Boston: Twayne, 1991.
Clinch, Thomas A. *Urban Populism and Free Silver in Montana: A Narrative of Ideology in Political Action.* Missoula: University of Montana Press, 1970.
Cook, James W. *The Arts of Deception: Playing with Fraud in the Age of Barnum.* Cambridge, MA: Harvard University Press, 2001.
Cordery, Simon. *Mother Jones: Raising Cain and Consciousness.* Albuquerque: University of New Mexico Press, 2010.
Davis, E. M. *The "Labor Reform" View of Money.* Philadelphia: O.P.Q., 1874.
Debord, Guy. *Society of the Spectacle.* New York: Rebel Press, 1967.
DePastino, Todd. *Citizen Hobo: How a Century of Homelessness Shaped America.* Chicago: University of Chicago Press, 2003.
Dungan, Nicholas. *Gallatin: America's Swiss Founding Father.* New York: New York University Press, 2010.
Feder, Leah Hannah. *Unemployment Relief in Periods of Depression.* New York: Russell Sage Foundation, 1966.
Fine, Sidney. *Laissez Faire and the General-Welfare State: A Study of Conflict in American Thought, 1865–1901.* Ann Arbor: University of Michigan Press, 1964.
Flanagan, Thomas. *Louis "David" Riel: Prophet of the New World.* Toronto: University of Toronto Press, 1996.
Franklin, Benjamin. *Memoirs.* Vol. 2. New York: Harper & Sons, 1839.
Franklin, Julia, ed. *Selections from the Works of Fourier.* London: S. Sonnenschein, 1901.
Garraty, John A. *Unemployment in History: Economic Thought and Public Policy.* New York: Harper & Row, 1978.
Gilbert, James. *Perfect Cities: Chicago's Utopias of 1893.* Chicago: University of Chicago Press, 1991.
Godwin, Joscelyn. *The Theosophical Enlightenment.* Albany: State University of New York Press, 1994.
Goldberg, Joseph, and William T. Moye. *The First Hundred Years of the Bureau of Labor Statistics, 1884–1994.* Washington, DC: Government Printing Office, 1984.
Goodman, Susan, and Carl Dawson. *William Dean Howells: A Writer's Life.* Berkeley: University of California Press, 2005.
Goodwyn, Lawrence. *Democratic Promise: The Populist Moment in America.* New York: Oxford University Press, 1976.
———. *The Populist Moment: A Short History of the Agrarian Revolt in America.* New York: Oxford University Press, 1978.
Green, Constance McLaughlin. *The Secret City.* Princeton, NJ: Princeton University Press, 1967.
———. *Washington: A History of the Capital 1800–1950.* Princeton: Princeton University Press, 1962.
———. *Washington: Capital City.* Princeton, NJ: Princeton University Press, 1962.
Green, James. *Death in the Haymarket.* New York: Random House, 2006.
Gutfreund, Owen D. *Twentieth-Century Sprawl: Highways and the Reshaping of the American Landscape.* New York: Oxford University Press, 2004.
Hicks, John Donald. *The Populist Revolt: A History of the Farmers' Alliance and the People's Party.* Lincoln: University of Nebraska Press, 1961.
Hild, Matthew. *Greenbackers, Knights of Labor, and Populists: Farmer-Labor Insurgency in the Late-Nineteenth-Century South.* Athens: University of Georgia Press, 2007.
Hill, Edwin Charles. *The Historical Register.* New York: E. C. Hill, 1919.

Hitchcock, Roswell D. *Socialism*. New York: Anson D. F. Randolph, 1879.

Hoffmann, Charles. *The Depression of the Nineties: An Economic History*. Westport, CT: Greenwood, 1970.

Hofstadter, Richard. *The Age of Reform*. New York: Vintage, 1960.

———. *Social Darwinism in American Thought*. Boston: Beacon Press, 1992.

Hoig, Stan Edward. *Fort Reno and the Indian Territory Frontier*. Fayetteville: University of Arkansas Press, 2005.

Hole, Reverend Reynolds S. *A Little Tour of America*. Carlisle, MA: Applewood Books, 1894.

Holli, Melvin G. *Reform in Detroit: Hazen S. Pingree and Urban Politics*. New York: Oxford University Press, 1969.

Hourwich, Isaac Aaronovich. *Immigration and Labor: The Economic Aspects of European Immigration to the United States*. New York: G. P. Putnam, 1922.

Howson, Embrey Bernard. *Jacob Sechler Coxey: A Biography of a Monetary Reformer*. New York: Arno Press, 1982.

James, Henry. *Richard Olney and His Public Service*. Boston: Houghton Mifflin, 1923.

Johnson, Rossiter, and John Howard Brown. *The Twentieth Century Biographical Dictionary of Notable Americans*. Boston: Biographical Society, 1904.

Kachun, Mitchell A. *Festivals of Freedom: Memory and Meaning in African American Emancipation Celebrations, 1808-1915*. Amherst: University of Massachusetts Press, 2003.

Kasson, John F. *Civilizing the Machine: Technology and Republican Values in America, 1776-1900*. New York: Macmillan, 1976.

Katz, Michael B. *In the Shadows of the Poorhouse: A Social History of Welfare in America*. New York: Basic Books, 1986.

Katz, Philip. *From Appomattox to Montmartre: Americans and the Paris Commune*. Cambridge, MA: Harvard University Press, 1998.

Kazin, Michael. *A Godly Hero: The Life of William Jennings Bryan*. New York: Alfred A. Knopf, 2006.

Kearney, Dennis. *Speeches of Dennis Kearney*. New York: Jesse Haney, 1878.

Kellogg, Edward. *A New Monetary System: The Only Means of Securing the Respective Rights of Labor and Property, and of Protecting the Public from Financial Revulsions*. New York: Rudd & Carleton, 1861.

Klatt, Wayne. *Chicago Journalism: A History*. Jefferson, NC: McFarland, 2009.

Kobre, Sidney. *The Yellow Press and Gilded Age Journalism*. Tallahassee: Florida State University, 1964.

Kusmer, Kenneth L. *Down and Out, on the Road: The Homeless in American History*. New York: Oxford University Press, 2003.

Larson, Erik. *The Devil in the White City: A Saga of Magic and Murder at the Fair That Changed America*. New York: Vintage, 2004.

Latham, Frank Brown. *The Panic of 1893: A Time of Strikes, Riots, Hobo Camps, Coxey's "Army," Starvation, Withering Droughts, and Fears of Revolution*. New York: F. Watts, 1971.

Lauck, W. Jett. *The Causes of the Panic of 1893*. Boston: Houghton Mifflin, 1907.

Lears, Jackson. *Fables of Abundance: A Cultural History of Advertising in America*. New York: Basic Books, 1995.

Masur, Kate. *An Example for All the Land: Emancipation and the Struggle for Equality in Washington D.C.* Chapel Hill: University of North Carolina Press, 2010.

McGerr, Michael. *A Fierce Discontent: The Rise and Fall of the Progressive Movement in America, 1870-1920*. New York: Oxford University Press, 2005.

McLoughlin, William Gerald. *Revivals, Awakenings, and Reform: An Essay on Religion and Social Change in America, 1607-1977*. Chicago: University of Chicago Press, 1980.

McMath, Robert C. *American Populism: A Social History, 1877-1898*. New York: Macmillan, 1993.

McMurry, Donald L. *Coxey's Army: A Study of the Industrial Army Movement of 1894*. Seattle: University of Washington Press, 1929.

Melder, Keith. *City of Magnificent Intentions: A History of Washington D.C.* Washington, DC: Intac, 1997.

Menand, Louis. *The Metaphysical Club: A Story of Ideas in America*. New York: Farrar, Straus & Giroux, 2002.

Miller, Donald. *The City of the Century: The Epic of Chicago and the Making of America*. New York: Simon & Shuster, 1991.

Molesworth, William Nassau. *The History of the Reform Bill of 1832*. London: Chapman & Hall, 1865.

Mott, Franklin Luther. *American Journalism: A History of Newspapers in the United States through 250 Years, 1690–1940*. New York: Macmillan, 1941.

National League for Good Roads. *National League for Good Roads*. Vol. 1. The League, 1892.

Nevins, Allan. *Grover Cleveland: A Study in Courage*. New York: Dodd, Mead, 1962.

Nye, Russel B. *A Baker's Dozen: Thirteen Unusual Americans*. East Lansing: Michigan State University Press, 1956.

O'Malley, Michael. *Face Value*. Chicago: University of Chicago Press, 2012.

Ordway, Albert. *Drill Regulations for Street Riot Duty: Including Lecture on Relations Between Military and Civil Authority: Rights and Duties of Military Officers: and Methods of Dealing with Riots*. Washington, DC: James J. Chapman, 1891.

Osborn, Norris Galpin. *Men of Mark in Connecticut: Ideals of American Life Told in Biographies and Autobiographies of Eminent Living Americans*. Hartford, CT: W. R. Goodspeed, 1904.

Paine, Albert Bigelow. *Thomas Nast: His Period and His Pictures*. New York: Macmillan, 1904.

Painter, Nell Irvin. *Standing at Armageddon: The United States, 1877–1919*. New York: W. W. Norton, 1987.

Partridge, Eric. *A Dictionary of Slang and Unreconstructed English*. New York: Macmillan, 1970.

Pittenger, Mark. *Class Unknown: Undercover Investigations of American Work from the Progressive Era to the Present*. New York: New York University Press, 2012.

Pollack, Norman. *The Populist Response to Industrial America*. Cambridge, MA: Harvard University Press, 1962.

Postel, Charles. *The Populist Vision*. New York: Oxford University Press, 2009.

Raymond, Rossiter Worthington. *Peter Cooper*. New York: Houghton, Mifflin, 1901.

Reef, Catherine. *Poverty in America*. New York: Facts on File, 2007.

Remini, Robert V. *The House: The History of the House of Representatives*. New York: HarperCollins, 2006.

Ricker, Ralph Ross. *The Greenback-Labor Movement in Pennsylvania*. Bellefonte: Pennsylvania Heritage, 1966.

Rigenbach, Paul T. *Tramps and Reformers, 1873–1916*. Westport, CT: Greenwood Press, 1973.

Ritter, Gretchen. *Goldbugs and Greenbacks: The Antimonopoly Tradition and the Politics of Finance in America*. Cambridge: Cambridge University Press, 1999.

Rosenberg, Vivian Graff. *Turn of the Century American Journalist, Home-Spun Philosopher: Ray Stannard Baker*. Published by author, 1977.

Salvatore, Nick. *Eugene V. Debs: Citizen and Socialist*. 2nd ed. Urbana: University of Illinois Press, 2007.

Sanders, Elizabeth. *Roots of Reform: Farmers, Workers, and the American State, 1877–1917*. Chicago: University of Chicago Press, 1999.

Sautter, Udo. *Three Cheers for the Unemployed: Government and Unemployment before the New Deal*. Cambridge: Cambridge University Press, 2001.

Sawrey, Robert Dixon. *Dubious Victory: The Reconstruction Debate in Ohio*. Lexington: University Press of Kentucky, 1992.

Schlereth, Thomas J. *Victorian America: Transformations in Everyday Life, 1876–1915*. New York: HarperCollins, 1992.

Schrag, Zachary M. *The Great Society Subway: A History of the Washington Metro*. Baltimore, MD: Johns Hopkins University Press, 2006.

Schudson, Michael. *Origins of the Ideal of Objectivity in the Professions: Studies in the History of American Journalism and American Law, 1830–1940*. Cambridge, MA: Harvard University Press, 1976.

Schwantes, Carlos A. *Coxey's Army: An American Odyssey*. Lincoln: University of Nebraska Press, 1985.

Searight, Thomas Brownfield. *The Old Pike: A History of the National Road*. Uniontown, PA: Thomas Brownfield Searight, 1894.

Semonche, John E. *Ray Stannard Baker*. Chapel Hill: University of North Carolina Press, 1969.

Slavishak, Edward. *Bodies of Work*. Durham, NC: Duke University Press, 2008.

Smith, Carl S. *Urban Disorder and the Shape of Belief: The Great Chicago Fire, the Haymarket Bomb, and the Model Town of Pullman*. Chicago: University of Chicago Press, 1995.

Smith, Donald B. *Honoré Jaxon: Prairie Visionary*. Regina, Saskatchewan: Coteau Books, 2007.

Smythe, Ted Curtis. *The Gilded Age Press, 1865–1900*. New York: Praeger, 2003.

Standiford, Les. *Meet You in Hell: Andrew Carnegie, Henry Clay Frick, and the Bitter Partnership That Transformed America*. New York: Random House Digital, 2005.

Stead, William T. *Chicago Today, or the Labour War in America*. London: Review of Reviews Office, 1894.

———. *If Christ Came to Chicago: A Plea for the Union of All Who Love in the Service of All Who Suffer.* Chicago: Laird & Lee, 1894.

Steeples, Douglas, and David O. Whitten. *Democracy in Desperation: The Depression of 1893.* Westport, CT: Greenwood Press, 1998.

Steffens, Lincoln. *The Autobiography of Lincoln Steffens.* New York: Harcourt, Brace & World, 1931.

Strouse, Jean. *Morgan: American Financier.* New York: HarperCollins, 2000.

Taylor, William Alexander, and Aubrey Clarence Taylor. *Ohio Statesmen and Annals of Progress: From the Year 1788 to the Year 1900.* Columbus, OH: Press at the Westphalia Co. State Printers, 1899.

Timberlake, Richard H. *Monetary Policy in the United States: An Intellectual and Institutional History.* Chicago: University of Chicago Press, 1978.

Tindall, George Brown. *A Populist Reader: Selections from the Works of American Populist Leaders.* New York: Harper & Row, 1966.

Trachtenberg, Alan. *The Incorporation of America: Culture and Society in the Gilded Age.* New York: Hill & Wang, 1982.

Tucker, David M. *Mugwumps: Public Moralists of the Gilded Age.* Columbia: University of Missouri Press, 1998.

Turner, Frederick Jackson. *The Frontier in American History.* New York: H. Holt, 1920.

Twain, Mark. *The Gilded Age.* Hartford, CT: American Publishing, 1884.

Unger, Irwin. *The Greenback Era: A Social and Political History of American Finance, 1865–1879.* Princeton, NJ: Princeton University Press, 1964.

Vincent, Henry. *The Story of the Commonweal.* Chicago: W. B. Conkey, 1894.

Vogt, Margy. *Towpath to Towpath: Massillon, Ohio: A History.* Massillon, OH: Bates Publishing, 2002.

Weingroff, Richard F. *Portrait of a General: General Roy Stone: Special Agent and Engineer for Road Inquiry, Office of Road Inquiry, Department of Agriculture, October 3, 1893–October 23, 1899.* Washington: Federal Highway Administration, 1993.

Whisenhunt, Donald W. *Utopian Movements and Ideas of the Great Depression: Dreamers, Believers, and Madmen.* Lanham: Lexington Books, 2013.

White, Richard. *Railroaded: The Transcontinentals and the Making of Modern America.* New York: W. W. Norton, 2011.

White, Ronald Cedric, Jr. *Liberty and Justice for All: Racial Reform and the Social Gospel (1877–1925).* Louisville, KY: Westminster John Knox Press, 2002.

Whyte, Frederic. *The Life of W. T. Stead.* 2 vols. New York: Houghton Mifflin, 1971.

Wilcox, Delos Franklin. *Great Cities in America: Their Problems and Their Government.* New York: MacMillan, 1913.

Wood, Amy Louise. *Lynching and Spectacle: Witnessing Racial Violence in America, 1890–1940.* Chapel Hill: University of North Carolina Press, 2011.

Woodward, C. Vann. *The Strange Career of Jim Crow.* New York: Oxford University Press, 1974.

Young, Alfred F. *The Shoemaker and the Tea Party: Memory and the American Revolution.* Boston: Beacon Press, 2000.

Dissertations and Theses

Hilles, William G. "The Good Roads Movement in the United States." Master's thesis, Duke University, 1958.

Mason, Philip P. "The League of American Wheelmen." PhD diss., University of Michigan, 1957.

Mills, Frederick C. "Contemporary Theories of Unemployment and Unemployment Relief." PhD diss., Columbia University, 1917.

Piehler, Harold Richard. "Henry Vincent: A Case Study in Political Deviancy." PhD diss., University of Kansas, 1975.

Interviews

Coxey, Jacob. "HBC Radio Story #98," April 16, 1951. Box 4, Folder 1. Jacob Sechler Coxey Sr. Papers, Massillon Museum, Massillon, OH.

"WHBC Interview by E. T. Heald," April 16, 1949. Clipping File. Massillon Public Library, Massillon, OH.

Journals and Magazines

Abbott, Carl. "Dimensions of Regional Change in Washington, D.C." *American Historical Review* 95, no. 5 (December 1, 1990): 1367–93.

Abrahams, Edward H. "Ignatius Donnelly and the Apocalyptic Style." *Minnesota History* 46, no. 3 (October 1, 1978): 102–11.

Allen, Howard W., and Robert Slagter. "Congress in Crisis: Changes in Personnel and the Legislative Agenda in the U.S. Congress in the 1890s." *Social Science History* 16, no. 3 (October 1, 1992): 401–20.

Argersinger, Peter H. "'A Place on the Ballot': Fusion Politics and Antifusion Laws." *American Historical Review* 85, no. 2 (April 1, 1980): 287–306.

"The Army of the Commonweal." *Harper's Weekly*, May 5, 1894.

Aronson, Sidney H. "The Sociology of the Bicycle." *Social Forces* 30, no. 3 (March 1, 1952): 305–12.

Austin, Shirley Plumer. "Coxey's Commonweal Army." *Chautauquan*, September 1894.

———. "The Downfall of Coxeyism." *Chautauquan*, September 1894.

Baack, Bennett D., and Edward John Ray. "Special Interests and the Adoption of the Income Tax in the United States." *Journal of Economic History* 45, no. 3 (1985): 607–25.

Baker, Ray Stannard. "Coxey and His Commonweal." *Tourney*, May 1894.

Bank, Rosemarie K. "Representing History: Performing the Columbian Exposition." *Theatre Journal* 54, no. 4 (December 1, 2002): 589–606.

Bard, Mitchell. "Ideology and Depression Politics I: Grover Cleveland (1893–97)." *Presidential Studies Quarterly* 15, no. 1 (January 1, 1985): 77–88.

Barkun, Michael. "Coxey's Army as a Millenial Movement." *Religion* 18, no. 4 (October 1988): 363–89.

Beik, William. "The Culture of Protest in Seventeenth-Century French Towns." *Social History* 15, no. 1 (January 1, 1990): 1–23.

Blavatsky, Madame, and H. P. Blavatsky. "Recent Progress in Theosophy." *North American Review* 151, no. 405 (1890): 173–86.

Bowling, Kenneth R. "From 'Federal Town' to 'National Capital': Ulysses S. Grant and the Reconstruction of Washington, D.C." *Washington History* 14, no. 1 (April 1, 2002): 8–25.

Browne, Junius Henri. "Succor for the Unemployed." *Harper's Weekly* 38 (January 6, 1894): 10.

Carruthers, Bruce G., and Sarah Babb. "The Color of Money and the Nature of Value: Greenbacks and Gold in Postbellum America." *American Journal of Sociology* 101, no. 6 (May 1, 1996): 1556–91.

Cawelti, John G. "Portrait of the Newsboy as a Young Man: Some Remarks on the Alger Stories." *Wisconsin Magazine of History* 45, no. 2 (December 1, 1961): 79–83.

Clanton, Gene. "'Hayseed Socialism' on the Hill: Congressional Populism, 1891–1895." *Western Historical Quarterly* 15, no. 2 (April 1, 1984): 139–62.

Clement, Priscilla Ferguson. "Nineteenth Century Welfare Policy Programs and Poor Women: Philadelphia as a Case Study." *Feminist Studies* 18, no. 1 (Spring 1992): 35–58.

Closson, Carlos C. "The Unemployed in American Cities." *Quarterly Journal of Economics* 8, no. 2 (January 1, 1894): 168–217.

Cohen, Daniel A. "Passing the Torch: Boston Firemen, 'Tea Party' Patriots, and the Burning of the Charlestown Convent." *Journal of the Early Republic* 24, no. 4 (December 1, 2004): 527–86.

Country Gentleman [pseud.]. "American Roads." *The New England Farmer, and Horticultural Register* 39, no. 16 (April 19, 1884): 1.

"Country Roads." *The American Farmer* 3, no. 19 (October 1, 1884): 270.

"Country Roads." *Century Illustrated Magazine*, April 1891.

"Country Roads." *Ohio Farmer* 68, no. 21 (November 21, 1885): 328.

"Coxey in Washington." *Harper's Weekly*, May 12, 1894.

"Coxeyism and the Interest Question." *Social Economist* 6, no. 6 (June 1894): 345.

"The Coxey Problem." *Nation*, May 17, 1894.

"Currency and Capital." *Harper's Weekly*, July 1, 1893.

Davis, Susan G. "Strike Parades and the Politics of Representing Class in Antebellum Philadelphia." *Drama Review* 29, no. 3 (October 1, 1985): 106–16.

Destler, Chester McA. "The Origin and Character of the Pendleton Plan." *Mississippi Valley Historical Review* 24, no. 2 (1937): 171–84.

Dewey, David R. "Irregularity of Employment." *Publications of the American Economic Association* 9, no. 5/6 (October–December 1894): 53–67.

"The Farm." *Michigan Farmer* 18, no. 24 (June 13, 1887): 2.

Ford, Lacy K. "Frontier Democracy: The Turner Thesis Revisited." *Journal of the Early Republic* 13, no. 2 (July 1, 1993): 144–63.

Foster, Susan Leigh. "Choreographies of Protest." *Theatre Journal* 55, no. 3 (October 1, 2003): 395–412.

Franklin, John Hope. "Edward Bellamy and the Nationalist Movement." *New England Quarterly* 11, no. 4 (December 1, 1938): 739–72.

Friedman, Milton. "The Crime of 1873." *Journal of Political Economy* 98, no. 16 (December 1990): 1159–193.

Gipe, George. "Rebel in a Wing Collar." *American Heritage* 18, no. 1 (December 1966).

Goldberg, Michael L. "Non-Partisan and All-Partisan: Rethinking Woman Suffrage and Party Politics in Gilded Age Kansas." *Western Historical Quarterly* 25, no. 1 (April 1, 1994): 21–44.

Griffin, Matthew F. "Secret Service Memories (Parts 1 and 2)." *Flynn's Weekly*, March 1926.

H. E. S. "National League of Good Roads." *American Farmer*, no. 28 (February 15, 1893): 5.

Hargrove, E. T. "Progress of Theosophy in the United States." *North American Review* 162, no. 475 (June 1, 1896): 698–704.

Hicks, John D. "The Legacy of Populism in the Western Middle West." *Agricultural History* 23, no. 4 (October 1, 1949): 225–36.

Holmes, William F. "Populism: In Search of Context." *Agricultural History* 64, no. 4 (October 1, 1990): 26–58.

Hooper, Osman C. "The Coxey Movement in Ohio." *Ohio Archaeological and Historical Quarterly*, n.d.

Howard, Oliver Otis, Thomas Byrnes, and Alvah H. Doty. "The Menace of 'Coxeyism.'" *North American Review* 158, no. 451 (June 1, 1894): 687–705.

Kauer, Ralph. "The Workingmen's Party of California." *Pacific Historical Review* 13, no. 3 (1944): 278–91.

Kerr, K. Austin. "Review: [untitled]." *Business History Review* 60, no. 3 (October 1, 1986): 497–98.

Kershaw, Baz. "Curiosity or Contempt: On Spectacle, the Human, and Activism." *Theatre Journal* 55, no. 4 (December 1, 2003): 591–611.

Kloppenberg, James T. "The Virtues of Liberalism: Christianity, Republicanism, and Ethics in Early American Political Discourse." *Journal of American History* 74, no. 1 (June 1, 1987): 9–33.

Kwiat, Joseph J. "The Newspaper Experience: Crane, Norris, and Dreiser." *Nineteenth-Century Fiction* 8, no. 2 (1953): 99–117.

Leonard, Frank. "Helping the Unemployed in the Nineteenth Century: The Case of the American Tramp." *Social Service Review* 40, no. 4 (December 1966): 431–32.

Levermore, Charles H. "Henry C. Carey and His Social System." *Political Science Quarterly* 5, no. 4 (December 1, 1890): 553–82.

Levi, Albert William. "Edward Bellamy: Utopian." *Ethics* 55, no. 2 (January 1, 1945): 131–44.

Lewis, William H. "General Jacob S. Coxey." *Glass Cutter* 20, no. 9 (March 1955).

London, Jack. "The March of Kelly's Army." *Cosmopolitan* 43, no. 6 (October 1907). http://carl-bell-2.baylor.edu/~bellc/JL/TheMarchOfKellysArmy.html.

Marcus, Irwin M., Jennie Bullard, and Rob Moore. "Change and Continuity: Steel Workers in Homestead, Pennsylvania, 1889–1895." *Pennsylvania Magazine of History and Biography* 111, no. 1 (January 1, 1987): 61–75.

McQuaid, Kim. "The Businessman as Reformer: Nelson O. Nelson and Late 19th Century Social Movements in America." *American Journal of Economics and Sociology* 33, no. 4 (October 1, 1974): 423–35.

Miller, Worth Robert. "The Lost World of Gilded Age Politics." *Journal of the Gilded Age and Progressive Era* 1, no. 1 (January 1, 2002): 49–67.

M'Kelvy, A. T. "Swinging Around the Circle." *Ohio Farmer* 83, no. 5 (February 2, 1893): 82.

Montgomery, David. "Wage Labor, Bondage, and Citizenship in Nineteenth-Century America." *International Labor and Working-Class History*, no. 48 (October 1, 1995): 6–27.

Moody, William Goodwin, and Laughlin, J. Laurence. "Workingmen's Grievances." *North American Review* 138, no. 330 (May 1884): 505.

Neckar, Ninon. "With the League of American Wheelmen at Washington." *Outing and the Wheelmen* 4, no. 6 (September 1884): 425.

Nelson, N. O. "Profit-Sharing." *North American Review* 144, no. 365 (April 1, 1887): 388–94.

Nugent, Walter. "Comments on Wyatt Wells 'Rhetoric of the Standards: The Debate over Gold and Silver in the 1890's.'" *Journal of the Gilded Age and Progressive Era* 14, no. 1 (2015): 69–76.

Nunis, Doyce B., Denis Kearney, and J. Bryce. "The Demagogue and the Demographer: Correspondence of Denis Kearney and Lord Bryce." *Pacific Historical Review* 36, no. 3 (1967): 269–88.

O'Malley, Michael. "Specie and Species: Race and the Money Question in Nineteenth-Century America." *American Historical Review* 99, no. 2 (April 1, 1994): 369–95.

Palmer, Stephanie C. "Realist Magic in the Fiction of William Dean Howells." *Nineteenth-Century Literature* 57, no. 2 (2002): 210–36.

Parsons, Stanley B., Karen Toombs Parsons, Walter Killilae, and Beverly Borgers. "The Role of Cooperatives in the Development of the Movement Culture of Populism." *Journal of American History* 69, no. 4 (March 1, 1983): 866–85.

Pierce, Michael. "Farmers and the Failure of Populism in Ohio, 1890–1891." *Agricultural History* 74, no. 1 (January 1, 2000): 58–85.

Plotz, John. "Crowd Power: Chartism, Carlyle, and the Victorian Public Sphere." *Representations*, no. 70 (April 1, 2000): 87–114.

Pomeroy, Benjamin, ed. Untitled. *Pomeroy's Advance Thought*, May 1894 in Jacob Sechler Coxey Sr. Papers, Box 4, Folder 35, Massillon Museum, Massillon, OH.

Pope, Andrew A. "An Industrial Revolution by Good Roads." *Forum* (March 1892): 115.

———. "Vox Populi: How to Raise Money to Improve Roads." *Daily Picayune*, October 18, 1893.

Rezneck, Samuel. "Unemployment, Unrest, and Relief in the United States during the Depression of 1893–97." *Journal of Political Economy* 61, no. 4 (1953): 324–45.

"Road Improvement." *Ohio Farmer* 83, no. 4 (January 26, 1893): 63.

Sautter, Udo. "Government and Unemployment: The Use of Public Works before the New Deal." *Journal of American History* 73, no. 1 (June 1, 1996): 59–86.

Schlabach, Theron F. "An Aristocrat on Trial: The Case of Richard T. Ely." *Wisconsin Magazine of History* 47, no. 2 (December 1, 1963): 146–59.

Schwantes, Carlos A. "The Concept of the Wageworkers' Frontier: A Framework for Future Research." *Western Historical Quarterly* 18, no. 1 (January 1, 1987): 39–55.

———. "Western Women in Coxey's Army in 1894." *Arizona and the West* 26, no. 1 (April 1, 1984): 5–20.

Shaw, Albert, and William Thomas Stead. "The Coxey Crusade." *Review of Reviews* 10 (July–December 1894): 63–65.

Skinner, Robert P. "The Coxey-Browne Crusade." *Harper's Weekly*, March 31, 1894.

"Social Economic and Educational." *Ohio Farmer* 83, no. 7 (February 16, 1893): 132.

"Social Unrest and Disorder." *Chautauquan* 19, no. 2 (May 1894).

Socolofsky, Homer E. "Jacob Coxey: Ohio's Fairly Respectable Populist." *Kansas Quarterly* 1, no. 4 (Fall 1969).

Speed, Jonathan Gilmer. "Common Highways." *Atlanta Constitution*, November 20, 1892.

———. "Common Roads as a Social Factor." *Chautauquan*, February 1883.

———. "Country Roads and Highways." *Lippincotts Monthly Magazine* 48 (September 1891).

Stead, William Thomas. "Coxeyism, a Character Sketch." *American Review of Reviews*, December 1894.

Sweeney, Michael S. "The Desire for the Sensational." *Journalism History* 23, no. 3 (Autumn 1997): 114–25.

Taussig, F. W. "The Tariff Act of 1894." *Political Science Quarterly* 9, no. 4 (December 1, 1894): 585–609.

Timberlake, Richard H. "Repeal of Silver Monetization in the Late Nineteenth Century." *Journal of Money, Credit and Banking* 10, no. 1 (February 1, 1978): 27–45.

Trier, James. "Guy Debord's 'The Society of the Spectacle.'" *Journal of Adolescent & Adult Literacy* 51, no. 1 (2007): 68–73.

Trimble, Steven, and Donald E. Winters. "Editor's Page: Warnings from the Past: 'Caesar's Column' and 'Nineteen-Eighty Four.'" *Minnesota History* 49, no. 3 (October 1, 1984): 109–14.

Turner, James. "Understanding the Populists." *Journal of American History* 67, no. 2 (1980): 354–73.

"Turnpikes." *Ohio Farmer* 62, no. 9 (September 2, 1882): 131.

Unger, Irwin. "Business Men and Specie Resumption." *Political Science Quarterly* 74, no. 1 (March 1, 1959): 46–70.

Vlahakis, Robert. "Ragged Dick by Horatio Alger Jr." *English Journal* 68, no. 2 (February 1, 1979): 40.

Wheeler, Chris. "The Meet of the Keystone Wheelmen in 1890." *Outing, an Illustrated Monthly Magazine of Recreation* 18, no. 2 (May 1891): 137.

Williams, Rhys H., and Susan M. Alexander. "Religious Rhetoric in American Populism: Civil Religion as Movement Ideology." *Journal for the Scientific Study of Religion* 33, no. 1 (March 1, 1994): 1–15.

Woodruff, W. "History and the Businessman." *Business History Review* 30, no. 3 (1956): 241–59.

"The Workingmen's Party of California, 1877–1882." *California Historical Quarterly* 55, no. 1 (April 1, 1976): 58–73.

Letters and Telegrams

Browne, Carl. "February 8, 1894 Letter to Jacob Coxey," February 8. Box 23, Reel 60. Ray Stannard Baker Papers, Library of Congress.

Coxey, Jacob. "To President-elect Franklin Roosevelt," November 15, 1932. Jacob Coxey Papers, Box 1, Folder 30, Massillon Museum.

Coxey, Jacob Sechler. "From Parlor 67 US Jail, Washington DC to Mr. F. D. Baldwin," May 24, 1894. Jacob Coxey Papers, Box 1, Folder 2, Massillon Museum.

Drummond, A. J. "To P. B. Olney, Attorney at Law," May 31, 1894. Papers of President Grover Cleveland, Reel 84, Series 2, Library of Congress.

———. "To Secretary of Agriculture J. Sterling Morton," May 7, 1894. Papers of President Grover Cleveland, Reel 84, Series 2, Library of Congress.

Hazen, William P. "To John G. Carlisle Secretary of the Treasury," April 20, 1894. Papers of President Grover Cleveland, Reel 84, Series 2, Library of Congress.

"Telegram from Secret Service at Capitol to Executive Mansion," May 1, 1894. Papers of President Grover Cleveland, Reel 84, Series 2, Library of Congress.

Government Documents

23 Congressional Record. March 29, 1892: 2632.

23 Congressional Record. July 5, 1892: 5765.

23 Congressional Record. July 27, 1892: 6846.

23 Congressional Record. July 29, 1892: 6941.

26 Congressional Record. March 19, 1894: 3076.

26 Congressional Record. April 2, 1894: 3382.

26 Congressional Record. June 13, 1894: 6193.

26 Congressional Record. May 2, 1894: 4335.

"The Message and Documents of Two Houses of Congress Beginning in the third session of the 53rd Congress," Report of the Secretary of Agriculture. Washington: Government Printing Office, 1895, 62.

Manuscripts

Browne, Carl. "Bulletin Number Three." February 28, 1894. Box 1. Massillon Museum, Massillon, OH.

Coxey, Jacob. "Bulletin Number One: Coxey Good Roads Association of the U.S." January 1893. Ray Stannard Baker Papers, Box 3, Reel 60, Library of Congress.

Coxey, Jacob Sechler. "The Coxey Plan." Jacob S. Coxey, Publisher, 1914. Jacob Sechler Coxey Papers, Massillon Museum, Massillon, OH.

Miller, Wilbur. "Coxey's Army Scrapbook." n.d. Wilbur Miller Papers, Ohio State Historical Society, Columbus, OH.

Wells, Guy McNeill. "Coxey's Motivation to March." June 30, 1924.

Newspapers

Alton Daily Telegraph (IL)
Atchison Globe (KS)
Atlanta Constitution
Baltimore American

Bangour Daily Whig and Courier (ME)
Bismarck Daily Tribune
Boston Daily Advertiser
Boston Daily Globe
Canton News Democrat
Carl's Campaign Cactus
Chicago Daily News
Chicago Daily Tribune
Chicago Inter Ocean
Chicago Record
Cincinnati Enquirer
Cleveland Plain Dealer
Daily Picayune (New Orleans)
Davenport Leader (IA)
Emporia Gazette (KS)
Galveston Daily News
Hamilton Daily Democrat (NY)
Janesville Gazette (WI)
Lebanon Daily News (PA)
Logansport Daily Journal (IN)
Los Angeles Times
Massillon Evening Independent
Mendocino Dispatch Democrat
Milwaukee Journal
Milwaukee Sentinel
Morning Oregonian
New York Commercial Advertiser
New York Journal
New York Times
New York World
North American (Philadelphia)
Oakland Times
Ogden Standard (UT)
The Penny Press (Minneapolis)
Pittsburgh Commercial Gazette
Pittsburgh Leader
Pittsburgh Post
Pittsburgh Times
Portsmouth Daily News
Raleigh News Observer
Rocky Mountain News
Sacramento Record Union
Salem Daily News
San Francisco Examiner
San Francisco Weekly Star
St. Paul Daily News
Washington Bee
Washington Post
Wisconsin State Register (Madison)

Index

Lightning Source UK Ltd.
Milton Keynes UK
UKHW010409110621
385256UK00010B/468